RACE, RHETORIC, AND IDENTITY:
THE ARCHITECTON OF SOUL

RACE, RHETORIC, AND IDENTITY:
THE ARCHITECTON OF SOUL

Molefi Kete Asante

Humanity Books

An Imprint of Prometheus Books

59 John Glenn Drive
Amherst, New York 14228-2119

Published 2005 by Humanity Books, an imprint of Prometheus Books

Inquiries should be addressed to
Humanity Books
59 John Glenn Drive
Amherst, New York 14228–2119
VOICE: 716–691–0133, ext. 210
FAX: 716–691–0137
WWW.PROMETHEUSBOOKS.COM

15 14   10 9 8

Library of Congress Cataloging-in-Publication Data

Asante, Molefi K., 1942–
    Race, rhetoric, and identity : the architecton of soul / Molefi Kete Asante.
        p. cm.
    Includes bibliographical references and index.
    ISBN 13: 978-159102-318-0
    ISBN 10: 1-59102-318-1 (alk. paper)

    1. African Americans—Race identity. 2. Afrocentrism. 3. African Americans—Intellectual life. 4. Rhetoric—Social aspects—United States. 5. Communication—Social aspects—United States. 6. Communication and culture—United States. 7. Racism—United States. 8. United States—Race relations. I. Title.

E185.625.A835 2005
305.896'073—dc22

                                                        2004030059

Printed in the United States on acid-free paper

To
ANA YENENGA ASANTE

Who knows what it is to be truly human, whose path from Africa to Jamaica to Costa Rica and the United States has been energized constantly by the spirit of her ancestors, and who shares with me her deepest and most profound insights into contemporary culture.

CONTENTS

Preface   9

Acknowledgments   17

1.   DuBois and *The Souls of Black Folk*   19

2.   De-racing the Media   25

3.   Trouble at the Gate: Identity Crisis   41

4.   The Rhetoric of Education   65

5.   The Preponderance of Bureaucracy   81

6.   The Continuing Prevalence of Racism   97

7.   A New Architecton of Images   111

8.   Communication, Culture, and Civilization   133

9.   Rhetoric and Myth   151

10.	Press Politics in a Racist Society	161
11.	Habermas and the Tyranny of Reason without Passion	169
12.	Literature and Criticism	179
13.	Afrocentricity, Sexism, and *Maat*	187
14.	Narrativity and the Rhetoric of Identity	199
15.	Reparations, Reasons, and Rhetoric	221
References		237
Index		243

PREFACE

This book has taken a long time to write. The length of its gestation period is a function of the changes within the themes, the debates with colleagues, and the dynamics of politics, over the years. I first considered writing a book that would examine communication in its rhetorical form in relationship to contemporary African American culture and race more than ten years ago. It had occurred to me, under the influence of the humanistic works of Kofi Asare Opoku, Kwame Gyekye, Marshall McLuhan, Maulana Karenga, Paulo Freire, Amilcar Cabral, Xing Lu, Miriam Ma'at Ka Re Monges, Katherine Bankole, Jack Daniel, Herbert Marcuse, Frantz Fanon, Ama Mazama, Paul Kurtz, George Gerbner, Alfred Opubor, Cornel West, Ronald Walters, Wade Nobles, Chenhamo Chimutengwende, Everett Rogers, and Paul Rosenthal to render a work that would bridge the chasm between what was imagined and what was real. I have read them all with enormous benefit. Indeed, the idea was to demonstrate how the imagined often morphed into the real where one could retain centeredness without losing ambiguity or irony. But over the intervening years the shifting political and cultural conditions for identity theory, Afrocentric analysis, intercultural communication, rhetorical discourse, and value analyses have caused me more than once to rethink some of the issues that I visited during the earlier days of manuscript development. I am now ready to offer the ideas and concepts in this manuscript for public scrutiny and evaluation.

What I have endeavored in this volume is to examine from an Afrocentric perspective several communication sites, such as culture, identity, leisure, bureaucracy, education, politics, and television, in an effort to produce alternative ways of understanding human interactions. I have defined communication rather broadly as both an arena of human discourse and a process of human interaction through the use of symbols. Thus, this is itself a rhetorical enterprise meant to prompt discussion and debate about some of the current issues in communication by applying the insights of what Prof. Ama Mazama calls in her work "the Afrocentric paradigm" to several critical subjects and themes that frame the philosophical and cultural structure of our society. The Afrocentric idea allows us to view issues, themes, topics, and situations from the standpoint of African people, on the continent and in the diaspora, as subjects of human experiences rather than as on the fringes of European experiences. It also allows one to examine Europe and European ideas from the perspective of African people. New insights and innovations are possible because of this reorientation to facts.

The most destructive force in a heterogeneous multicultural industrial society is the doctrine of racial domination because it distorts relationships, undermines the authenticity of human communication, and complicates the intersections of class, gender, and sexuality. It wobbles the natural orbits of human communication and interaction, creating a chaotic vortex. Therefore, as a humanist, I present this work as an inquiry into the nature of our lives and as an assault on chaos. The tradition is African in the sense that the objective, as the ancient Egyptians understood *Maat*, is to hold back chaos.

As I pursue this line of inquiry and declaration, I am attesting to the strength of harmony, order, balance, righteousness, justice, truth, reciprocity—that is, *Maat*. Whatever is necessary as an attack on chaos is also an argument against disharmony and disunity. But no notion of coherence or transformation can exist without mutual respect and appreciation; this is the lesson of history. Thus, I seek to launch an architectonics of soul, an investigation into rhetoric and identity in contemporary society in order to arrange what we know into a coherent pattern. I realize that this is contrary to the antistructuralist positions of much of contemporary postmodernism. As an Afrocentrist, I am opposed to the notion of ruin; I detest the idea that it is necessary to fragment the world in order to interrogate phenomena. I do not covet the rubble left over from the violent assaults on humanity. The walking dead, weary and directionless, cannot be what was envisioned by the visionaries of postmodernism. The forms of deconstruction often suggested by many postmodernist thinkers leave nothing in the process but unadulterated individualistic narcissism that undermines the human capacity to feel solidarity with others. Thus, the idea of an *architecton* of soul is a thrust into chaos in order to move toward the world not away from it, in order to construct, to build, even if it means to enthrone a new *constructural* adjustment in our relationships with each other. In some ways it is a neoclassical idea in the neo-Kemetic sense of advancing *Maat*, order, harmony, balance, and reciprocity. Life as a random collage or free association of images may invoke an isolationist individuality, but it is never cohesive enough to deal with the reality of community and communities, that is, groups of people who are bound together by similar historical experiences and who are developed by common phenomenological responses.

Such an examination should yield moments of interrogation that open up new avenues for understanding how humans react in communication situations where identity is created by innovative discourse and existing cultural institutions. How to modify those situations and institutions becomes a crucial point of departure for developing any unifying narrative. Why is such an *architecton* as a unifying narrative even necessary? I think it is found in the fact that within the past, which is gone, and the future, which is to come, we human beings must devote our time to the middle moment, which is now, so that we can more properly deal with the endless opportunities for human peace and goodwill. We are capable of responding to variations in human situations, in perceptual realities, and in multifarious relationships without destroying each other. Thus, this book is an optimistic work, devoted to the idea that only when the African person views himself or herself and is viewed by others as subject or agent will a transformation occur that will unlock the potential evolution in our cultural and social relationships.

I have approached the structure of this book by dealing first with the intellectual work of William E. B. DuBois, the major African American scholar of the twentieth century. Chapter 1 suggests that DuBois's famous book *The Souls of Black Folk* was a response to the architectonics built by the ideology of white supremacy and the first real attempt by an African American to define the response to this ideology by offering a discourse on African American identity.

In chapter 2, "De-racing the Media," I attempt to demonstrate that the media institutions of American society are constructed out of racist cultural materials. What DuBois responded to in 1903 remains an issue more than one hundred years later when African Americans must counter the images, symbols, and signs erected by white society to advance the notion of white dominance. My objective in this chapter is to dramatize the enormous obstacles African Americans find in the layered construction of a racist society.

Subsequently, in chapter 3, "Trouble at the Gate: Identity Crisis," I suggest that the problems found in DuBois and discovered in the media itself from the earliest appearance of written literature about the presence of Africans in America produced a psychological dislocation that introduced identity confusion among African Americans. The resultant crisis is the issue that Afrocentrists have addressed for the past twenty years in critical studies, essays, and books. They have found this problem to be centered in the way children are educated.

Chapter 4, "The Rhetoric of Education," delves into the nature of the educational process in America with special interest and emphasis on the exchange and interchange of ideas. It may be necessary to reconceptualize education in the context of modern issues and problems. To an important degree the political environment dictates the type of education that will exist in a society. Our task must be to reorient the education of students toward a more humanistic interaction.

In chapter 5, "The Preponderance of Bureaucracy," I am concerned with the endeavors in organizations to stratify the function of communication in order to insure efficiency and to demonstrate how it is often a product of the industrial society in a racist era. Much of bureaucracy, especially in the United States, is now hopelessly entangled in the tentacles of postmodern technology. Rather than eliminating bureaucracy, technocracy has made space for more virile levels of bureaucracy, and therefore humans are exploited in an even more diverse array of ways.

Chapter 6, "The Continuing Prevalence of Racism," seeks to examine the persistence of racial logic in the modern and postmodern age. How is it possible that racism, an ethical and moral issue, retains its provocative and negative impact in society? It is possible that we have missed the point of racism by claiming it as some abnormality of human interaction rather than as a deep moral depravity.

My intention in chapter 7, "A New Architecton of Images," is to deal with the new techniques of developing structures that are perceived as a part of the general racist organization of society. Indeed, the architectonics of modern society, while based on more advanced technologies, often reflect the deep-seated racial attitudes of a society developed on the slave trade.

Chapter 8, "Communication, Culture, and Civilization," is an exploration of the convergence of these concepts in contemporary issues of rhetoric and race. How we confront the novelties of ethnic and multiethnic cultural expressions in the context of a diverse civilizing ethos is really the front door of the new era of human relations.

Chapter 9, "Rhetoric and Myth," suggests that we are in the process of defining tactics and strategies for human communication that, in the end, will constitute an approach to myth. Perhaps it is possible that the terminology of interests and the ethical foundation of a society can form the basis of a new rhetoric of myth. This chapter explores the dimensions of rhetoric and myth.

Chapter 10, "Press Politics in a Racist Society," provides the reader with one of the clearest modern examples of how racism distorted the function of the press and demonstrated how a press embedded in a political administration can be used to serve the interests of politics. Given the fact that South Africa under the white minority regime sought to keep the black majority in a state of subjugation, the government's aim was to use the press as an instrument of state policy.

In chapter 11, "Habermas and the Tyranny of Reason without Passion," I contend that Jürgen Habermas, one of the most popular European philosophers, is at once engaging in his defense of rationality and at the same time frightening in his commitment to the most awesome demons of transcendental reason. In many ways, like the French philosophers Jacques Derrida and Michel Foucault, the German philosopher Habermas has influenced the way Americans think about modern culture. What we have come to know is that rationality does not prevent racism, violence, patriarchy, or gender discrimination. Yet since Habermas is one of the leading contemporary philosophers, it is important to examine a key element in his thinking.

Chapter 12, "Literature and Criticism," establishes the idea that African writers who have become known to the world outside of Africa have usually worked within the context of the signs and significations of Europe. This has created the odd literature where Africans write against themselves or write outside of the framework of their own liberation. One problem is that the African or African American writer rarely uses his or her own language.

Chapter 13, "Afrocentricity, Sexism, and *Maat*," recognizes the profusion of discourses on centeredness, gender, and sex, and advances *Maat* as the ancient concept for unifying all discourse. The aim of *Maat* is to hold back chaos with balance, harmony, order, and justice.

Chapter 14, "Narrativity and the Rhetoric of Identity," is an analysis of a couple of writers who seek to advance a narrativity that compounds the problems of the architectonics of our society because it draws upon the constricting forms of the past.

Finally, in chapter 15, "Reparations, Reasons, and Rhetoric," I once again interrogate the warrants for reparations. The chapter supports the thesis for reparations and argues that the historical and ethical demands of a just society would have to include reparations. Reparations are symbolic of the culmination of the discourse of liberty, equality, and community and the defeat of the rhetoric of slavery and inequality.

Taken together, the chapters in this book are designed to constitute a family, a resemblance to each other, in the way that they treat the centrality of the Afrocentric idea in interrogations of diverse themes and subjects. Since communication is a constant in human interactions, I have been able to demonstrate its relevance over and over again. If one lives in society, one cannot escape the inevitability of communicating, and this is so regardless of one's identity.

ACKNOWLEDGMENTS

I owe acknowledgments to too many people to name. This book is like all the rest of my works in that I owe a lot of people for their ideas, arguments, and criticisms. Some I have accepted and others I have not, but ultimately I am a beneficiary of the profound insights of many of my students, colleagues, and contemporaries.

This book could not have been developed without the discussions I have had with my Temple colleagues, Profs. Ama Mazama and Emeka Nwadiora, two intellectuals committed to a thorough reorientation of our cultural and political consciousness. Former students and friends such as Mark Christian, Yoshitaka Miiki, Suzuko Morikawa, Troy Allen, Adisa Alkebulan, Ana Monteiro Ferreira, Daryl Zizwe Poe, Kwame Botwe-Asamoah, FeFe Dunham, Katherine Bankole, Cecil Blake, Reiland Rabaka, and Yuan Ji have assisted me immensely. They have enlarged my perspective on human cultures and communication and demonstrated the need for *centric* studies in many societies.

I must also acknowledge the *Journal of Black Studies* and the *Howard Journal of Communication* for previously publishing, though not in the same form, some of the ideas that are contained in the present book.

chapter 1
DuBois and *The Souls of Black Folk*

*T*he Souls of Black Folk was first published in 1903.[1]

It has remained the most popular book of W. E. B. DuBois, the greatest African American scholar of the twentieth century. The turn of the century was the African American nadir; no time had been any crueler nor yet had any place in the world seemed so unwelcoming as the United States to people who had actually been on the land for three hundred years.

Our adversity was matched only by our will to overcome adversity. More open brutality, racial exclusions in employment and at leisure, occurred during this era than ever in previous years. Gender and class were both bound up in the totalizing racial attack on the African American person. We were neither rich nor poor, neither male nor female; we were black as in African black, and the rhetoric of the day was anti-African. One's economic status or gender status did not matter; the irreducible commonality was race.

We were victimized at every instance, and there was little satisfaction coming from the halls of government. White Americans were feeling the itch for empire, and in the South this meant more terror for those who opposed the march of white supremacy. DuBois was the lion out of the lair who stood squarely in the road to equality, fighting and defending a people just up from enslavement.

19

The lynching of black men and women reached its highest point during the early part of the twentieth century.[2] DuBois brought a new interpretation of our experience to the forefront, expounding in the most eloquent way the meaning of our cultural forms and at the same time placing into perspective the leading thinking of the day in the African American community. Thus, his forays into art and music as well as into the meaning of Booker T. Washington's concentration on industrial education made *The Souls of Black Folk* one of the most important works by an American in the twentieth century.

When the book was written, African Americans had been just thirty-eight years in physical freedom from enslavement. Our mental enslavement, in a sense, had only just begun because even in the twenty-first century there are indications of mental dislocation and psychological displacement. Some African Americans have, in effect, become victims of their own self-contempt and can write books suggesting their appreciation for the enslavement. When Keith Richburg wrote *Out of America* (1997) he showed how confused African Americans could be. The year 2005 is forty years from the death of Malcolm X, the preeminent proponent of black consciousness. DuBois wrote *The Souls of Black Folk* just twenty-six years after the collapse of Reconstruction. This juxtaposition shows how brief the time was between the end of Reconstruction and DuBois and how far we are from Malcolm X. As a product of its time, a statement of hope, *The Souls of Black Folk* was a timely book, one meant to underscore the coming to be of a people, not so much as Booker T. Washington's *Up from Slavery* had been, but more fundamentally as a book that captured the soul, in DuBois's own words, of the African American people.

It was forward thinking of him to use the phrase "Black Folk" in 1903 when most African Americans were still frightened of the term, much like many are frightened of the term "Afrocentric" today. DuBois knew or believed that in time there would be a transformation in the people's conception of themselves. It was almost a Darwinian notion that "progress" would have to come to the descendents of enslaved persons just as it came to others.

Possibly DuBois's German education directed him toward the

grand idealism of a national spirit for the African American people. It was DuBois's understanding of the nature of peoplehood, the pathway to being adequate within one's own framework of being, that brought him to this point of view. There was the profound sense that justice demanded movement, change—that is, transformation toward a more humanistic conception of the world. Africans were no longer simply the products of white people but were black people with our own "souls" in the DuBoisian construction. We had to assume the burden of our own souls and to take flight within the limits of our destiny. Of course, DuBois would be followed by a host of authors such as Benjamin Brawley (1937) who would contend that "the Negro genius" was equal to that of any other race. In DuBois's own construction of a defense of the race, however, one would see his firm conviction in crushing the racist arguments for white domination.

Undoubtedly, it is from his German education that DuBois came to believe in the Hegelian idea of "souls" or "spirits" of nations. So powerful had been the idea of the German *spirit* as an essential marker of distinction in the writing of many German scholars that DuBois was mightily influenced to arrive at some notion of the African spirit, particularly as it resided in the collective sense of consciousness of the African American.

In this way of thinking, he had been a precursor voice to the Negritude philosophers—Léopold Senghor, Aimé Césaire, and Léon Damas—who would find later a need to express in French the difference between the African culture and that of the European. Senghor would make an unfortunate comment to the effect that "reason is European, emotion is black" and set back the philosophical advancement of the Negritude movement. His simplification of the cultural contexts would disrupt black thought and create friction between Francophone and Anglophone Africans. Wole Soyinka would misunderstand the nature of the Negritude movement by virtue of Senghor's dictum and offer his own dictum to the effect that a "tiger does not declare its tigertude." Of course, a tiger makes no declaration whatsoever; it is only humans who can consciously declare something. Nevertheless, the Negritude school had shot itself in the foot and could never regain the momentum it promised.

The presence of African students in Paris had been a provocative statement and symbol that Africans were ready to reassume their place in the discourse on culture. But since Negritude was simply an aesthetic and literary movement, it could have no overall impact on the economic, political, and cultural conditions of the African people. It would take a more inclusive theory to impact the totality of the African experience.

I believe that because DuBois had a disciplined historical mind he avoided some of the mistakes of the African and African American literati. His commentaries were made with an eye to chronology and facts, allowing him to provide for his readers a more intelligent way of grasping the evolution of the African American "soul" in the midst of a white supremacist state. He is clearly encouraged by the attitude of the African in America. There is nothing unclear about his position on the significance and magnificence of the cultural achievements of a mistreated and resilient people. While he did not conceive of a theoretical viewpoint that explained the possibility of reenforcing an African perspective, he did interrogate the historical and sociological issues that were at the root of black oppression.

In his mind what could be any more classic than the great master songs, the spirituals, and who could be any more beautiful than the African woman? There was always in his writings the necessity to defend the humanity of Africans since such enmity had been built against our existence. The times called forth a heroic rhetorician capable of expressing in words what black people genuinely lived. The beauty, grace, and strength of the long-suffering masses emerge from DuBois's prose, and the reader is looking straight into the face of a people full of gravity of manner but who also possess considerable flexibility and ease of humor.[3]

There was in DuBois's stance toward African Americans a considerable admiration for the way the masses of people had stood against the imposition of racism.[4] What people could have maintained their lives during so many pogroms, massacres, lynchings, and what he called in 1903 the "holocaust of violence" against Africans? Yet maintenance was not enough and the people's soul did not rest with simple survival; it thrived with arts, education, and culture. If there was evidence of backwardness, so much of it had to be laid at the door of religion. No people had ever saved themselves by choosing the religion of their oppressors. DuBois understood this and his understanding of it caused him to mistrust the preachers and the churches that sought to "save the souls" of black folk while leaving their bodies exposed to economic exploitation and political manipulation. He once walked out of a chapel at Wilberforce College when asked to give a public prayer. Of course he lost his job, but his vision was always clear on the nature of religion as a restraint on the freedom of the mind (Broderick 1959).

Finally, DuBois knew what we all come to know, sooner or later, as Africans in America, that our past, however shallow or deep, leads back to the West African savannas and forests. Deep cultural responses to the environment created the context for songs that spoke of the intense relationship of Africans with resistance, survival, and transformation (Fisher 1990). This was connected to the pathos of the Middle Passage and the African continent. Therefore, this is not to deny our recent history or to cast aspersions on anyone else's past but to state a fact for African Americans. Running away from the past has meant the death of our souls. Thus, what DuBois did in *The Souls of Black Folk* was to set in motion the inevitable Afrocentric transformation that would occur in the latter part of the twentieth century. Indeed, a new reality was invoked; a new vision was introduced. In fact, it became the first and only reality for African people in America; it was simply rediscovery. Our eyes became new, or rather what we saw became clearer. Already we have seen the explosion of Afrocentricity in every walk of life affecting African people. The arts, education, architecture, communication studies, psychology, science, information technology, symbolism, and spirituality are just a few of the areas where this consciousness has invaded our spaces as measures of recovery. Discovery, in this case, leads directly to recovery. We are inheritors of a new future, one not predicted by those who, at the turn of the twentieth century, sought our death.

NOTES

1. It was considered by many to be an essay in defense of the African American people.

2. See Asante and Mattson (1998) for a discussion of the terror of lynching.

3. It had barely been thirty years from the time of the great betrayal when the North had allowed the Southern whites to regain power over the black masses, and those who had longed for their "chilluns" who had been sent to different regions of the country during the enslavement gathered to sing the songs of optimism and tell the stories that poked fun at the masters. DuBois knew these people; he had seen their resilience in the South and he had paid homage to them in Tennessee and Georgia. There was no question about their flexibility and survivability.

4. DuBois saw these people as "sturdy, uncouth country folk, good natured and simple, talkative to a degree, and yet far more silent and brooding than the crowds of the Rhine-pfalfz, or Naples, or Cracow. They drink considerable quantities of whiskey, but do not get very drunk, they talk and laugh loudly at times, but seldom quarrel or fight" (DuBois, 1903).

chapter 2
DE-RACING THE MEDIA

A nation is not merely the aggregation of individuals within given borders. Nor is a nation simply the political institutions that govern a society. Indeed, to know *this* American nation one must ask questions of origin. What is necessary to create a nation? Are there organic conditions that secure a national will?

The answer to these questions also touches on what makes a society hold together. It seems to me that the real task for those who wish for a cohesive future of the nation must be the utilization of the media at our disposal to continue the creation of nation. A nation is not a static idea. It must be dynamic, ongoing.

The United States today is not what it was one hundred years ago, and it will not be same one hundred years from now. So the process of creating the United States of America, at the level of the people, involves finding in the multiplicity of cultures and histories the most useful commonalities among us. They must emerge, not be imposed; they may not represent one or the other ethnic group but must be seen to represent shared values and sentiments that establish bonds of respect and honor. Indeed, these must be values that one is willing to give up personal possession and even life to maintain for the rest of the society.

History seems to teach us that nations are ultimately the creations of the rhetorical and historical processes that constitute groups with common visions. Here we are on the verge of understanding something about the nature of the American nation. It is not by blood alone that nations are created, but something more authentic, more genuine, more lasting than blood; nations are founded ultimately on the commonly shared spiritual and emotional experiences of a people. It is not even by rationality that nations are created. They often have common responses to social, economic, political, and cultural conditions. Those entities are maintained, that is, sustained by cultural symbols and ritualized behaviors supported by the apparatus of media. The African American response to nation is no different.

Over the past four hundred years this creative ritualized process has been at work within the context of ever-present doctrines of white cultural domination, often adopted consciously, to advance white superiority. This has complicated the creation of the nation. It means that the media that sustains this ideology must be de-racialized. To an extent, the attempt to dominate and suppress the African population has made a reaction formation necessary, although this reaction has often been the leading edge of the national energy of the African American people. What I mean is that the 246 years of enslavement and the nearly 150 years of discrimination created, inter alia, a people, a nation, out of the various African ethnic groups that were initially brought to the English colonies, and this people has been made into a collective body, fundamentally united against racism. Lewis Gordon is correct to state that "race has emerged, throughout its history, as the question fundamentally of 'the blacks' as it has for no other group" (Gordon 2000, 12). The implications of this concentrated energy are numerous, but one stands out in the creation of nation. On a mass scale, spiritual and emotional experiences are always nation-creating phenomena; this is the reality of the African American situation. From Martin Delany, one of the founders of Black Nationalism, to Michael Dawson, one of the chroniclers of the political landscape among African Americans, intellectuals have always known that the collective reality of the group experience could not be overcome simply by individual examples of psychological or economic escape.

Prior to this American experience, African Americans were

Yoruba, Sherbro, Wolof, Mandinka, Ibo, Ewe, Asante, Congo, Baule, Ga, and so forth, but with the meshing of the different ethnicities into a common situation vis-à-vis the productive and expressive energies of the American society, these groups became one group: black people. Whether mixed with whites or Indians, the African American people saw themselves as one people by virtue of the emotional and spiritual experiences maintained by the rituals of society.

There were no black people in Africa; there were only the various ethnic groups. There were no white people in Europe, only nationalities—German, French, Irish, and so forth—as it has always been. The ideology of white privilege over blacks in the United States made whiteness possible as a people but created also blackness as a people. White racial domination as expressed by the racist media in an aggressive stance against Africans promoted the notion of race and elevated the idea as an essentialist characteristic, a condition unknown among Africans, of white people. Nation meant, for the votarists of such a view, white nation. Almost all categorization of Africans in America was the function of a white system of privilege. Hence, ideas such as "minority," "disadvantaged," and "cultural or social deprivation" are conceptually the products of white thinkers.[1]

A ready capacity to set the political and cultural agenda through rhetorical discourse made it possible for the American people to produce marginalized people of Africans and therefore to encourage the separateness that now is disparaged. Preachers, teachers, professors, and journalists used the logic of race to establish whites as both separate and superior to the African population. That whites were separate and different, no one doubted, but Africans struggled mightily from the beginning against the corrupt notion that difference meant that whites were better.[2]

The contemporary political and economic situation of black folk developed in relation to the rhetoric of privilege in a way that could not have been anticipated by even the genius of W. E. B. DuBois. The discourse about race, racism, white privilege, and white domination has permeated the media. Unquestionably, DuBois had an impact on African American identity apart from the media of his day. We became *Negroes* after *The Souls of Black Folk* and quickly turned to *Colored People* and then to *Afro-Americans* and then to *Black* and *African Americans* almost simultaneously. All of these changes in nomenclature referred to the same objective group of people. Our economic or political situations did not immediately change because there was a change in the language of our identity. Nevertheless, we understood, as expressed by our opinion makers and thinkers, that it was necessary to change the way we perceived ourselves in order to raise a new level of consciousness about what we could do for ourselves.

In a similar vein, African American philosophers have always seen the need for a constructive engagement with the media, contending that we must have a new relationship with ourselves before there could be a positive relationship with the media. We are the arbiters of our stories, the tellers of the tales, the makers of the myths, and whenever we leave these functions to the protectors of white privilege, we see the confusion in the African American population, political backtracking among white politicians, and ignorance in the general public. What is more damaging, however, is the lack of ethics in relationship to a common humanity (see Karenga 1990).

Any new relationship to the media, like much of the old, would have to be mediated by television, books, articles, CDs, and movies. Arguments would be advanced, criticized, debated, and made a part of the ongoing discourse about the nature, not just of the African American but also of American society. But at this level of debate African Americans would engage the discourse around identity with understanding of the critical need for transformation. We would create out of our own condition and situation a new approach to ethics, society, and values that would overcome many of the racial and social obstacles to community.

McLuhan's Table

I once had dinner with Marshall McLuhan, the twentieth-century media guru and author of *Understanding Media* (1994), in an old ornate Mexican restaurant in the city of Monterey. We had been invited in the late 1970s by the Monterey Institute of Technology to discuss communication and media for the next decade. I was teaching communication at the State University of New York at Buffalo and Jorge Garcia, the coordinator of the conference, had spent a summer studying with me. So when he got back to Monterey, Mexico, where he was teaching, he organized a remarkable international conference with Canadian, American, and Mexican participants.

At dinner and in the presence of a couple of Mexican graduate students, McLuhan (I was sitting across the table from him), with his dark eyes looking down the avenue of his angular face, leaned forward and teased me with a question, "Molefi, what do you see on the table?"

I meditated momentarily on the array of cutlery, bowls, plates, salt and pepper shakers, glasses, napkins, and a couple of ballpoint pens and said triumphantly, "Human creations, instruments for service and personal use."

McLuhan loved the pun, aphorisms, teasers, puzzles, and anything out of the ordinary. I had heard him in the 1970s in his seminar at the University of Toronto during the visit of Paulo Freire, and I knew that something was up his sleeve. He said, "That's not what I see." Then he paused, a great long pause, a beckoning sort of pause, like, ask me what I see. "What do you see Professor McLuhan?" I took the bait.

"I see a multitude of people, the army, the bureaucrats, black people, white people, Mexicans, rich and poor people, short and tall people. Look at the table, can't you see that the arrangement is almost martial, but it has infinite metaphorical possibilities for peace, racial harmony?"

Politics and the media are conjoined to produce a conundrum of the spirit in our most ordinary lives. We are all stimulated by this combination of the media and race, connected and intertwined, by the groans for personal and national engagement around race. But we are not helpless. Like diners around a table of food, we are eagerly eyeing the most appealing condiments of culture, waiting to gobble them up. Race has always been the most difficult piece of our history for white Americans to digest. The reason for this has a lot to do with the feeling of guilt. I don't believe for one minute that we would need to discuss race so much if whites would simply admit the wrong that they have done to black and other people. We could move beyond the falsification of data, the distortion of images, the hiding behind myths, and the managing of the news that have come to constitute the most powerful tools in the arsenal of racism. But whites fear the admission of any guilt because it would mean that they would have to act differently.

Of course, the issue in the media has become the effective management of the technologies of communication in an era of quickening cyberspace change and transcultural and transcontinental interactions. What can we do to transform the management of the technologies as well as to provide new content? We live with an incredible aura of preposterous science fiction that influences the major social and political decisions of our daily lives, from new forms of address to cellular worlds away from wires and the old technology of mechanics. And now that the genome scientists have conquered the complete human genome, giving us an entire genetic code, we have edged closer to knowing who we are genetically, what we can do to conquer diseases, and how related we really are to each other. Indeed, we are on the verge of a much more preposterous science.

The tall, gangly McLuhan would have called this the era of digital charisma. I am able to see the dramatic pace of the changes as I walk through any airport in the world or down the Champs Élysées or Michigan Avenue or Walnut Street and see my fellow travelers using their cell phones as easily as a generation ago people used their watches. This is the real flesh of history in the making. As such, it is the time of technological interfaces between human beings with their palm pilots and other accessories of postmodernity. As products of a new cultural and communication climate, we are in the process of adjusting our psychological thermostats to reflect the new social situation abruptly upon us. It now becomes essential to know exactly how all media transforms our attitudes and behaviors. Otherwise we are lost amid the influx of media magic, victims of electronic Houdinism.

It is as clear to me now as ever that those who control the instruments of communication also control political power. There have rarely been cases in world history where the two were separated for long. Political power is image-making power because politics is like a giant assembly line in that whatever is placed on the conveyor belt is touched or tampered with by those who shape public opinion. The combination of the media and computers will reorient our thinking about all kinds of politics within the next century.

What any of us think about New York City, Abidjan, a Palestinian state, French politics, globalization, Afrocentricity, or Japanese schools is to a large extent a factor of where our ideas were touched by the agenda setters. But we cannot look for people in blue or gray suits as the agenda setters. There are no conspiracies in this regard except the conspiracy of a system set in motion to operate like a time machine moving inexorably ahead. Thus we stereotype others and by our stereotypes create prisons that keep some in and others out. The universal attachment of names to our attitudes, beliefs, and values has made communication more difficult to achieve while simultaneously making it easier for researchers to operationalize their studies. Furthermore, the political influences of the media are clouded by our views of politics, politicians, and the political process. So much of what we think of these aspects of our national life are mediated and influenced by media managers who may not even be known. I can now read many books written ostensibly by the author whose name appears on the book cover only to later discover that the name on the book cover did not write the book. In fact, the name on the book may have recorded a narrative that was then written by someone whom I will never know—at least, I will never know the name of the person. Image making is the largest commercial trade going on at this time.

Mass images are the clues to how we see others and ourselves. Show me an image and I can tell you something about its maker and the audience for whom it is made. In the United States, people of African descent have waged heroic battles against the pseudotheories of race, origin of man, evolution, nature of intelligence, and the doctrine of white supremacy. Such is also the case with Indians in Peru, Mexico, and Bolivia, and oppressed people everywhere. But these are often losing battles because we do not control the instruments of communication. How do you change the image of Africa today?

The African American has had hundreds of years of stout propaganda hostile to African identity that has corrupted the national consciousness and created feelings of inferiority in many African Americans. Designed to buttress the feelings of white racial supremacy, such hostile propaganda contributed to psychological dislocation and cultural disorientation among blacks. Communication has been and is being used culturally and politically to define the African American reality, indeed, even to dictate the nature of the African American identity. I know from my own experiences that to deal with ontological identity in this age of multiple consciousnesses requires a new response to the media of communication. There is a history to this problem.

When the first American announcements advertising Africans as slaves were made and the notices nailed to posts and placed in small gazettes, the use of the media as an American instrument to stereotype Africans had arrived. Only with the understanding of the media's delinquent past will we be able to erase much of the previous markings on the intellectual and social pages of US history.

It goes without saying that many people have fought an incessant struggle against racism in America because the history of the country is one in which racial minorities have been oppressed and suppressed and the most heroic national activity ought to be antiracism. The great presidents of this nation have always been on the side of the downtrodden, and despite the temporary popularity of those who counsel against human rights, they will not be remembered as great leaders of social transformation. Moral leadership is always tricky, but in the arena of race in America we are threatened by the lack of leaders who see racism as an ethical problem rather than as a mere nuisance of the personality.

Antiracism, not war, is genuinely the American contribution to heroism. This is why David Walker remains an icon of revolutionary thought. This is why John Brown lingers in the American soul as the conscience of a people thrusting about for direction. This is why Lucretia Mott's name and fame resound even till this day in the suburbs of Philadelphia. If we African Americans have been able to prevent the total devouring of our labor, the exploitation of our minds and bodies, the extermination of our culture, it has been because we have appealed to the common documents of the nation. What is it that constitutes community anyway if it is not common values, common symbols, and common struggles?

These are documents that are often disputed and challenged by those who would deny the call for diversity and acceptance of all nationalities and races into the American body politic. Racism prevails regardless of the efforts of the heroes of diversity and will, so long as victims remain (Bell 1992). Although Derrick Bell warned of the permanence of racism, it is still worthwhile for us to consider renegotiation of the national compact so that victims disappear.

What is called for is the complete reorientation of the media on the question of racism. This cannot be accomplished apart from a thorough societal transformation, which means it is a people problem. If it cannot be achieved, and there is ample doubt, then we are doomed to endless bitterness wrought by the clash of cultures and philosophies. Our task is to set right what we know, that is, to do right what we know.

I believe that the elimination of racial discrimination is one thing but the elimination of racism is altogether something different and must be tackled in the front yard. This is the media issue. Whenever racism raises its head, it must be smashed, not just by black people, but by all people in American society. Arriving at this point—that is, the point where blacks and whites are closer to each other's perspective on the critical discourses of the day—will be difficult, but it can be achieved with constant debate and discussion. I do not believe that this nation is permanently stuck in the frame of two nations, however much it appears that way when we discuss issues like O. J. Simpson, Kobe Bryant, affirmative action, or reparations.

Eradication of the images caused by the manipulation of the early gazettes, broadsides, pamphlets, and other media in America is no easy task.

After seeing the Stephen Spielberg movie *Amistad*, I had the impression that nothing would ever be able to change the image of Africans as dependent upon the good graces of whites. There is limited African agency in this film. Once again a movie about a black revolt on the high seas turns on the benevolence of whites who remained for all other purposes wedded to a system of privilege that espoused the infe-riority of Africans. What makes it possible for a good filmmaker to make a bad film when it comes to black people? I believe that it is the society itself that dictates the way the filmmaker will respond to the artistic and entertainment environment. There could not have been a movie about black men revolting against white people who sought to enslave them without the benevolence of some white man. There would not have been a place of entry for the white audience in America. This we know, from Spike Lee's beautiful film *Malcolm X*, is important because whites do not like to see serious films about racism that do not have points of entry for them. It is not the art but the entertainment value that is significant to the white audiences in these cases.

However, it remains for Africans in a contemporary sense to accept the African past.[3] Such acceptance will produce an unprece-dented era of African American cultural, political, and economic pro-ductivity, and it will help to change the nature of interracial relations.

The acceptance of Africa by African Americans is social pressure because the acceptance of Africa—not merely as symbol, but as his-toric fact—is the single most important happening in the African American experience. Even if one rejects Africa, it remains the most important element in the life of the African American person, because the rejection itself is a testimony of the loss of place. There are other important realities, to be sure, but as an intellectual concept nothing has equaled, nor can equal, the singularity of this fact. It is the one fact that we have heretofore refused to accept, and its truth has been denied so frequently that even now there are faint reactions against it.

Not only will this acceptance transform social life in the United States, but it will concretely and substantively alter the quality of life on the African continent. Media responses to socioevolutionary processes and acceptance of Africa will rival the transformation that moved us from a rural to an urban society on this continent.

To begin to understand this phenomenon it is necessary to recog-nize its characteristics and to chart its effects. The first task requires attention to immediate description; the latter requires perhaps a bit of prophecy. But in neither case is the fact so obscure as to distort our perception.

Newspapers and books created a sort of African American fatalism and produced what W. E. B. DuBois properly understood in his time not as double consciousness but as our spiritual strivings against the African holocaust. It is precisely the rejection of this negation that must be achieved by a more perfect communication. The media are the barometers to acceptance and rejection of images. This knowledge is the source of concentrated skill and disciplined productivity, socially and intellectually, and African Americans must always seek to minimize our contradictions to Afrocentricity by capturing the initiative against marginality. For me to say "initiative against marginality" implies making some first steps or taking aggressive action to gain sanity, to fight back insanity, to lift the veil.

The idea that African Americans could be integrated into America by becoming whiter was a monstrous lie. Even as a child growing up in the verdant regions of the Deep South I did not believe it, but I knew too many people who did. They felt if they were lighter in complexion, even to the point of bleaching their skin, they would be more acceptable. They believed that if they "processed" their kinky hair and talked "proper" English they would be more acceptable to whites. It was all a lie in the first place. Our rejection, persecution, and oppression by whites had little to do with us, which means that there was nothing that we could do to change it. It was preeminently a problem of white people's psychology. This had been the predominant theme of the abolitionists during the enslavement in the nineteenth century, and later in the twentieth it had emerged again with the liberals during the civil rights era.

European Americans have always been divided on the question of African participation in America, and so very early different whites were expounding different doctrines about participation. In my community as a child I knew some Africans who underwent a metamorphosis from African to European in their minds and thus assumed Americanization like the settlers from Europe. All they had to do was to forgo Africanism in fashion, habits, styles, language, and politics. Few whites were fooled by this alchemy. Yet there was a tradition to this type of transformation that went back to the days of slavery.

During the period of slavery, political leaders and academics expounded this theory of racial transformation through print and by platform. Even abolitionists such as Benjamin Lundy and Wendell Phillips preached of a time when blacks would assume their places, after passing through the whitewashing machines, alongside whites. Abolitionists participated in another form of robbery. Their robbery of the African was paternalistic; they would dispense with Africa and Africanity to make Africans acceptable to the European majority. Thus when Africans assumed white habits, language, customs, dress, and modes of operation—that is, the more white and less African they became—the more American they would be and thereby more acceptable.

This was not only a lie; it was a mystery. In some quasi-magical way Africans would be knighted with whiteness and made Americans. The truth is that we blacks believed that myth more than we believed the voices of Martin Delany, Edward Blyden, Marcus Garvey, and Henry Turner. The media had propagandized us well to believe the lie because not to believe meant we had to accept Africa. Such acceptance was difficult and nearly impossible. We found our images of Africa to be negative products of the media. Christianity with its parading missionaries had taught us that Africans were heathens; we, that is, ordinary African Americans, had not yet come to know of the ancient African kingdoms of Egypt, Nubia, Kush, Zimbabwe, Mali, Songhay, and Ghana.

Tripped by our own ignorance, the images of the white media held us down. For this reason acceptance of Africa was difficult and almost impossible for us. Compounding the mystery was the limited knowledge whites had of Africans and the African past despite centuries of interaction with the continent. If one imagined what whites of the eighteenth and nineteenth centuries knew about Africa and then imagined what their enslaved Africans knew about it, the near impossibility of the African American to accept Africa as a positive place is understandable. We desired to be American in the fashion of the European American. Such desire was not unique to us because people from eastern and southern Europe were willing to shed their customs, languages, and names in order to be more perfectly fitted for the American society. Africans, too, stepped into this arena, and when all the participants had been chosen, we alone stood in the center of the arena as unchosen, nonparticipants. Our uniqueness was only in our separateness. This separateness nurtured strength. Whatever manifestation of power ventured from this separateness was to be a rejection of fatalism.

Black Power was therefore an attack on fatalism. To say attack is to underscore the violence inherent in such declaration. Kwame Toure, then Stokely Carmichael, made a historic discovery with his call for "Black Power." That discovery was that words could transform people as they perceived themselves as powerful and acted upon that belief (Carmichael and Hamilton 1967). When whites reacted negatively against the concept because they identified it with violence, they understood more than they knew. While it did not necessarily mean physical violence as many had supposed, it did mean the death of fatalism. To bring about the end of a tradition we renounced cultural paternalism in order to create cultural maturity. Don't call me "boy" and don't call me "uncle" were signs that the revolution had finally come home.

The sixties were the surreal dramatic stage upon which all verbs were played out. In a typical thievery of irony, white-controlled media attempted to show that Maulana Karenga, the eloquent philosopher of cultural maturity and creator of Kwanzaa, was insane. His pronouncements were indications that blacks intended to be actors, no longer simply acted upon. The stage became total action in our own acceptance of ourselves; self-definition is a verb. When a suppressed people seize the communication advantage by the exploitation of new arrangements of images, they are on their way to cultural maturity. Such knowledge was not merely unusual but judged to be insane as well.

The political situation of the first part of the twentieth century demanded the most agile intellectual feats to explain why many of us believed the black-into-white evolutionary theory of society. The brilliant book *The Souls of Black Folk* made a remarkable place for DuBois, establishing him as one of the most often quoted thinkers of the twentieth century. But the duality he expressed has caused the grossest errors in interpreting black presence in American society.

The description is adequate in its psychological implications if the duality itself was indeed an unavoidable condition as DuBois argued. However, the inadequacy of the description results from a lack of understanding of the role of communication in the shaping of attitudes and the forming of opinions. Simply put, there can be no dilemma of duality as the DuBoisians would have it. The most that can be said for it is that it was an adequate and precise intellectual interpretation of what could happen to African Americans who believed media propaganda.

Breaking the grip of fatalism or any other psychological illness takes a determined countermovement of symbols. This was the symbolic meaning of Watts, of Newark, of Detroit on a mass scale, and the Afro hairstyle on an individual level. In fact, there are no limits to its manifestation. The coming to terms with welfare, black-on-black crime, victim psychosis, and narcotics is the resolve to renounce dependencies and change images. Thus when the Crips and the Blackstone Rangers in Chicago resolved to paint houses instead of holding rumbles, they had defined a new image. Nevertheless, fatalism can be broken only by separation, which is inherently violent. Resolve is the first action. As the addict who would be unhooked can find no easy-off solution but must have a separation, which is the essence of violence, so a people cannot jive out of fatalism. It does not, nor will it, simply happen. One makes it happen. The politics of communication means that the possibilities for changing the grounds of community are held by the people themselves.

The fires of Western paternalism and racism have been fed by columnists, writers, academics, and in recent times the creators of television dramas. African American communities frequently adjust to those sentiments as expressed by the media. Adjustment is the sine qua non of fatalism. For us African Americans, adjustment is a direct result of belief in the view that the closer we approach whites in color, customs, language, and so on, which means the less African we are, the more acceptable we will become to European Americans. This intellectual madness led to the most sustained period of mental adjustment in American history.

NOTES

1. See the introduction in Ama Mazama, ed., *The Afrocentric Paradigm* (Trenton: Africa World Press, 2002).

2. Remi Kapo has written an insightful analysis of this notion of superiority in his book, *A Savage Culture* (London: Quartet Books, 1981). Of the British insistence on white superiority over the black, Kapo says, "Britain's blithe spirit, grounded in condescension, is being demolished brick by brick. With black equality, of every kind slapping him in the face, his (the British) new question is, 'If this savage is as talented as I am, then what have I been all along?'"

3. This is the point of my book *Afrocentricity* (2003a). The only way that African Americans can advance is to have an appreciation of the past to the degree that we accept our ancestors' attempt to change their reality. America produces memory lapses ad nauseam. This is something that must be fought.

chapter 3
TROUBLE AT THE GATE
Identity Crisis

The year 1816 was the most critical year in the history of African identity in America. Such were the political and economic twists of events that during that year several influential whites got the idea that Africans should be returned to Africa. And thus they formed the American Colonization Society. The free Africans' negative response, though understandable, was also lamentable for several reasons. In the first place, it fueled the smoldering fires of white supremacy, the cousin to white paternalism. Second, it was an acceptance of social and cultural fatalism. Third, it produced the most pronounced brainwashing that had ever been perpetrated on Africans in America. The overpowering penetration of false conceptions about Africa and African Americans is one example of a sustained campaign to obliterate the actual truth of a situation and to alter a nation's perceptions. While it is true as they say that we survived, it is arguable whether our survival could have been positively better had our ancestors known how to counteract the negative media.

Survival is often an immediate activity. A person makes his accord with the powers and principalities on the terms presented to him in the manner he can best afford. Nevertheless, the response of Africans in America toward the creation of the American Colonization Society in 1816 was to initiate perhaps the most serious flaw in African American political and cultural history.

A nation's use of every available means of persuasion to convince an audience, a specific audience, to accept a certain perspective is awesome. At another level the use of all channels available to an organization can also be powerful. The American Colonization Society was resisted by blacks. The resistance was an empty victory. Every conceivable abolitionist supported the idea, and so did politicians and editors. Blacks in positions of influence refused to accept the proposal even though it had been expounded through every communication channel.

How did the tough resistance of Africans to the philanthropic intentions of whites in the American Colonization Society support white supremacist ideas? It did so by rejecting the idea that blacks were capable of maintaining a colony in Africa. Peter Williams and James Forten called a mass meeting of free blacks in Philadelphia in 1817 to oppose the colonization scheme. Whatever the real reasons for opposition, they gave the following as reasons: (1) emancipation is presently proceeding; (2) the slave is not fitted by habit to maintain a government; (3) the slave owners would send their most belligerent slaves and retain the most servile; (4) it would stretch the bonds of brotherhood across the sea; and (5) it would take too long (Smith 1969). The mass meeting adopted these reasons as valid for opposition and went on record to fight repatriation at every opportunity. Leading abolitionists were afraid to support the American Colonization Society for fear Americans would be offended. One segment of the abolitionist movement, white, had accepted the proposal; the other, black, had rejected it.

When one analyzes the reasons given for opposing colonization, it becomes clear that these were only superficial reasons supporting a much more basic belief about Africa. It was an acceptance of fatalism. Africans had, after 198 years, been beguiled by the overpowering media to believe that acceptance into American society was possible if no traces of Africa remained. These nineteenth-century African Americans' vision was futuristic, and somewhat naive, but they had faith, like their peers of that era, in the perfectibility of man generally and of whites and blacks in America particularly. The whites would adhere to the edicts, sacred documents, and moral doctrines of their divines and holies; and the blacks would become increasingly white—

thus both groups would arrive at their respective perfectibility. The truth, of course, has been frequently told. Man's perfectibility is at best relative. In the case of most people, the stuff in the books and even in the spirit is not necessarily translated into action. On the other hand, those of us who accepted the myth could never really fulfill its demands. And if we partially fulfilled them, we became unwitting participants in white racism because we believed, like the bigoted whites, that unless blacks whitened in speech and habits they could never achieve acceptability in white America. Thus, in rejecting one white proposal such blacks unwittingly accepted another.

Consistent with their own view of the American social context, some of these blacks embarked upon the most determined propaganda movement in African American history. Their endeavor was to convince Americans that blacks were not Africans. The lament begins with the free blacks in the North (not slaves in the field), who vigorously insisted that they were not Africans but colored Americans. This is the beginning of DuBois's dilemma.

The result of this media declaration has been to compromise the black masses. Those blacks who moved according to their perceptions renounced Africa and started the treadmill of the dilemma. Until this period blacks had been content with and considerably proud of their Africanness. As a consequence, from 1619 to 1817 many organizations and fellowships had been formed encouraging this Africanity.

There was the establishment of the African Free School in New York City, the African Benevolent Societies, and various African lodges and brotherhoods. The most remarkable achievement during this period was the beginning of the African Methodist Episcopal (AME) Church by Richard Allen in 1793. The AME remains one of the oldest effective organizations in African America and at one time was the principal supplier of teachers, preachers, and lawyers.

A parade of outstanding bishops with fiery temperaments made the AME the seat of protest. My contention is that Richard Allen's response to the white Methodist church's refusal to allow him and his followers to pray is indicative of the contemporary rejection of some white standards and values by African Americans. This means that despite the press and the pressure to the contrary, Allen drew upon his separateness from the whites to find his strength. Once accomplished, he had discovered, as others had before and many would afterward, that disparagement of Africa is not necessary for a healthy psyche; instead, rejection of ancestral heritage can constitute an adherence to fatalism, which could actually be a form of *menticide*, the killing of the mind.

It is no wonder libations are poured even today by some African Americans as a proper gesture in memory of our ancestors. What had been arranged by the collective power of the media of the day was nothing less than the complete obliteration of Africanity. Thus Richard Allen's rejection is neither a rejection of the press nor of America but rather a strike against injustice perpetrated by false images and distorted perceptions. He could never accept European America as absolute teacher. Allen's adjustment was made in the name of his church, African Methodist Episcopal. It was made distinctive by "African" in the title and by adjusting the classical European Methodist liturgy to express the black lifestyle. So what develops is a denial and rejection of European American tendencies that are contrary to the African personality. Therefore, to reject fatalism it is only necessary for us to deny those symbols that are antithetical to our person. It is actually the case with anyone who seeks liberation.

Numerous symbols in American society (which are the result of a symbolic hegemony over other races by European Americans) have to be rejected by African Americans. This is the true minimizing of contradictions. Indeed, it is the only way African Americans can find sanity within society; otherwise it means a rejection of one's self—self-hatred, anomie, nihilism, death.

Richard Allen's response was, in fact, *a rejection to rejection*; he sought an alternative to European American churches and started what became an African American church. He could argue as he did that his church was not European because Christianity was a world religion. He would not accept white governance or religious guidance; his was an independent black-controlled fellowship. It is conceivable, however, that so long as blacks and whites share the same geography, institutions will be proposed to reflect that geographical sharing. But for Richard Allen such was not his choice. It had been dictated by white power as expressed in a racist religion and upheld by the communication monopoly controlled by the same power. Allen did not see his church as an oppositional alternative; that would not come until Elijah Muhammad in the twentieth century. What he did see, however, was the limited ability of the church to save anybody. Elijah would simply dispense with the church and try to conceive another vehicle for salvation only to find that it, too, was lacking in the necessary freedom.

There is no reason to burden this account with a total recount of black response to the media in America. It is, however, necessary to demonstrate the extent of the rhetorical efforts to indoctrinate African Americans in the rejection of the African past. When David Walker wrote his bitter antislavery document in 1829, twelve years after the Philadelphia mass meeting organized by the Reverend Peter Williams and James Forten, he chose to call it *An Appeal to the Colored Citizens of the World*. Why was the angriest pamphleteer in antebellum black history inclined to write to the colored citizens and not to the Africans? Probably because he had accepted the idea of blacks in America having a "colored" identity. This is not to say that Walker does not refer to blacks as Africans also, but the propaganda of free blacks was directed toward bettering the condition of persons living in the United States.

An African identity left a person open to the argument of the American Colonization Society that he should be sent back to Africa. When DuBois found his way to Africa late in his life, he was completing the journey that he set out upon in 1903. He did not see the end of his life in Ghana when he wrote *The Souls of Black Folk*, but there was within his own consciousness an overwhelming attraction to the continent of Africa, and his 1903 book was a shout in the direction of Africa.

Explorations of identity have been the themes of plays by August Wilson, Charles Fuller, and Ntozake Shange. Indeed Ntozake Shange's play *For Colored Girls Who've Considered Suicide/ When the Rainbow Is Not Enough* is instructive. It is not for African girls or black girls or African American girls; it is for girls whose personalities and identities are confused. Ntozake Shange's choice reflects the black American's dilemma in addressing audiences, particularly when the subjects are black people. Toni Morrison has made a career out of writing novels that interrogate the relationship of African people in America to identity, history, and each other.

The nineteenth-century blacks saw themselves in an American context, not as Africa's sons and daughters temporarily domiciled in a strange land. There was nothing so repelling to them than the insistence by some that they were Africans. Their sights were clear, but they seemed to be looking at the wrong object. What they hoped to achieve would have been, as time has shown, extremely expensive in psychical and physical suffering. More painful, as we now know, is the fact that the leaders of this propaganda against Africa were really peddling suicide. Liberation is never achieved by self-destructive methods.

They hoped to lop off the offending parts of themselves in a sort of what-you-need-what-you-get way. If it was their speech that offended whites, they would discontinue its use; if whites were offended by their clothes, they had to conform to white styles and colors; if they were offended by the black sensual swagger, the gait had to be modified, and some "members" even learned to yodel and forgot how to sing the spirituals because they wanted to be accepted. This was the death caused by the controlling use of the media. Furthermore, for us it is the legacy of the Philadelphia meeting of 1817.

The renunciation of Africanness was to be a progressive death; what was begun by the reaction to the American Colonization Society quickly careened through history touching every institution and twisting every concept so that in the end communication media presented both a distorted view of history and the existential situation. The blues were indicative of black fatalism. The more we believed, the sadder our songs became. Ma Rainey, Bessie Smith, Jasbo Brown, Leadbelly, and Billie Holiday wailed our blues into musical history. Poets reflected this sadness in poignant questions: Why do you make a poet black? Why do you hate me so? And so forth. Can you imagine Dead Prez, KRS One, or Common asking such questions? Perhaps they do not experience DuBois's dilemma because they have decided. To decide is to close the discussion by conscious action. There is always finality to a decision; even if one has to make another decision at another moment, the present decision is done.

Decision always prevails over ambivalence, and from it emerges the recharged response to contemporary media. Politics designs the communication theme and determines how much attention should be paid to what themes. A decisive rejection of white-dominated images of blacks has resulted in new fields of inquiry into art, religion, economics, and technology. Understanding the new grammar of the media must begin as a first step to accept the past as consciousness. Print and television media have become the godfathers of our most elemental desires and wishes. They organize our lives, set our agendas, define our standards of beauty, and teach our children to believe that the Greeks existed before the Chinese, Jews, or Egyptians. Even myths, presumably out of our own cultural soil, appear to be affected by media.

The myth of messianism as seen in black America is a direct descendant of the politics of communication operating within the community. Such a view, all encompassing in its present focus, is nothing more than the transformation of individual missions into collective ones. The messiah is mission oriented and feels a moral or suprarational need to deliver people. DuBois resisted the temptation to declare himself the African American savior. In fact, his unfortunate personal assaults on Marcus Garvey came because he believed Garvey represented the messianic spirit (Clarke 1974). Garvey's life was devoted to teaching Africans to love themselves; DuBois's life was dedicated to defending the humanity of Africans. They clashed on the best possible way to advance the cause of the African people. For DuBois, this could not be found in the messiah.

Our tenure in the United States is replete with acts of valor and individual sacrifice for the whole people. Few of these acts ever resulted in major victories, but their frequent happening is fact enough to demonstrate the internal thrust for group, and even national, salvation.

All *messianism* is pregnant with the idea of deliverance.[1] This means that there must be someone or something that is worthy of deliverance or at least so considered by the would-be deliverer. Our spokespersons have frequently indicated their sense of mission in the dynamism of their rhetorical style; their force of speech has given substance to hope for something better. To say "something better" is to indicate the source and origin of mission as a concept. In varying degrees and by different means, leaders have attempted to provide "something better" for the people at the expense of themselves. "Something better" is descriptive and comparative.

Messianism uses communication exceptionally well because it is concerned with present and future. Beyond that, however, it builds on the past because *messianism* is like an artificial environment, totally encompassing of its messiah. Those who do not understand mission may never understand *messianism.* We are programmed to react to missions and collective themes. The media organize us as audiences. The essence of all successful movements is emotionalism; and two of the most effective vehicles for emotionalism are powerful slogans and spokespersons with messianic complexes.

It is impossible to divorce the spirit from the body, the heart from the head. Thus we contend that the media show us for the first time the collectivization of mission, the acceptance by the black masses of a will to deliverance. This is, therefore, the translation of the messianic complex from an individual to a group concept.

Historically, the need to deliver the people motivated many Africans to rise up to kill their masters on the plantations. Usually these murders only involved the death of one or two white people, but the slave who was sure to die often could not control his urge to slay the oppressors, and, by so doing, if only for a short while, to become the deliverer. Mission was here internalized and individualized.

The most methodically conceived assassinations were those carried out by Nat Turner. When nearly sixty whites fell at the hands of Turner and his men, the event rearranged the symbols of security, and the South shook as never before. This marauding African believed that he was the vicar of vengeance sent to rid the earth of sin and devils. Such was his sense of direction that he said he had been chosen from the womb for the work of death carried out against whites around Jerusalem, Virginia. There were the telltale signs of his chosenness—the blood, the angels struggling, the den, and his extraordinary wisdom and intelligence. These were unmistakable signals that he was the chosen leader of the suffering people. He became the moment's Chaka.

Nat Turner exemplified the purest form of messianism. Chosenness is problematic with messiahs, and Turner was in direct contrast to those who had accepted fatalism as preached by the media. His situation spoke only one action, and no other conduct could adequately befit a person born into the disadvantages of enslavement and indoctrinated by the limited information he had received. Turner's acceptance of what he thought was the "call of Providence" was made possible by his limited communication environment.

In less dramatic fashion but in a similar sense, many other spokespersons have demonstrated messianic action as the resort of sanity. Failure to be chosen or to be self-choosing, which is really to be chosen, causes pain, and consistent invisibility leads to nothing but resignation, that is, fatalism. It is this power to determine choice, or to influence one's choosing, that separates the victors from the victims of the media. The reinforcing factors of personal acceptance and mass adherence are principal reasons for determined messianism. As a case in point, we can look at Marcus Garvey's Back to Africa movement (Cronon 1968).

What factors contributed to Garvey's messianism? The two forces working on the mission-oriented person are personal acceptance and mass public adherence. Mass public adherence is related to all the media of communication. Adherence presupposes a certain attraction. Without a belief in the efficacy of the person, which is tantamount to personal attraction, there can be no reinforcing of the messianic complex. Marcus Garvey received from his followers rigorous support for his personality appeals. He was king, emperor, president, and it was his mission to direct the African world toward its salvation. Thus the followers gave the kind of reassurance Garvey sought for his chosen role. He had asked himself, Where is the black man's government? Where is his army? Where is his president? and he had answered, I will lead them and I will build the government, the army, and the navy. Belief in himself was a prerequisite to his success as the chosen leader. Such self-belief had to do with his concept of mission. Did he believe in himself as chosen leader to perform a certain task? Further, did the task involve the deliverance of a people? Marcus Garvey answered both questions in the affirmative. In the first question we are concerned with personal capability, and in the second we are concerned with salvation. There is a third element that is not necessarily best put in question form, but which underlies the affirmative answer to the aforementioned questions. That element is the principle of divine selection. The messianic complex can be developed in conjunction with extraordinary events or feats or unique experiences or visions. Thus Nat Turner's call came in the fields with various signs indicating a suprarational wish for him to assume leadership. In Marcus Garvey's case it was his travels around South and Central America that convinced him of the need for a deliverer, but it was the response to those who heard him speak that convinced him of *his* chosenness to lead. Classically, Garvey convinced himself through his own rhetoric as well as convincing those who heard him. He was the mass propagandist believing and acting upon his own propaganda. His call for self-determination and self-definition was the basis for later nationalist rhetoric in the African American community. No one who had seen the condition of blacks in the banana plantations of Costa Rica or the sugar cane farms of Panama and Jamaica could disagree with Garvey's rational eloquence.

We may recall that Martin Luther King Jr. expressed his sense of mission in biblical terms: "I have seen the glory of the coming of the Lord." He had seen other things as well. At Selma and Montgomery he had seen the people mesmerized by his spoken words; at Albany he had lost a battle and yet because of television emerged an embattled but more legendary figure; and he had seen more than 250,000 people galvanized by his visionary rhetoric—so there was no reason for him not to believe in his chosenness as the spokesman of black America. The press had made him more than a spokesman; he was the leader.

In the twentieth century, King was perhaps the last of the great men with messianic complexes to stand out and beyond the masses as a directing star. His charisma, and that of Malcolm X, Kwame Toure, Maulana Karenga, and Huey Newton–Bobby Seale, made possible the transformation of individual purposes and missions into more collective missions for the African American people. We shared a collective messianic complex more than at any other time in history. The belief was that we were now capable of assertions for our salvation and ultimately salvation for the United States. Messianism always rises out of degradation. This makes it a fundamental necessity for oppressed people.

On the individual level, there are those who have internalized deliverance. They do not aspire to national reputations, nor yet to individual leadership or mass salvation, but only to the task of securing the betterment of their communities. They aspire to significant social and economic contributions. The media no longer seek them out and they no longer care to be sought out. The media are tired like old worn hats waiting to be unwrinkled by new owners.

This development is very much in line with the rejection of fatalism. When the history of this era is undertaken, it will be demonstrated that the collectivization of the messianic complex, a product of the media's rejection of the mass leader, gave rise to unparalleled cultural, intellectual, and political thought. And in its turn this evolution will stimulate the national life and will impact upon the African continent that has yet to find the solution to eroding factionalisms. More than anything, however, will the consequent intellectual power generated in African America be as a result of the rejection of fatalism.

A collective will—in this context, the will to mission—employs the best intention and capabilities of the people. No longer are the people's skills and energies appropriated for the defense of an impossible situation. The media will have restructured the symbols of the society to reflect the possible.

The African American's rejection of fatalism and the concomitant transcension of oppression means that the entire presenile American society could be reinvigorated. It has been my view that African Americans have demonstrated through the willingness to challenge the most sclerotic elements in the society that we can transcend oppression. Achieving self-respect as a member of a discriminated group is difficult but not impossible if one joins the assertion for freedom.

Racism is like a magic spell—it has to be perfectly maintained to have the proper demoralizing effect on the recipient. One leak and the spell is broken. It truly is a case of the mirror of reality replacing the broken mirror. We have awakened from the orgy of self-hatred that confronted both Marcus Garvey and W. E. B. DuBois. However, we are not out of the woods yet; there are still too many African

Americans who have deep-seated feelings of hatred for themselves and their culture. As a nation, we must do something about this in order to bring about a more normal order of human interaction; indeed, it is essential for a united nation.

Few cultural inventions have ever been charged with so much power for an oppressed people constantly bombarded with negative messages about themselves and negative images of themselves as the "Black is beautiful" slogan of the late twentieth century. It represented both a cultural and a political transformation. This dual transformation is what the new *messianism* is founded upon. Alongside this declaration was the Afro hair style, the most revolutionary cultural statement made by the African American community since Marcus Garvey's announcement that the white man's religion meant death to the African.

We must ask, "Are we confounded by the potential directions of this collective messianism?" We do not have to be confused because its outline is clearly set before us in the dynamics of the spirit. Happiness, regrets, various social courtesies, magnanimity, goodwill, and faith—these are the materials out of which the mission must be accomplished. It becomes a struggle of the heart, not just of the head, but an emotional involvement with destiny. Unlike the movement led by Martin Luther King, collective messianism takes the concept of mission from a single leader and redistributes it throughout the group so that each person releases whatever potential is possessed for leadership and group salvation (King 1958; 1964). After all, salvation is the end of *messianism*. It obliterates the need for a messiah.

The collectivization of the messianic complex has merit for all people, and the historical fact that we are in an unprecedented media era means that we must all assume a messianic concern for others. During the 1990s the press, electronic and print, failed to capture the agony of African Americans, Puerto Ricans, and Mexican Americans. Rather, our pain has been characterized by patience and brotherly kindness. It may be argued, and with some validity, that the peculiar captivity imposed upon us in this country forces us to seek the moral ground. Thus, after King, while Ralph Abernathy and Jesse Jackson carved out their respective moral positions for nonviolence, Huey

Newton and Bobby Seale staked out their moral positions for revolutionary action, particularly if attacked by the police, the occupying forces in the African American community. Both these cases were predicated upon an entrapment. Every argument for violence rested upon the moral right of an oppressed people to throw off tyrants, and every argument for nonviolence rested upon the grounds that the oppressed had to demonstrate a higher law than the oppressors. In essence, therefore, both positions were based upon the African American predicament as communicated by the media.

We were in a fishbowl, exposed to the media, living in its environment, and interpreted by its information. Furthermore, the media instructed the oppressed in patience. As a virtue, it is a symbol of the oppressed. But symbolic patience breeds frustration, and frustration is a mother of violent reaction. Whether it was William Whipple in 1837 preaching nonresistance to aggression or Martin Luther King in 1957 saying that the oppressed had to love the enemy to death, the result has always been the same: inculcation of brotherly kindness. Black media are as guilty as white media.

Radical democrats like Manning Marable and Cornel West have called for an alliance of poor whites and blacks; this again, some cynic has said, is an appeal that cannot be reciprocated by poor whites because the media have rejected the idea.

This is really no conundrum. It expresses itself in the collectivization of the messianic complex because messianism has been a significant part of our existence in America. Situationally, we had to come to this point. For if leaders, who by their assumed or given roles, possess traits that link them to the past and future—thus understanding what has been and capable of anticipating what is to come—then the masses, who have more than ever been mediarized, are capable of similar kinds of judgments. We are not leaderless nor can we ever be leaderless because now our mission is indeed a mass phenomenon. *1984* is passé. George Orwell is real. George Bush uses doublespeak. We are terrorized in our bodies and spirits.

In one sense, namely, historical, the United States has been moving in the direction of the mass phenomenon where the consciousness is so raised that any person is leader. As late as James

Baldwin's *The Fire Next Time* (1964) and, at least, as early as David Walker's address to the national convention of colored citizens in Boston in 1827, major thinkers have predicted, although sometimes vaguely, that the masses would become knowledgeable and articulate about life in these United States. It is important to understand what happens in a situation such as this.

Times change, role expectations are modified, economics shift, but the media exercise their unending role as agenda setters. They are enduring institutions creating a sort of collectivization, a community of consumers. Garvey's revolt could never have been a collective messianic movement because he dominated it too thoroughly with his charisma.

Could it have been a collective and personal movement? Probably not. At least not as it came to exist with Garvey's leadership; he was, as his power showed, the media of his movement. With Garvey there was no distributive charisma—a phenomenon that awaited the advent of television as an instrument of exposure.

Extending images and concepts into every corner of society, the television provided us with the same exposure to the defeat of the melting pot theory and thus offered the way for the decline of fatalism. During the civil rights era we saw what could not be and raised our hopes on what now had to be. Even now the geography of television makes it possible for a contemporary black sharecropper in Alabama and a black judge in Philadelphia to participate in the same pathos of suffering on the six o'clock news. Vicarious suffering can be picked up, like a baton, twirled, handled, and set down. In the 1960s what television showed Birmingham, Plaquemine, Louisiana, Selma, Boston, and Albany, Georgia, was what we suspected to be true about our country but had never really wanted to accept, expecting all the time some regeneration or sanctification that would allow relaxation of tension. Television's version of drama at six o'clock in the evening shattered peace dreams with bombs and screaming parents. Now the events surrounding police beatings are dramatized in the same way. We become participants, experiencing the deaths of the dead or mutilated Africans in confrontations with the police. In some strange way we are victimized again by the crimes against the civil rights movement when we see the brutality measured out to Africans on the streets of our cities.

At one time in this society what was being erected were the scaffoldings of a collective messianism, a mass rising, brought on by the expanding geographies of the image being transmitted throughout the nation and the world. Society was being transformed into something different. Individuals in their own way reacted to the displaying of social drama. Americans were galvanized by the substantive rhetoric of victory and consequently became, each in his own turn, a part of the mass mission. Even white children learned to say "Black Power," "black is beautiful," and "I am somebody," and to lay the groundwork for "reverse discrimination" as a political concept as well as ethnic minorities and women as deprived groups. In black America we heard the voices of a hundred Gabriels, Douglasses, Washingtons, Garveys, and Randolphs saying that the time had come for the nation to stand beside its past and assume a collective mission for social justice.

> I want to be ready
> to walk in Jerusalem just like John.

Television could conceivably advance specific nationalistic objectives that are essential to the capability of internalizing social justice. There is nothing mysterious about this phenomenon. It is the destiny of the machine to enhance the objectives of its maker, at least, for the foreseeable future. Intellectuals in and out of the business will play an important role in the making and projecting of theme and symbol. It is the crystallization of purpose, individual and private, into a collective sense of justice that will emerge with the effective management of communication technologies.

One has to understand the distributive nature of Louis Farrakhan's Million Man March speech, echoed a million times and sent into more than a million homes. Whatever the emotions one may have about Minister Farrakhan, it is impossible to deny his significant impact on the nature of the African American challenge to racism. Whether a person agrees with him or not, it is impossible not to have an opinion because television, more than any other media, has made that so.

As African Americans we are victimized by the legacy of commercial advertisements in the press. Inasmuch as our role in the capitalist economy is minuscule, we do not exercise any real influence on the press. Quite simply, the press is the pressure because its pressure is both one of commission and one of omission. Black people assume that the press intends to remain illegitimate in black communities.

American news reporting is all too frequently symbolic posturing. During roundtable after roundtable white reporters assemble to discuss the political problems of the day. The line is clear, predictable, and stale. Americans can do no wrong, and anything that is wrong with the world is the result of bad governance on the part of some nation's "dictator" but not on the part of America's foreign policy. Such reporting leaves an audience dumber than the reporters found it, particularly if it is an issue involving Liberia, Iraq, Haiti, Cuba, Venezuela, North Korea, or Cuba. Is it impossible to be just and fair in reporting events in those nations? What are the possibilities of having a fair discussion of the Palestinian plight? There is rarely any discussion of the humanitarian interest in a political situation.

The conservative black press often follows the agenda set by the white press. They emphasize the same ideas, support the same politics, praise the same black people, and condemn the same international leaders. In the end those newspapers, like their white counterparts, are illegitimate also. They are usually devoid of African consciousness or history. Consequently, they add to the burden borne by black people and constitute a negative influence on economic, cultural, and social development. Racism, the dominant factor in the relationship of Americans with each other, has so infected the conservative black press that it cannot exercise judgment independent of the racist domination under which it labors. To break out of this bind, the conservative black press must become radical and wage war against the system that cripples it and the American people. At that point the black press will become a true ally to the psychological health of African people. Only accidentally do the media controlled by whites serve the purposes of black people. The conservative black press could be a force for creative change if it were not so steeped in provincialism. Even in South Africa the white press accidentally aided the cause of black liberation. Therefore, we cannot praise the black press when it supports the black community by default, for even racists fall into that pit.

Chimutengwende (1978, 105) understands that the media may be helpful to racially oppressed people because it unwittingly gives them psychological victories. Whenever the oppressors must retreat from their racist positions because of the resistance of the oppressed, the press announces the retreats. Thus the press becomes an ally of the oppressed in ways never intended by the press owners or the government. When Chimutengwende says that the government propaganda of South Africa helps the African to understand the mind of the racist enemy, he is referring to the need of racist propagandists to report their activities against the liberation forces. Yet in their reports are also reports of sabotage, losses of soldiers, rallies against the government, and other difficulties experienced by government forces. These are usually cryptically reported, however. One hears that a law has been changed, a military action undertaken, police have broken up demonstrations.

Those who know the political habits of the oppressor can usually read behind the propaganda in order to gather facts. During apartheid whites owned and controlled the media in South Africa, and consequently they were in a position to print those views that were supportive of their social and economic privilege. Africans who recognized this pattern took a jaded view of the media in South Africa. It has changed only a little since 1994. Whites still retain a disproportionate share of media influence and power in South Africa. Progressive black media moguls such as Thami Mazwai of Mafube Publishing often try to educate the masses. They discover black media executives who continue some of the practices of the old apartheid press. The reason for this is that they fear losing their sponsors.

Freedom of the press has little meaning when the press tramples on the rights of the majority of the people because it is controlled by a fascist ideology. What does freedom mean in a context where the majority of the people are denied access to the press in their own country? What meaning can be attributed to freedom, such a holy term, when the unholy fetish of white racism is the guiding totem of the erstwhile *ruling* class? Political habits, sanctified by racist laws, were denials of liberties for Africans in South Africa. Racism affected the intellectual air inhaled by the people of South Africa. Although it is much better now, it still remains a problem in those sectors of the media where blacks working for white-owned companies or in their own companies censor themselves because of the threat of the loss of commercial sponsorship.

In Western heterogeneous industrial nations, the endemic nature of racism in the media is an inherent technological reality, as all technology assumes the motif dictated by its special mythological history. Therefore, racism is the result of a disjunctive articulation between reality and the technological manifestations white people create to fill the spaces of their existence. It is aetiological on one hand; and on the other, axiological. What exists as the absence of Africa exists as the presence of Europe. For the racists, conscious or ignorant, there is never the possibility of sharing equally. The presence of Europe is the absence of Africa and vice versa. I use Africa and Europe here symbolically.

We are confronted by the widespread assault of the absence of Africa in every conceivable media. Airports, airplanes, trains, buses, and other instruments of transportation regularly advertise, but in America it is as if we remain until now Ralph Ellison's invisible man. So even with billions of dollars annually as consumers we do not make a change in the racist presentations of the media. We make a mistake to think, however cleverly, that our problem is merely a lack of visibility in ads on or about travel and transportation. An interacting racism networking the society leads a conspiracy of conscience against the best communication interests of all those who do not look like the corporate owners, producers, and directors. Ours is a predictable condition, but the way to extricate ourselves is also predictable.

Although technical knowledge has expanded in the United States, its universal expansion has been slowed by racist practices. Everywhere the African is uprooted from communication traditions valuable to society. This is seen clearly in the fact that the rate of black usage of computers lags far behind that of whites. While it is true that a large part has to do with economics, a great deal of this difference is placed at the feet of the racist construction of the economy.

Individuals as well as groups can contribute to the expansions of technical communications by their passionate and committed posture toward knowledge. There have been many such people. Njoya, the Bamun king who created an alphabet and made numerous inventions and scientific discoveries, stands as a symbol of what individuals can do to facilitate communication. King Njoya was not the first human being to speed the stream of communication; he followed in a tradition established by Imhotep and Johannes Gutenberg and Noah Webster and W. E. B. DuBois. Thousands have traveled the same road. Njoya in the early nineteenth century developed a script in order to preserve in writing the teachings of the kingdom. Like a harmattan wind he covered vast areas of knowledge and stamped a legend on the Cameroonian people.

The varieties of our responses to phenomena constitute the possibility for facilitating communication in creative ways. Blacks in the United States see and hear differently. I once stood on the banks of the fabled Congo River and saw fishermen throwing their nets into the water and envisioned them feeding a nation. A friend of mine said this would make a great place for a shopping center. We got into a long discussion unnecessary to repeat here. My only point is the variety of responses to phenomena. The Nubians built pyramids in what is now Sudan and Egypt; the Zimbabweans built Zimbabwe. The Mayas built pyramids, the Aztecs built pyramids, and the Khmer erected edifices of stone in response to their environments. Most instances of these great achievements were symbolic, even to the point of representing themselves as the center of the universe. The pharaohs were regarded to have such central auras. Our entire systems of writing and communicating with lesser symbols or principal symbols (Smith 1973) is predicated upon responses to the environment. Obenga (1980, 107) tells us that the diverse word *wen* designates writing, design, literature, and civilization. In diverse history the literature of the emperor's court was considered the classical, the proverbial, the relevant to government functioning and stability in the realm. Thus, *wen* was a response to the environmental conditions of Chinese, mainly Han, culture. Among the Yoruba the Alaafin of Oyo has *ilari*, ambassadors, who are given names that represent the king's message.

Thus, an Alaafin's ambassadors may be named "Obakosetan," the king is not ready; "Obagbori," the king triumphs; and "Madaarikan," do not oppose the king. These person-symbols may also carry a message, but the principal message is always the name of the *ilari*. Yoruba names, like many African names, possess significance in the context of society. Racism has distorted even the naming process in America. Africans no longer understand their connection to names. We have been struck by the lightning of slavery and are only now recovering from the shock. We can receive no help from the white press or the white media. Our sanity rests squarely on the shoulders of our own intellectuals who must reinstitute a cultural criticism and science that shall speak to the essential outline of this rearmament.

Unable to name oneself after the manner of one's cultural and historic heritage, a person becomes a wanderer, not fully recognizing, not to speak of understanding the psychological invasion. Our names are Lincoln, Jefferson, Washington, Williams, Jones, Johnson, and Smith as express symbols of our slave past, not our past prior to slavery. We often have no memory longer than 1619, the date the first Africans were indentured in North America. Obviously our history goes beyond the interference of slavery, and the names of the African continent beckon to us.

An unforgivable ignorance of Africa and therefore African Americans grips contemporary American journalists. They wrestle with their limited knowledge and are often defeated by issues of history, culture, and mythology. While the average black American carries Stagolee, Shine, and Simple with him each day, the white journalist lives in a world devoid of African American mythology, and consequently to report or comment on what seems to be a fact may be the exhibition of the greatest ignorance.

A white journalist who had heard of the arrest of two black suspects for a theft wrote her story without any appreciation of African American culture, and the story was incomplete. It seems that two teenage black males had been apprehended by the police as suspects in a theft. They told the police they were on their way to a party. They had no invitations, it was after midnight, and they did not know the name of the party giver. Although these boys were suspects to the police and in the mind of the journalist, most blacks would have seen nothing wrong with the facts. No invitation, after midnight, and ignorance of the host's name are not factors that should incriminate youths. As a culturalist, I had been asked to testify on behalf of the youths. They were exonerated.

The illegitimacy of the American press as it relates to Africans is reiterated daily within the black community. Like the police departments in major cities, the white press is to be tolerated and used for whatever you can use it for, but never can it be considered credible. It can clearly be identified as opposed to the genuine interest of the black masses.

The great majority of our people are out of synchrony with the daily press on domestic, racial, political, and policy issues. Articles especially on Africa are frequently insulting, often in contradiction to our own experiences and views. Our voices and opinions are hardly heard. The broken bottle of American journalism often snags our sensibilities. The press functions as an information instrument for the white population. As marginal audiences for the white press, black readers seldom find their interests expressed. Whether in the reporting of trivia or in the foreign policy opinions expressed, the press is decidedly anti-African and consequently is a tool of the same racist oppression condemned in many other institutions of American life. Even trivial reporting often found as fillers in newspapers seldom is of information relevant to Africa or African peoples. This marginality highlighted by the absence of black-oriented trivia underscores the illegitimacy of the general American press for a black audience.

Evidence is so overwhelming that the press remains unable or incapable of covering and appealing to the African audiences in America that to speak of it is to indict almost every major newspaper in America. The only way to understand how the press functions in American society is to see African Americans as a colonized people. A colony is reported only if it is of interest to the metropole. What is reported by the press about the colony is nothing that enhances the colonized peoples but everything that advances the interest of the colonizing power. If information is of a political nature, there is every reason on the part of the colonial press to suppress such information.

At the founding convention of the National Black Independent Political Party in Gary, Indiana, in 1972, some three thousand blacks gathered to create a national party. The white press reported variously that there was anywhere from seven hundred to two thousand persons gathered. Those in attendance at the historic event in which state delegations were counted and recorded wondered how such reporting could occur. The evidence is striking in many other aspects of the press reporting that what is factual and real to Africans is often not real to the white press. Those who write for the press make every effort to minimize stories or information that might threaten the stability of the institutions. This is the protective, stabilizing function of the racist press.

It is much like any other sector of society in that regard. Education is a case in point. Professors who are only drawing a salary, sitting at a desk, and otherwise being noncreative are allowed to remain in universities while creative, politically conscious, and humanitarian professors who exhibit a sense of ethical value are often hounded out of the university prior to reaching tenure. The aim in the university, as in the press, is to stabilize, to protect. The objective cannot be to destabilize to create change to challenge the status quo.

The level of press sophistication reflects the level of sophistication within a society. Because the press is a social institution and consequently of the same weave as the society's fabric, to unravel the press is to unravel the society. The American press, electronic and traditional, has often been opposed to the interests of African Americans and Africans in general. The press sees us the same way as the police, the educational institutions, the judiciary, and the financial institutions. There is no such thing as an institution more liberal than any other; they are all of the same fabric. If the major institutions of a society do not support the political structure, a disastrous conflict will probably ensue. History supports this view as seen in the confrontations of the American colonists through the *Boston Gazette* with the British occupiers. Whenever the press can no longer accept the political order of a society, the conflict can be far-reaching. That is why in most cases the press has supported the government and the government has given tacit support to press freedom since the eighteenth century.

English newspapers were often subsidized by the government in the eighteenth century; newspapers are still subsidized in certain developing nations. Only with the coming of advertisements in Western industrial nations did the press find a measure of independence. The move to secure independent financing was one of the most urgent in the Western press, particularly in England and France. Taxpayers began to raise complaints about the maintenance of papers that frequently were used to attack private individuals.

Thus, in the nineteenth century securing of commercial advertisement was considered one of the foremost blessings of capitalism. But it became increasingly difficult for the press in capitalist societies to attack or question the practices of large commercial houses. The prevailing ideas of state became the prevailing ideas of press.

The role of the press, the most highly active intellectual institution, is the expansive and general awakening of its audience to human potential. In our view, such crystallization of purpose will come as a result of aggressive, independent social and political forces. The independence of the press is essential to the investigation and appraisal of political and social actions. In the United States the fact that the Federal Bureau of Investigation could and did authorize a letter threatening Martin Luther King demonstrates what happens when the press finds sacrosanct some institutions, persons, and subjects. This is not so much an attack on the press as an indication that the US press has often participated in melodramatic reporting.

Because television is simple and straightforward, even the illiterate can "get the news message" and there are fewer and fewer people who aren't "literate" in television. So television is an instrumental arm of the realization of social goals. Furthermore, its work is accomplished not by special programming but because an in-depth portrayal of life in general can sustain and enhance the collective good. However, television's capacity to portray is also a capacity to distort. Literary and creative licenses are abused when distortions are presented as if they are truths. Audiences are frequently caught, encapsulated by dull images, plotting their escape. Freedom can come only when audiences are antagonistic, belligerent, and sassy. Those who may have failed to become literate in television because of historical discontinuities brought on by the cleavage between print and television will participate in the future because the future is in electronic media.

There are two ways in which the masses will become clients of this new visual literacy: (1) they will be reinforced by the political influences of the technological state, and (2) they will take part in the general cultural resurrection of contemporary society in a new key. In the first instance, the intellectuals will begin to forge a union representative of common interests focused on priorities mutually established. Visual literacy is the key to political maturity and the very beginning of mass education. The political forum is of importance only insofar as it transmits the wishes and wills of the people. The politics of communication should address essence rather than shape or kind. Essence is substantive, comprised of the social, economic, and cultural indices of a complex society. The resultant political condition will be significant; in fact, it is likely to change forever the character of race, media, and politics.

I can imagine what DuBois would have thought about all of this because he believed in the possibility of human transformation and insisted, as I do, on an optimistic future.

NOTE

1. Nat Turner was a classic case of the African American deliverer. It was his belief that he was the instrument by which the enslaved Africans in his region of Virginia would be freed. Given the limited information available to enslaved Africans, most of whom could not read or write, it was exceptional that Nat Turner interpreted his life in the context of messianism. He was the one chosen to strike the blow at enslavement and therefore in August 1831 he put his life on the line for the freedom of his brothers and sisters in one of the most dramatic revolt episodes in American history.

chapter 4
THE RHETORIC OF EDUCATION

I cannot honestly say that I have ever found a school in the United States run by whites that adequately prepares black children to enter the world as sane human beings. This is a sad admission, but a true one. Only recently have I discovered schools run by blacks that, in my opinion, adequately educate children. These are also few and scattered. Furthermore, they are not supported by society at the level of the failing schools.

The reason for this situation has little to do with the integrity or interest of teachers and even less to do with intentions. It has a lot to do with the fact that the educational structure in a racist society is, inter alia, racist, just as an educational system in a liberal polity would be liberal or a conservative society would produce an educational system that is in line with the political philosophy. A Marxist system produces Marxist education, and in the United States an exploitative, capitalist system that enshrines plantation owners as saints and national heroes cannot possibly create sane black children.

What is more damaging in the educational arena is the rhetoric used to justify the failure of the educational system itself. Abigail and Stephan Thernstrom, two of the leading conservative commentators on education, have argued in their book *No Excuses: Closing the Racial Gap in Learning* (2003) that black Americans are hopelessly behind in higher education and drop out of college as a result of poor preparation at the K–12 level. They also contend that the academic gap between blacks and whites is worse than it was in 1990. The problem with the Thernstroms is that they refuse to attribute any of the educational deficits to the racism that is prevalent in the educational system from the teachers to the school boards. They do not see that the curricula are themselves the promoters of white racism. They have limited appreciation for the overwhelming legacy of ruinous psychological damage done to black families. They do not consider the fact that economic status, particularly in generational terms, has a lot to do with school performance. This means that their analysis is neither accurate nor useful in understanding the complexity of the dropout situation. Theodore Cross, in an important essay "The Good News that the Thernstroms Neglected to Tell" published in the *Journal of Blacks in Higher Education*, argues that the Thernstroms fail to tell the story "of the often brilliant, and now apparently unstoppable progress" that black students are making in the college years and at the graduate level (Cross 2003/2004).

What Cross demonstrates is the fact that the economic gap between whites and blacks is directly related to the dropout rate in college. Cross shows that the nationwide difference between black and white college dropouts is twenty-one percentage points. However, the economic gap is thirty-seven percentage points. While this large difference in family income might not be the sole contributor to the difference in college dropout rates, black families are crippled by college costs at a far greater rate than white families. In effect, the racial penalty continues to operate in the arena of educational access in a racist society. In my judgment, Cross's position has more integrity than that articulated by the Thernstroms because it takes into consideration factors other than biology, although as we have seen the biological question is at the heart of so much of the educational doctrine and economic chances.

Clearly, to argue from statistics is not the best way to capture the impact of racism on education, but it is one way to show that economics plays a major role in what people can and cannot do.

Of course, the issue of curriculum—that is, what is taught and who is teaching with what objective—is critical to the process of adequate education. Carter Woodson once wrote that Africans were deliberately being miseducated (Woodson 1991). His examples remain powerful after more than fifty years. Blacks are taught, even in historically black universities and colleges, to appreciate European culture more than they are taught to know African culture. Most African Americans know far more about the ethnic diversity of Europe than they know about the ethnic composition of Africa. Most African Americans know more about European art, history, and music than they know about African art, history, and music. While Woodson has seldom been challenged on his thesis, some conservative writers have attacked the contemporary neoliberal education of blacks. Unfortunately, the conservative approach they recommend is as detrimental to black children's education as the approach they attack. I have come to believe that the pioneering work of George Sefa Dei of the University of Toronto may hold some value for education in multiracial, heterogeneous, industrialized societies. Dei (1996) has conceptualized an idea that is radical in its application to a racist society; he has argued that education should be antiracist.

Africans in America cannot depend upon white institutions filled with notions of white supremacy and Western civilization dominance to instill either motivation or values in African American children. Any institution that successfully educates black students will by definition cease being white. This is the burden of American education. At this juncture in American history I see little evidence that most elementary and high schools are willing to cease being white in their perspective. Certainly the Harvards, Yales, Berkeleys, and Stony Brooks have no intention, on their own accord, of diluting their fundamentally European orientations despite the increasing numbers of African, Asian, and Hispanic students entering those institutions. *This is true even though the only way for those institutions to be truly American is to cease being white.* On the other hand, those institutions that seek to become white or whiter are seeking to become less American. The nation is profoundly mixed.

Given circumstances of racism, which quite correctly are different from circumstances of intelligence, we can assume that entrance and maintenance in American institutions of learning will continue to rest upon the ethnocentric provincialism of a European worldview. Such an educational perspective may not be altogether incorrect in a monoethnic nation, though even there one must be careful to demonstrate the possibilities of intercultural interactions. But a multiethnic nation demands, by its inherent diversity, an educational philosophy that can accommodate cultural pluralism. Obviously, however, these "demands" have been less than imperative in the United States.

Traditionally African American institutions carry the same Eurocentric bale of cotton around their philosophical shoulders as the white institutions. Without a clearly developed African worldview, these institutions are destined to be alien to themselves while providing shelter from the direct blows of white ethnocentric symbolism found in nonblack institutions. Ensconced in an educational context that seeks certain "marks," ritual academic scarifications, that attest to one's achievement, these African American institutions are mere facsimiles of white institutions. The group therapy given to black students by the togetherness of the brothers and sisters provides camaraderie and opportunities for lasting relationships not found in the white colleges. But camaraderie alone cannot furnish the psychological and philosophical materials necessary for the survival of Africans in an alien cultural context.[1]

The educational system is arrayed in constant battle formation against the intellectual well-being of Africans in the United States. Journals, symposia, panels, and research projects are the principal ammunition used to attack and destroy the Africans' spirit. It remains so long after the initial forays issued against blacks in the colonial period. When admittance to the now-ivyed colleges came for blacks, it came with a very high price: the absolute renunciation of African history, culture, and civilization. Periodically, some J. Phillipe Rushton or Arthur Jensen, white warriors marching valiantly in their own cause, attempt to strengthen the weaker flanks of their racist positions. Their works, in the media tradition of American education, become additional monuments to a base science. A vigorous debate normally ensues involving African American scientists and some non-African scholar or popularizer debating the merits of anti-Africanism.

I have always understood these debates as media phenomena, contemporary popular dramas, similar in ethos to the cowboy and Indian genre of movies in the late forties. They pit two clearly definable and recognizable sides against each other in mock battle when the conclusion is already drawn in the minds of the black and white audiences.

Embattled by its monoethnicity and cultural iconoclasm, the American education system must be redefined. Academic inquiry, already undergoing changes, must be transformed, enlarging its geographic and philosophical sphere. Education is the transmission of a society's rules for coping. In effect, education is the communication of culture, the propagation of certain more specific knowledge and a hierarchy of values. As an American enterprise it has always possessed the deep and abiding racism inherent in other American institutions. From the early days at William and Mary College and at Harvard, the white fathers of American education endeavored to teach, to transmit, to propagate only the culture and values of Europe, and, of course, in the process to formulate values developing in America. Africans were present within the society, but the ignorance surrounding the presence or the history of my ancestors was phenomenal, and indeed little has changed since the seventeenth century. US political leaders still speak of white societies as civilized and others, nonwhite, as barbarian.

Education should be a radical communication process that involves in a fundamental sense a commitment to make deals with environment and time for the sake of the pupil. To be radical, in this sense, means to engage in a comprehensive attempt to restructure the learning reality for all children. I mean, can anyone really explain how a white child can enter American educational institutions as a racist in elementary school and then leave as a racist in the twelfth grade? Of course, on one level we can explain it, but does it really make sense in a multicultural society?

A practicable relationship among the pupil, environment, and time captures the essence of communication in the classroom. It defines the relationship of people to time and environment in a learning community and as such is a holistic and systemic view of the teaching-learning process that takes into account the total vocal-visual context of the particular classroom. Whatever the relationship of one person to another is in an interactive situation, the transaction within the educational environment should be a reciprocal process. Only in this way can we minimize the insidious racist nature of American education.

Education is dynamic. In a properly ordered educational environment the pupil becomes the catalyst for the transaction. At the time of entry into the classroom situation the pupil becomes the focus of whatever the teacher seeks to do. Nothing is to be transacted without consideration of the role of the pupil. If the environment is to be altered, walls posted, mirrors erected, desks changed, floors carpeted, or chairs rearranged, it is to be accomplished with the pupil as the essential fixture. In effect, the pupil becomes the center of the environment. Temporal factors are typically pupil oriented: how much time for recess, what time shall be spent on reading or writing, how shall I divide the time of my modules, and so on. The dynamic, therefore, of the educational environment is in a substantial way dependent upon the pupil as the catalytic agent. When the teacher respects the environmental and temporal aspects of education as supportive to the student, the radicalization of education has begun. Education is communication.

The teacher coordinates, orchestrates, and directs the various factors converging in the classroom, but it is the pupil who should be the center of these factors. The child provides a peculiarly significant dynamic to the learning community because of traditions and culture. In order to instruct successfully, the teacher must be able to respond to numerous behavior patterns and folk styles. The teacher who did not know how to react to the first grader who told her that his name was "sweet thing" was not aware of the significance of nicknames among black inner-city children. To say, as she did, that it was pathetic that he did not know his name was to miss the point. He knew his name as he had always heard it and when asked to give his name responded as he had always responded to his peers and parents.

Elementary classrooms are designed to foster specific kinds of learning behaviors. They are program laboratories designed to prepare pupils for society. How we structure the learning community influences the learning behavior of pupils. An environment-centered school emphasizes location and newness of buildings, facilities, equipment, and supplies. These are servants of the school; they do not comprise the school. Neither possession nor nonpossession of such paraphernalia really matters in terms of a school. Those who contend that we need a new learning environment with no walls and no equipment are also environment centered, although they want a denuded situation. What we really need are learning communities where the culture of children is not dominated by a corporate society that emphasizes monoethnic norms.

A school is not an institution though there exist certain institutional aspects. A school is a type of relationship among pupils, teachers, administrators, and parents. If the relationship existing among these real people is conducive to a learning community, then a school exists. Whatever the quota of pupil bodies, the modernity of educational facilities, or the degrees of the instructors, it matters little if a relationship has not been established among the entities that produce a cooperative and meaningful learning experience for students. Student teachers must be made profoundly aware of the communicative purpose for which they are training.

A school must be a network of communication bringing the best values of the society to bear on the methods of instruction. This, however, can be done only if we have some precise sense of where the community's values are and where society is going. This is not to say that objectives are to be established and religiously adhered to regardless of necessity but rather to note that teachers must be aware of how their instructional approaches relate to the general society. In this sense the transaction between teacher and learning community is constant, with the pupil being fed and nourished at every level of classroom activity. Radicalization of education also means that teachers must restructure the time element in the classroom so that it becomes a servant rather than a master. Communicative education demands that the teacher see the need for having several objectives instead of one in an hour block. Conceivably, a teacher might develop several behavioral competencies to be mastered by the pupils within hour blocks.

If each hour were so structured and the activities so varied to accomplish a single competency requirement, the element of time would be mastered and the learning community sufficiently opened so as to constitute a transaction with time. As long as the pupil is the center of the process and the teacher manages time and environment in such a way as to enhance the learning relationship, the educational enterprise is healthy. Orthodoxy becomes orthopraxy.

When the teacher has accomplished the task of orchestrating substance, time, and environment in relationship to the pupil, there should be a move toward total community awareness. At this point other actors must appear on the stage in addition to the teacher and pupil. The parents and administrators of a school are key factors in the success of the learning community.

Parental involvement at the elementary level of education is a necessary component for changing the learning community. Without input and vigilance from parents, the most competent teachers and administrators may fail to commit time and environment to the pupil. The teacher, as facilitator of the learning community, has to actively seek parental input and contact. Some parents may reject the advances made by the facilitator at first because of inadequate communication channels and prior exclusion. But how does a teacher transmit her interest to parents? What are the peculiar guidelines for communicative success? Answering these questions will give us insight into the complexities of parental involvement at all levels. African American parents are wary of teachers and administrators who consistently miseducate, misguide, and miscounsel their children. Forming communication communities where teacher-facilitators demonstrate their commitment of time to pupils and parents is one answer to the deafening questions of process.

Education is a communicative act in its most essential sense. If you were to think of it as a simple communication system with encoders, messages, channels, and decoders, it would be possible to see that the educative process is a transactional system. The basic communication model assumes that messages are sent and received. A sender of the message encodes, and a receiver of the message decodes. Vocal and visual stimuli constitute the message. As in any communication situation, the interaction in education takes place on several levels and within several contexts over space and time. How to manage those levels and regulate the effective flow of information is the principal task of the teacher, who stands at the hub of the transactional vortex. What messages to send, what messages to respond to, and what time and environment need to be coordinated for the pupils' ultimate benefit are the essential issues. To exist, therefore, in a communication setting means that one will have to attend to how that setting is influenced externally and how others within the transaction try to influence it and are influenced by it.

In efforts to explain the education of inner-city children, numerous authors have concentrated on the classroom experience between teacher and pupil to the exclusion of anything or anyone else. This is a linear view. In this model, the teacher transmits messages in a straight line to the pupil, and the pupil transmits messages in a straight line to the teacher. In such a model the answer to the question, what is two and two? might be predicted. The student would give an answer of either "I don't know" or "It is four" or an incorrect answer of some other sum. However, the student who responds, "Ask two" or "Suppose I don't know" or "What is it to you?" would create a transactional problem. A linear perspective is convenient, teacher reassuring, and frequently inoperative in the inner-city schools. It does not take into account the student's optional predispositions that may add several levels to the transaction. "What is two and two?" does not have to lead to either "four" or "I don't know." It may well lead to "I don't give a shit" or "Ask two" or "Suppose I don't know?" These optional predispositions must be dealt with on a transactional level.

In any communicative act such as the education process the transactional scene is marked by language strategies. Just as we know how to respond to our children and friends when they ask, "How are you?" or when they ask, "What caused you to lie to me?" we should know when a pupil has moved from one level to another. Quite conventionally, teachers have generally participated only at the A level. Fluidity is a definitional part of the communication experience. Openness to modification is the key to effectiveness in the classroom. The tendency to condescend to students, fear of misjudgment, and lack of awareness of communication levels plague new teachers. As the transaction chart shows, it is possible for either the teacher or the pupil to interact with the other across space and time at any level. Thus a teacher at level B may interact with a pupil at D or E. The most effective communication in education or elsewhere takes place in a one-to-one correspondence between two people, usually utilizing the same linguistic code, in the same place, and at the same or nearly the same time. Such an easy fact has recommended the linear approach to education. However, openness provides the teacher with a choice among the various levels, depending upon the code and demands of the situation in the communication. The most effective communication occurs when people interact at the same level, yet there are instances when our interaction with people, even of our own age and station, must be at another level than the one we are accustomed to employing in conversation.

The concept of transaction education can be achieved within the framework of the present educational resources, both personnel and facilities, available within the various inner-city schools. Additionally, mature teachers, as well as recent graduates of teacher-training institutions, will find *transactionalism* practicable and practical. The intervening factor in the teaching process becomes the recognition of transactional levels and the projection of language strategies relative to the particular level. Most teachers are capable of discerning the difference between an interrogative and a declaratory statement, and most know or can be taught the appropriate response to both types of statements.

The first type of responder is that of the *refuser*, who refuses to get involved with other people. A typical *refuser* will avoid as much as possible communicative interaction with the teacher or fellow pupils. When asked a question, the *refuser* will not respond vocally or will respond with "Leave me alone" or "I don't want to answer" or some similar noncommittal expression. His total concern is to keep his anonymity. Thus when the teacher or another pupil makes statements to him, he responds with as little vocal interaction as possible. The results are that the *refuser* maintains his distance from the other participants in the interaction. To transact with him, one will have to do it at a distance. This is not always physical distance but rather communicative distance, which is a process of language behavior. Many African American students do not fail in school; they assume the role of *refusers*—they refuse to learn without even taking on the role of mastering information that might be harmful to their psychological health.

The second transactional type found among students is the *signifier*. The *signifier* is constantly on the alert for weaknesses in the teacher or his peers. When he sees an advantage, he pounces upon it vocally, frequently to the surprise of the teacher and sometimes to the shock of the students. He is not vicious in the sense that he can be classified as a student needing the supervision of a principal or other administrator. The *signifier* never engages in physical attacks on teachers or pupils. He is merely an insinuator, willing to back down if the appropriate response is made by the teacher. His major weapon is the returned question. This type of response is usually marked by the *signifier* turning a question asked him to the querist. For example, if the teacher asked, "What is five times 127?" instead of attempting to answer, the *signifier* might respond, "What do you think?" It is the audacity of the respondent that tends to surprise teachers working in the inner city. The *signifier*'s forte is surprise.

The third transactional type is the *general*, who directs and orders. He seeks to avoid all direct involvement with the teacher or his fellow pupils unless he is in charge of the interactive situation. Seeing his role as one who delegates, he tries to assume a command position vis-à-vis others. Thus when the teacher asks him, "Who is the secretary of state of the United States of America?" he refers the question to a peer, "Tony, answer that question." Of course, he might also elect to give the teacher an order, "Ask Mary, let's see if she knows." The *general* is able to direct and order because he usually knows the answers to the questions. His skills and abilities as a student are used to avoid responding to questions he decides not to answer and to engage in communication where he assumes leadership. The *general*, therefore, seeks to demonstrate power.

A final transactional type is the *mediator*. He is adept at bargaining. The mediator seeks to obtain trade-offs with the teacher or with other pupils. He is the champion of the quid pro quo. Quite literally, the teacher who is not aware of this communication type may find herself highly distressed at the language behavior of the mediator. In reply to a question he is likely to respond, "If you give me your telephone number" or "What is it to you?" or "If I answer that question, can I go home for the day?" His purpose is to make certain that everything he does counts for something. The *mediator* is willing to make a verbal deal even though the deal may be challenged by the teacher. It is the posing of the bargain that is essential in this transaction. Therefore, the *mediator* is interested in striking a bargain.

These communication types are not hard-and-fast molds, but rather characteristic approaches to language behavior in the classroom. Teachers can be generally classified along similar lines. Teachers can and do exhibit characteristics of the four types of transactions.

As *refuser*, the teacher communicates as little as possible with the students in the classroom. Rolls are taken, instructions are given, and students are examined, but there is no attempt to initiate discussion with them beyond what is required for basic instruction. In this case, the teacher becomes an initiator under obligation, not a creator or imaginative facilitator. Furthermore, if the teacher considers a particular student to be threatening, the communication with that student is apt to be brief, strained, and difficult. Additionally, on this level the teacher finds the role of disciplinarian to be unusually trying and will try to keep from making basic decisions related to class problems. The teacher as *refuser*, like the pupil as *refuser*, seeks to maintain distance. Teachers on this level do not possess interactive humanism. As a style, interactive humanism involves initiating and supporting conversation with students by references to their personal or community activities, interests, and resources. The teacher as *refuser* cannot demonstrate this type of interaction because the inability to relate is based upon the inability to use language. When we say that a person does not or cannot relate well, we are saying that he or she does not use verbal or physical language well. This is the least interactive type of classroom behavior.

The teacher as *signifier* seeks to intimidate students by reference to their racial, cultural, environmental, or personal background.

Teachers, like other human beings, possess the ability to react in a negative manner toward others. One of the things that we have learned from the multicultural expert James A. Banks is that in multiethnic education it is necessary for the teacher to pay close attention to diversity in a positive sense (1981). A teacher does not have to be a negative *signifier*, yet it happens often enough to create classroom disaster. The teacher as *signifier* is fond of showing students that they are not intellectually competent on a certain point or in a certain way. For example, the teacher who says to a student "You don't know the answer? I knew you wouldn't know" is engaging in the *signifier's* combat. What is significant in this case is the teacher's disregard for the traditional role of facilitator to become an attacker. The student becomes an object to be taught a lesson about his intelligence vis-à-vis that of the teacher. Another case might involve the teacher saying to the student in the presence of the whole class, "Your breath is awful" or "John, didn't I tell you to get your arithmetic assignment done?" In either case if the student responds, the teacher is prepared to verbally annihilate him before the class. This is the arena of the *signifier*.

As a *general* the teacher operates in an authoritarian manner. Because the *general* directs and orders, many teachers have seen this as their traditional role. The classroom is the battlefield and the students are the soldiers to be ordered around and directed at the will of the *general*. Disobedience on the part of the student will result in punishment. At one time in the American school system most punishment was physical; now it is mostly verbal or psychological. The result of the teacher's *general* attitude is perhaps a well-ordered class but not a creative class. In such instances discipline is rewarded but individuality, as expressed by the student, is frequently suppressed. Thus, the *general* is in charge of the situation from beginning to end—directing, ordering, making statements, and asking questions. One might say that the *general* operates as an interviewer while the student is the interviewee; or the *general* acts as a tutor while the student is being tutored. When a teacher interacts on this level, the students must submit or be ostracized from the learning experience within the class.

As *mediator* the teacher seeks to establish an atmosphere for negotiations that would enhance pupil communicativeness. Any motivational methods or strategies may be employed to attain the objective. Therefore, the teacher frequently fails to respond to pupil needs, individually or collectively, because he is concerned only with getting the students to communicate. Communication is a worthy goal, but many teachers use methods to motivate pupils that may impede communication. A teacher who constantly urges pupils to "interact," to "talk," to "respond," or to "discuss" exposes himself to the danger of emphasizing the objective to the detriment of more immediate, perhaps, affective needs of the pupils. Managing is the style of the *mediator*. The classroom is viewed as a game of skill where the diligent *mediator* can move the players toward a predetermined objective. In this sense it is a persuasive task that confronts the teacher. To be able to orchestrate the various intellectual aptitudes, behavior patterns, and natural communicativeness of the pupils in a classroom is no small task. Thus a teacher who can establish an atmosphere for give-and-take sessions considers himself effective. In fact, the *mediator* may only be successful at getting class interaction but not at teaching. Interaction and teaching are different, and one is not necessarily related to the other. While learning is usually thought of as occurring in an interaction situation, such situations may occur and no real learning take place. Of course, this probably strains the point. My concern is that the *mediator* understands that an atmosphere for communication is not the end of his teaching function; the objective should be learning by the pupil. The old adage still holds: the teacher has not taught until the pupil has learned.

Education is a pervasive symbol. It exists everywhere and takes a multiplicity of forms. The education of children in American high schools has reached a point of epochal embarrassment. Never in any age since the beginning of formalized education have so many teachers lost a sense of purpose as in the present. This is not to say that there are no committed teachers dedicated to the art of teaching; there are many. Yet, taken as a whole, the institutions of education in our urban centers are in dire need of revolution. This much has been said before in other councils and by other authors. In the preceding pages I have laid out a workable framework for radical communication in the classroom.

High school education, as presently conceived, rests upon the assumption that high school is preparatory for college. It further assumes that duly selected and unionized teachers will be committed to teaching. However, like other arts and crafts in American society, we seem to have lost the primitive notion that what we are is communicated through what we do. Teachers are no different. Diversity, anonymity, and legal protection have shielded them from a confrontation with their work. Refuge in the teachers' lounge during the academic day and refuge in the social club in some suburb during the night makes the teacher no more than a visitor who drops in to chat with students for a while and then leaves for the real business.

Innovators have had to set up their own schools out of frustration with changing the educational institutions of Western societies. A key problem is the distinct gulf between teachers and pupils. Lack of effective communication skills threatens the whole enterprise.

We know that culture cannot be called into existence by a nationally endowed commission or a council of learned and scholarly types. It creates itself out of freedom, indeed out of nothing more than the needs of people living together in society. Culture often stems from necessities. Ancient Egypt, as the source of African traditions; China, as the fountainhead of Asian traditions; and Greece, as the *alpha* of Western traditions—all these represent highly developed classical systems of culture. Yet no Egyptian pharaoh, however great and charismatic, could have commanded that geometry or astronomy be discovered or writing invented or tools made. Cultural values are never the result of political dictates. Political leaders may guide the integration of cultural values into political or social purposes, much like John F. Kennedy did with the space program in America or Nikita Khrushchev did in the old Soviet Union with the Sputnik program. Like ancient political leaders, contemporary heads of state appropriate the people's development and often make them serve the political ends of the government. In a similar fashion we now know that the radical transformation of education will take place only as a result of the transformation of society as we manage the subjectivity of ourselves and the rationality of the world.

NOTE

1. A number of fraternal and sororal organizations exist in the African American community. Most of these call themselves "Greek organization," which immediately creates problems with "real" Greeks. Caught up in the fraternal organizations of the early twentieth century, many organizations took on European names as standards. This is because they have little understanding of Africa.

chapter 5
THE PREPONDERANCE OF BUREAUCRACY

As an African American in the twenty-first century, I am one of the most institutionalized human beings in the world. My history is the history of institutions. I am the descendant of those who gave the institution of slavery its identity in modern times. And even today I am not unknown to institutions.

Nearly one million of my brothers and sisters are institutionalized in the prisons of America. One in four of all African Americans are engaged in some way with the federal, state, or local criminal or juridical bureaucracy. We are involved in every level of the welfare bureaucracy. Hospitals and schools are often the institutions of last resort for those broken in spirit or too poor to run away. Our children are victimized by a Eurocentric curriculum that causes them to hate themselves, to believe in white supremacy, and to become little white supremacists themselves fighting for the privilege of being at the top of an oppressive bureaucracy. The most pathetic examples (Condelezza Rice, Clarence Thomas) receive limited social and economic benefits from cultural denial and become the opposite of what their ancestors would have wished. There are cases in educational and cultural institutions where rewards are handed out to black incompetents who participate in white supremacy. These individuals have little or no recognition within the community of progressives; they are victims who are made to believe that they are partners. In the end, they are like the unfortunate black police under the old apartheid regime in South Africa who were told to "go arrest your mother" when they presented themselves to the whites for a job. Those African Americans who have denied their own birthrights to defend justice, to struggle against all forms of oppression, individual and collective, and to stand with the downtrodden against the corporate and institutional powers have become the mad cows of bureaucracy. They are the operatives, the defenders of the oppression, and when it came to it, they have arrested their own mothers.

Richard Wright knew more about the native sons of Africa here in this wilderness of bureaucracy than did many bureaucrats of his day. As the novelist of his era, Richard Wright eschewed the abstract, cold, isolated, detached pieces of individualism that he found in much of the literature in America and sought to find in the reality a principle to express the African American desire for freedom. There is in Wright a hatred for the insanity that parades as race relations between blacks and whites, where whites are able, through the bureaucracy, to control the aims and objectives of blacks. One must see bureaucracy as a form of oppression whenever it is in the hands of malevolent individuals. As a cover for promoting incompetence, nothing has been more effective than bureaucracy.

Bureaucracy, the endeavor in organizations to stratify the function of communication in order to insure efficiency, is a product of industrial society. It is now hopelessly entangled in the tentacles of postmodern technology and often racist ideology. Rather than eliminating bureaucracy, the technocracy has made a space for more levels of bureaucracy; indeed, the computer has made everyone potentially equal to the captains, at least, as far as information is concerned. What is more, the revolution in technology has made it possible for corporations headquartered in the state of Delaware to use hundreds of college-educated Indian citizens as account counselors.

The capture of communication by the bureau of contemporary organizations is among the most critical problems facing the twenty-first century management of industry. Herbert Marcuse understood well how "a sort of well-being, the productive superstructure over the unhappy base of society, permeates the 'media' which mediate between the masters and their dependents." For "its publicity agents shape the universe of communication in which a dimensional behavior expresses itself" (Marcuse 1971). While Marcuse concentrates on a macroanalysis, one could easily see how the same analysis might be made at the microlevel—that is, a bureaucracy shares the same elements of designation, force, power, imitation, and above all efficiency that one finds in superstructures of government. Indeed these smaller bureaucracies may be said to constitute the superstructure. They are like stepping-stones to an infinite web of entrapment.

I seek to attack bureaucracy whenever I can. It is not only a stifling reality of our society but a dehumanizing experience that exercises itself in the American society as anti-African. This is not to say that it does not affect other people; it does so. Yet African Americans possess all of the characteristics that threaten bureaucracy.

For bureaucracy to hold absolute sway, the people must not ask questions; they must not write intelligent letters. They must acquiesce. But I have never been one to acquiesce in what I thought was incorrect, wrong, unjust, cruel, vengeful, or petty. It has meant many battles with those who would avoid answering the hard questions with diversionary tactics. You ask them why a certain action was not considered, and they tell you the sun is not shining. I have come to believe that a bureaucracy feeds on its own stupidity until it collapses. It becomes dysfunctional by virtue of the inability of those who are its managers to manage human communication. They are often the least capable individuals from a communication standpoint in an institution. The problem, of course, is that African American people are often the clients of such bureaucracies.

In the United States African Americans occupy much of the lower stratum of economic life, and consequently we are pushed around by the indignities of traffic courts, welfare departments, prisons, judiciary hearing rooms, special federal programs, and the police. Thus, we bring an intense temperament of impatience to disrespect, personal slight, and ignorant arrogance. If anything, the African American's historical memory creates antagonism against bureaucracy because there is a sense of being haunted by the impersonal buying and selling of humans during the enslavement.

In 2001, just after 9/11, I was invited to speak at Graterford Prison in Pennsylvania. The NAACP on the yard had asked me to come and speak about African American history. I did so with joy. Having been there several years earlier and having had such a powerful experience on that occasion, I was eager to visit the prison. I have always found the black prisoners to be astute, knowledgeable, and often quite intelligent, many having educated themselves while in prison. They learn to read, study numerous foreign languages, and master the sciences, since they have an unlimited amount of free time.

After going through security, my wife, Ana Yenenga, a friend, Joey Temple, and I were escorted by armed guards to an auditorium where forty or fifty prisoners, members of the NAACP, waited for me. I noticed that two white men with weapons sat in the back. They were of higher status than the guards who had ushered us to the auditorium. I detected that they must have been the chief overseers because they told the other guards that it was all right for them to leave. After I spoke, there were, as always, many questions. I answered them as truthfully and forcefully as I could. I noticed that the two white men were becoming nervous. When I finished speaking, I gave the president of the NAACP four books that I had written. One of the white men came and immediately took the books from the brother. I thought that he was simply making certain that they would all have access to the books.

A few days later I received a rude awakening when the books were mailed back to me with a note that the prisoners could not read my books. This created an intense volcano of anger in me, and I wrote to the superintendent of the prison complaining about the attitude of this white man who had intercepted the books and then mailed them back to me. The superintendent's office asked me to return the books to them and they would allow the prisoners to have them. I have spent many days wondering what was wrong with the white man who took the books from the prisoners. Obviously he was a stooge for bureaucracy.

Blurring lines appear between real and fictitious, reason and feeling, fact and process, and we become victims of a system that refuses to answer our questions. By historical habit we become suspicious of whites, who mostly people the bureaucracies, peering into our business, getting into our faces, and demanding this or that. Here I am going to the courtroom with my teenage son to hear what the judge will say about his youthful prank of throwing eggs on Halloween night. But before we could enter, a burly red, white man with a scowl on his face hollers, "Take that hat off!" to the man entering behind us. It was startling, jarring, and totally uncalled for in any courtroom decorum. But here he was a white man in charge of a room full of blacks, and he must be a white man in that situation—acting, posturing, and shouting like the overseer he fashioned himself to be. I still say how communication is managed will determine whether there can be peace between the managers and the managed.

Quite directly, I must be fully engaged, militant and confrontational, to take my place in the resolution of bureaucratic conflict in order to alleviate the inequities built into archaic bureaucracies that subordinate both the bureaucrat and the client to the organization. Such action will help politics and society to adapt to new human realities. We all must be so engaged as we wait for the bureaucracy to straighten out the twisted knots of our circumstances. Each time you tell a bureaucrat "I want this cleared up right now," "Give me the person in charge," "Don't tell me it cannot be done," or "Show me the rule you are applying," you make a dent in the armor of this seemingly impregnable machine.

This is only a stage in the general revamping of the institutions that have been built to reflect efficiency. It is not, by any means, the sounding of the death knell for the bureaucratic system; it is rather a new spirit, one inherent even in the best thoughts of Herbert Schiller, Marshall McLuhan, and Philip Slater. When this occurs, we shall expect different questions to be raised and different answers to be given. No more shall our managers ask the first questions: What will it cost? Or how can we do it for less money and with less labor? The new communication demands a respect for human beings without regard to continental origin.

Two historical developments have sustained the legitimacy of

Western bureaucracies. Neither occurred on the North American continent nor in this century, yet they have legitimized the procedure employed by all institutions in American society and are particularly relevant where the media are concerned. Both developments relate to the concept of proof. Originally perceived in relation to public discourse in ancient Egypt, Sicily, and Greece, proof was a rhetorical idea meant to serve the interest of persuasion. Speakers who effectively used the constituents of proof secured adherence to their positions. *Logos, pathos,* and *ethos* were the pillars of proof for the ancients. The Egyptian mysteries had relied heavily upon these methods of proof. Priestly training emphasized skills in knowledge and rational explanation, the proper use of emotions, the modulation of the voice in reading the sacred texts, sincerity, and good character. A person who combined these traits could prove to be a wise priest, perhaps get to be even a *kheri-heb*, as Imhotep was, and be considered a magician. Aristotle, who first introduced these proofs in Greek, said that logos referred to logical appeals, pathos to emotional appeals, and ethos to character appeals. Aristotle had probably acquired his African collection of books through his close association with Alexander the Great.

The first development was the renunciation of these "pagan" ideas of proof and the institutionalization of Western notions of proof during the Middle Ages. The influence of the barbarians was widespread. Entry of the Germanic tribes—Visigoths, Ostrogoths, and Vandals—into the remnants of the Roman Empire and the Holy Roman Empire pressured the existing Christian pedagogical system inherited from the pagan Romans to adopt new concepts of proof. The Holy Roman Church, eager to extend its influence, bent to the demands of its new adherents, who brought with them an extensive system of proof derived from their history. The Germans introduced oaths, ordeals, and duels as the triune divinities of proof and in the process dethroned the pre-Christian ideas of logos, pathos, and ethos. A major factor in the later European Renaissance was a return to the "pagan" proofs.

In the interim, however, the church acquiesced and permitted priests to serve as mediators, judges, and officials in matters of proof. With the institutionalization of this trinity of proof, a person who was accused of a crime had the burden of proving himself innocent by one of the legitimate proofs: oath, ordeal, or duel.

No longer was it sufficient for a person to use mere logic, emotion, and character in a defense; he must demonstrate his innocence by successfully going through the trials. This concept of proof so enthusiastically adopted by the church was an attempt to circumscribe and conquer the barbaric German gods by allowing the new Christian deity to assume the burden of protecting the innocent. Thus when one chose to prove his innocence, what he was saying in effect was that his deity would allow him to pass the trial because a good god could not punish an innocent person. Many innocent persons were maimed for life.

Oaths required witnesses to the degree of the crime's severity and the accused's social status. All accused persons could choose compurgators to bear witness to their oath taking. If the accused should stumble or slip or forget the words of the oath, he was judged guilty. An innocent person would speak the words of the oath flawlessly.

Ordeals were physical tests involving only the accused and usually were tests in extreme hot or cold. A person would be required to retrieve a pebble from a container of boiling water. If the hand manifested any type of burn, the accused was adjudged guilty as charged. Sometimes the ordeal would require the accused to be tied with a rope and dropped into a body of water. If he sank, he was innocent; on the other hand, floaters were truly guilty because the nature of water, being purified by the priest and thereby holy, refused to receive a guilty, and therefore evil, body into itself. How many innocent persons who were tried by this proof lived to celebrate their innocence is hard to say. Duels required the accused and the accuser to engage in a physical contest against each other. Again, the idea was the inevitability of innocence being protected by Providence.

When Pope Innocent called the Fourth Lateran Council in 1215, he explicitly forbade priests to officiate at ordeals and duels. Proof of guilt or innocence was to be discovered in the proper application of the Scriptures. Only the priests in England obeyed, probably at the behest of King John, who owed Innocent a favor for his declaration annulling the Magna Carta. Three years later, however, when both

John and Innocent were dead, the Magna Carta was reinstated by the English barons. Throughout the Holy Roman Empire the decline in combative proofs was felt as the church imposed Christian culture with its Hebraic-Greco-Roman ethos over the whole of Europe. Nevertheless, by this time the impact of the flirtation with competitive and combative proofs had left an indelible imprint on Western notions of legitimacy.

The second historical development that helped to sustain the legitimacy of bureaucracy, media institutions, is the publication of Bishop Richard Whatley's *Elements of Logic* and *Essentials of Rhetoric*, in 1826 and 1828, respectively. Whatley spent a lifetime defending Christian evidence. From his belief that the proof of the divine needed no demonstration but that the disproof the divine's existence needed demonstration, he evolved the doctrines of presumption and burden of proof. Perhaps no two notions have aided and abetted the maintenance of the status quo and the sustenance of institutional legitimacy more than presumption and burden of proof. These notions, imbedded in Western thought as they are, have created presumption for Westerners in argument with others.

Presumption is the preoccupation of the ground. It is presumed to be true unless arguments are adduced against it. The burden of proof rests with the person who would move the presumption. Changing the presumption from existing media institutions has become increasingly more difficult as the media institutions have acquired new techniques for managing impressions. In addition to operating as mere institutions preoccupying ground and thus establishing their legitimacy and presumption, the new media have gone on the offensive with the best traditions of oaths, ordeals, and duels.

They present their own people as the best possible institutions to do what they do and that there are no reasonable alternatives to be chosen. Consequently, even legitimizing agencies are no match for the institutions that have assumed the presumption by their existence. In America, to be in the process of doing, that is, performing an activity, even though it may be illegal or illegitimate, gives you the occupation of the ground. In fact, on a personal level of involvement, individuals often find it to their advantage to be engaged in an activity in order to substantiate the need for it or the value of their effort. They do what they must, and prove it afterward. Proving and verifying become functions of the bureaucracy.

There really is no need to underscore the search for a novel approach to communication in bureaucracies. It is not so much novelty that is necessary as it is a different approach to how we relate to each other. I do not mean to imply a totally new metaphysical or philosophical system, simply the application of what all of us already understand as necessary for human communication. Humility, not merely as a sentiment, but as an action, in the type of relationship one person shares with another, must be the lodestone. This introduces, as it should, the substance of what bureaucracy ought to be, which is only a type of relationship, a quality of association. But it is a managed relationship. In industrial situations it is organized for economic value.

I can now say that the interrelationship between the past and the contemporary moment is influenced by economics and communication. Economics forms the superstructure and communication the cornerstone. But so long as intellectuals seek to promulgate the essential contemporary world outlook, they will contribute to the promotion of benign bureaucracy. What this society needs is a corps of intellectuals who will abandon the bureaucratic notion and embrace communication as the sine qua non of organizational management, thus overturning any reliance on race as a category for discrimination just as the Internet has overturned gatekeepers.

Bureaucracies need to be audited for communication as much as they are audited financially. Communication audits would record and analyze the flow of communication between different units of an organization. This involves, to a significant degree, practical considerations that play a part in organizational survival. Communication audits can tell us more than what exists; they should also tell us how to perfect our communication with persons of cultures other than our own.

In spite of various technological advances to assist in bureaucratic communication, the institutions seem to be in the midst of a perpetual cycle of mediocrity. Bureaucrats have become tragically commercial; functionaries have multiplied while ideas have diminished. This is not a lament but an assessment. Such a dire organizational situation is set to usher in, at the prompting of a new conception of communication, a reorganization of bureaucracies. This new shift, a modification in conception, cannot be subjected to public relations stunts by academics and advertisers but must be solidly founded upon substantive human values.

One continues to see that the fundamental character of Western informational societies is organizational bureaucracy. Almost every facet of an individual's life is mediated by agencies whose sole purpose is to manage the affairs of individuals. They see to it, or claim to see to it, that pensions are delivered, goods are transmitted, services are rendered, and duties are performed. In fact, how happy or sad a person is can depend upon how well she believes the bureaucracies are functioning in her situation. When the unemployment people, the tax people, the school people, the housing people, the welfare people, the lottery people, and the health people satisfy us as individuals, we do not become frustrated. The fact that access to goods can be denied by bureaucracies gives them a central place in the structure of Western societies.

Any encounter with a bureaucracy represents a collision, and collision creates temporary chaos. Resolution can only come about when the parts of one perfectly match the parts of the other. Forcing the parts to fit is much like the mechanic forcing one piece of equipment to do another's work: it may not stand up under objective scrutiny. Yet it is probably such makeshift measures that are needed to bring humanism into Western bureaucracies. When a person goes to the welfare office in the United States, he is usually required to stand in line with other people who are there to initiate a communicative episode with the bureaucracy. It is usually a brief encounter between the individual and the agency. Such episodes rarely last beyond thirty minutes, and in most cases where people are seeking help from the agency, the encounter lasts less than fifteen minutes. There is not much said on either side.

The communicative situation is classic. The seeker sits or stands on one side of the counter; the potential giver or rejector on the other side. Under normal conditions of bureaucracy, the evaluator represents all the rules, guidelines, and traditions of the agency. Thus it is the agency person's responsibility to determine the validity of requests, the appropriateness of the match between the need of the seeker and the coverage of the agency. The communication may be briefer than the preliminaries, which may include filling out certain forms, answering particular questions, and having papers processed before the meeting with the key agency personnel who will either reject or accept.

Once a decision is made by the agency, the individual may initiate further contacts or discontinue contact with the agency. In one study done by a student of mine, whites averaged three minutes at a welfare agency and blacks seventy seconds.

I think what is needed by bureaucracies is a notion of metavalue, which will allow planners of bureaucracies to question all values that interdict the human spirit and violate human needs in an effort at efficiency. The Third Reich epitomized in its military operations the concept of efficiency, using even the skins of its victims for lamp shades. No time was lost, no materials were wasted, and no mercy was granted. Such is the end of military efficiency. A metavalue would not necessarily obliterate values but would allow human beings an opportunity to look beyond immediate bureaucratic values to broader human values.

The communicative encounter with the agency provides the seeker with an opportunity to make her own evaluation. In making this evaluation the seeker is influenced by previous encounters with the agency, by the propaganda materials emanating from the agency, and by network conversations provided by other seekers. What is determined is how she will respond to the larger political system of which the particular bureau is a part. The politics of communication between bureaucracies and their clients must seek to establish mechanisms for the survival of the clients in the twenty-first century. It must form a mechanism that will not destroy or subjugate the human personality to mere efficiency. Bureaus must abandon the ethic that reduces everything to how much you can do with what you have in a specified amount of time in favor of a more personal concern with helping clients and thereby themselves.

Bureaucracy in Western societies will find it difficult to shed the ethic of procedure because our total social and political environment is controlled by analogues. These master concepts spin the wheel of our thought. Two of the most obvious analogues affecting the bureaucracy are the process analogue and the cavity analogue.

Process as a dynamic analogue has occupied the center stage for the last one hundred years. Its origin is in the revolution of physics and thermodynamics. It is responsible for the emphasis on action in American society. Elementary school children are taught to read fast. It is not enough for a child to learn how to read, but teachers require students to learn under pressure of time. To accomplish this type of learning, it becomes vital for teachers to understand teaching as a process. So it is with bureaucracy, an understanding of process supposedly creates a hospitable climate for efficiency. Involved in the understanding, of course, is an appreciation of speed. The rationale for process is therefore both speed and efficiency. What is presumed in such cases is that once a person knows process or "technique," he will be able to perform quickly and accurately. Bureaucrats normally learn the system well and assume their places at the gates. They seek to employ communication skills to quietly and accurately move information and people. These communication brokers, like others, stand at the gate to who shall eat and who shall be sheltered. The idea of gatekeeper is a process concept. Process as an analogue in human relations has distorted the fundamental nature of human interactions. An attempt to get away from architectons produces well-meaning but mistaken notions about human beings. Motion is at the center of process. Certainly there is motion when we interact, but there is also reality; we see each other at a given moment in time, but within all time that moment is stationary. Like a tree standing in a forest growing, it is both motion and reality. In fact, a great part of its reality is motion but motion so imperceptible as to be unnoticed. It is so with us very human beings.

Process as an analogue complicates our understanding of the reality confrontation when we just "do it" or "say it" or "relate." Process is a complement of bureaucracy. People in the United States, India, and Nigeria complain about bureaucracy, but few people complain about process. The functioning of the bureaucracy depends upon process analogues. If you do not follow the right process, then you cannot achieve the intended objective. Whether what you do is significant or not is irrelevant unless the process is completed. In this way John Dewey's pragmatism has become a new process orientation. Means are elevated; objectives are minimized. Process becomes the materialization of quest.

In universities the committees who decide who shall receive tenure and who shall not have tenure epitomize the process orientation. Their actions are cryptic. The icons of success and academic growth are paraded in front of the committee. A committee is usually comprised of white males who if they did not come from antiseptic backgrounds of white suburbs have always aspired to them. Members of such a committee see a Native American professor who understands the communicative significance of the wampum belt and is able to turn students on to the drama of native culture as a threat to their view of their institution. The process allows them to keep the institution like themselves. It makes it possible for these brokers to decide who shall eat and who shall not.

Clearly the bifurcation extends to any *explanandum*. Explanation can be nomological or teleological. The first refers to causes producing the explanation, and the latter refers to ends determining the cause of the explanation. Emphasis on acceptance of future events distorts a true teleological position that resides in the stability and maintenance of an institution or situation. Ends are not necessarily agents in their own realization. Rather it is the present that determines explanation on the basis of contributing to the survival of the institution. There is an operant marginalism in problem solutions that goes hand in hand with the process orientation, or the "nomological" mind-set toward society. Changes are conservative, piecemeal, incremental, and slow. This marginalism is the direct result of the process analogue. Access to process is synonymous with access to decision making. Blacks, women, and Spanish-surnamed persons are normally excluded from process. If they are included, they bring a culturally distinct attitude toward process. They bring impatience, the one quality that process finds impossible to accept. To be successful in the Western sense is to adapt to a certain orientation.

Western ideology, contrary to some opinions, does not assault merely by its technology but also by its success orientation. Communication technology developed in the West and extended by Japan, the most imitative of the non-Western societies, is an outgrowth of an individualistic reliance on success. Human beings are more or less restricted by their cultural inclinations. A Nigerian mother would think it "savage" to deny a child food as a method of punishment. In the United States parents have been known to deny children the right to eat a meal as punishment. It is a matter of cultural behavior. Yet even in our limited spheres, and we are limited as Herbert Marcuse ably told us a few years ago, we are participants in the Great Western Drama. It is hardly possible for anyone in any place from Abu Dhabi to Ouagadougou to minimize the insistence of Western technology. There seems to be an inexorable march. But behind the technology is a basic Western cultural driveshaft—the need to succeed. Success is an individual commodity that can only become collective if other individuals put in their fair share. Individuals seek to stand out as politicians, educators, military leaders, business people, or even spiritualists. The naming of names, a sort of hall of fame identity guide, can be called as the African invokes the names of the ancestors. Thus, the "dropping of names" of important persons is an indication of one's own success. The names dropped are usually those of persons considered successful. In the end, then, it is the instance of success, the force of competition, and not the insistence of technology, which accounts for Western ideology's assault on other societies. The truth of the matter is that all human activity counts about the same in the ethical and moral dimensions of actions. Who is to say that success in the military is more "valuable" than success as a street sweeper? In fact, as Jean-Paul Sartre told us in his example of the drunkard and the leader of a nation, the valuableness of the activity may well be in favor of the person less readily recognized as important. At least, such an individual does not cause as much human pain by the mistakes he may make.

The cavity analogue helps dictate the style of bureaucracy and contemporary art. We seek to remove, replace, and say, "It's finished." Yet the disintegration and decay in bureaucracy and modern art are not dealt with by removing and replacing. Blatant crassness, audience abuse, and immature symbology, devoid of meaningful references, hinder the growth of culture and management. The cavity analogue represents movement and change in the contemporary bureaucracy. It is the constant need to reorganize and modify. Notions of decadence and repair, holes and fillings, gaps and fixtures dominate the thinking in this area. This analogue creates decisionism, decision for the sake of decision—communication meant as a repair or stopgap measure proliferates. Bureaucrats decide in order to give the impression of action.

In his *Dehumanization of Art*, Ortega (1976) suggested in his morphological view of art that some art is incomprehensible to the masses. However, the reason for the lack of understanding may rest more with the artist than with the masses. Operating from the cavity analogue, many artists use their works to fill in personal gaps. This may be done by drawing a series of lines on a white canvas or by leaning a pole against a door. The audience is supposed to provide its own answers. In this respect, not only has art been dehumanized but the masses have been saddled with the artist's own inadequacies.

But it is in bureaucracy where the cavity analogue finds its greatest impact on society. Here the insatiable desires of the bureaucracy are fed by an ever-flowing supply of persons, money, and problems. We see a cycle of demand and supply that never ends nor can ever end. Bureaucracy must receive forever; that is essentially its nature, its life. If we recognize the analogic assumptions upon which bureaucracy stands, then it is clear that any message originating from the bureaucracy is a message which demands that whether the bureaucracy deals with domestic or foreign affairs, social or economic issues, it has the same character and the same purpose: to receive. Bureaucracy astutely achieves this purpose while appearing to give. Understanding this idea, it is easier to decipher the message of foreign aid and the transfer of technology.

Foreign aid is a complex message. Rich nations have long sought to send messages to weaker nations through the medium of foreign aid. These messages have frequently been distorted, misinterpreted, or ignored. What a nation does with its economic largesse has always been an indication of what it thinks of itself and other nations. To get an accurate account of any modern nation, take a look at the countries it has aided and the causes it has supported. These are communicative items that color our perceptions of nations. The miser nations are known and are discussed in diplomatic halls. Some Western nations demand to know what they are going to get for their aid. Will we have more friends because of aid, demands an American woman of her senator. Foreign aid becomes tied to interest instead of altruism in most political circles. Its intent is not to heal the sick or make the lame to walk or bring happiness to the hearts of the sad, but to insure the power of the giver in world opinion. When a smaller nation fails to understand that message, it runs the risk of being a victim of foreign aid neglect. Tractors, tanks, and schools are clear messages, and the receiver must acknowledge his debt to the giver. Bureaucrats in the giver nation look for evidence that receiver nations reciprocate by their political actions. Receiver nations that do not get the message soon get another message that discontinues aid.

Finally, two characteristics of Western bureaucracies project a pessimistic prognosis for Western societies. On the one hand, there is an enormous bureaucratic establishment; on the other hand, there is almost complete isolation and alienation of the individual, even within the bureaucracy. We do not know very much about how this bifurcation of masses and isolated individuals fits into the total fabric of how life is lived in the major conurbations of our time. But surely there are many alienated people. The bureaucracy, with its separate offices, carrels, desks, and keys to toilets, can be experienced as lonely places whose hostility strikes the most dedicated bureaucrat, and although there is increased communication channels—newspapers, bulletin boards, video aids, and teleconferencing facilities—they merely add to the confusion, frustration, and loneliness. Indeed, the communication aids have aided in the din. Perhaps the most enduring legacy of the contemporary bureaucracy is the fact that we are unable to communicate because everyone is trying to talk at the same time and no one is able to hear anyone else.

chapter 6
THE CONTINUING PREVALENCE OF RACISM

In his controversial book *The Declining Significance of Race*, William Julius Wilson, the Harvard professor, formerly of Chicago, writes, "Race relations in America have undergone fundamental changes in recent years, so much so that now the life chances of individual blacks have more to do with their economic class position than with their day to day encounters with whites" (Wilson 1979). But what Wilson omits or dismisses is the fact that inasmuch as racism is systemic, and operates as process, it is unnecessary for blacks to encounter whites daily in the United States in order to have limited life chances.[1] Furthermore, the economic class position of blacks generally is directly related to race.[2]

Perhaps Lewis R. Gordon understood the situation best when he described the condition of problematic people, suggesting that in a racist society people with problems can simply become to the oppressor problematic people. In other words, we become, as African Americans, not just people who experience crime, poor education, lack of decent housing, or unemployment, but rather we become, to the oppressive system, crime, unemployment, licentiousness, and other social pathologies (Gordon 2000, 69).

Given how easily this becomes the case in the United States, one can also see how the media become instruments for the dissemination of political and social information as materiality and the transmission of cultural values that reinforce negative beliefs about African Americans. Indeed, the other problem is the removal of African values, styles, and cultures, in their most potent and powerful forms, from the media. It matters little that protests have been mounted and petitions signed; the process seems inexorable in its exclusion of blacks from truly substantive roles and images. Notwithstanding the few actors and actresses hired and the limited but growing number of writers and directors, media in all forms remains essentially a white enterprise for the promotion of white cultural values, which tend to be racist and exclusivist in nature. In the communication media, class arguments notwithstanding, blacks still are racially discriminated against in many companies. For blacks in America, race is more primary for our life chances than class or gender, although both gender and class are important at the intersection of racial progress and identity. We are certainly victims of all these exploitations, but it is the peculiar history of Africans and Europeans in America that makes race the fundamental contradiction.

If America can be humanized within the foreseeable future, the obliteration of racism must be the fundamental task. In America, it is possible for one to change classes but virtually impossible for one to change races. Yet the assumptions of class distinctions have always been based on race or ethnic distinctions. The imperative of race is the myth that stands guard over the injustices perpetrated by class or gender distinctions.

I am happy to be able to distinguish the modalities at work in any construction of a discourse on race. For me to say, as I have just written, that it is possible for "one to change classes but virtually impossible to change races" does not mean that there is some implied value in changing races like when a poor person becomes a well-to-do person. However, when we discuss race, we cannot assume that becoming white is an advance despite the fact that this position has been taken by many immigrants and African Americans intoxicated by the thought of privilege in a racist society. This is merely an illusion because race itself remains a scientific illusion, much like ether, and in some future time it, too, will disappear from our discussions as new forms of human groupings become ascendant. Yet it remains a major myth in our society.

The language of revolution must become the persuasive instrument for change in the governing myth of Western capitalism, and only with the collective force of public opinion can we achieve success. It was necessary, of course, to indict Western communism for being guilty, just like capitalism, of racism. Mistreatment of ethnic and racial minorities has not been confined to consumer economies, although it is most prevalent in such societies. As an underlying factor in the oppression of the world's masses, racism, in its most virulent form, is a general category of class.

The separation of race and class cannot be made on any permanent basis in racist societies. What one must understand is that while race is fundamental, it becomes also a criterion for class discrimination and oppression. By claiming an end to racism, reactionary forces seek to pronounce the end to antiracist campaigns. Yet I remain convinced that the human passion to freedom will always overcome the human will to oppress. However, it is clear that solidarity with other oppressed peoples, whether their oppression begins with color, economics, or gender, is predicated upon common struggle. Setting up economics as the basic criterion of human acceptability, Western society defined human value through productivity. The enslavement of Africans found its practical roots in economic output and its theoretical basis in psychological aberrations (Davis 1966).

The doctrine of economic power as the determiner of political and social relations grows more prevalent each day. It is only a partially correct view of the scope of political affairs. Deeply embedded in Western political doctrine is the idea that if all people are landlords, then a commonwealth exists. This view, carried to the level of collective land ownership where the state becomes the sole landlord, is as much a part of the contemporary world as it was a part of the Western past. Economic determinism is at its base a spiritless philosophy that enshrines positivism in the heart of American social thought. Without this view, America would have been farther along on the path to equal justice. America is burdened with its European concept of landlords and nobility. The weight of this idea oppresses the poor and retards social justice (Willhelm 1983). Whereas the traditional African concept of community is generally more egalitarian because of communal land ownership, in America the clash of cultures continues to produce conflict. Economic power, however enshrined, stands in the middle of all social and political progress in the United States. To a large extent, however, it is still the racism of individuals that decides how justice will live in American society.

Personal racism is unabated. The evil that has plagued this nation for more than a quarter of a millennium has adjusted rather comfortably to the last round of public agitation. The signs of the next round are already emerging in the North and the South. In almost every sphere of human activity in the nation, adjustment to grievances expressed by African Americans in the 1960s has been painfully achieved. Therein lies the next round.

During the 1960s personal racism was manifest most intensely against African Americans in either de facto or de jure institutional racism. White racist adjustment took the form of "opening the doors" of educational, religious, social, and philanthropic institutions only to "clog the corridors" with process mechanisms that effectively controlled the numbers of blacks who achieved success.

Affirmative action programs were mandated by governments, agencies, and churches as responses to the overwhelming inequality in society. Institutional racism was on its way to being stamped out. The indignation of whites whose own personal racism had perpetuated institutional racism seemed to match the anger of blacks. What resulted was a hiatus for all of us who had marched, been clubbed, and been jailed in the 1960s. Expressions heard in the community were somehow different now because our demands were being addressed in democratic fashion. We could "go on vacation," "take five," "be fraternal," and "climb on in."

The times are fluid again. Personal racism continues as strong or stronger than in the 1950s according to the proliferation of white supremacist groups, whose activities are rarely seen in a terrorist light. In addition, something else has happened, however; institutional racism, while almost nonexistent from a legal standpoint at this time, has given way to the novel racist stratagem of process racism.

Instead of barring the African American outright through custom or law as in institutional racism, process racism concentrates on "getting you" in procedures, a creative and novel adjustment mechanism. A case in point was the changing process that was put into place by a university dean of a large northeastern university when an outstanding black professor came up for promotion to full professorship. The professor had five books and thirty-five articles published, numerous extraordinary recommendations, superb student evaluations, and a record of community service. The professor was approved by the departmental committee and recommended by four full professors at other institutions but got caught in the dean's Machiavellian actions to prevent the professor from advancing. First, the dean said that the professor had to translate two books, published by the professor but written in French, into English. Then the dean suggested that the external reviewers should have been from Ivy League institutions, and finally, the dean protested that the professor had not accepted the dean's recommendation to postpone the promotion request. What was at work in this case was process racism. It was revealed in the changing of the rules, the modification of the standards, and the ease with which personal racism was permitted to cloud the promotion process. Clearly the guidelines, affirmative action plans, elaborate committee systems, and screening panels are nothing short of an innovative level in the dialectics of racism.

Former president Jimmy Carter's church was a case par excellence; it embodied the personal racism of its members in a process—a screening committee. Previously, the church exercised institutional racism, the group manifestation of most of its members. Process racism replaced institutional racism in direct response to Rev. Clemon King's agitation in the form of black worshipers. But neither King nor the white racists in President Carter's church expected that the screening committee would ever screen Clemon King into the church. The church's adjustment was a page from other American institutions, affirming their racism by assuming a process orientation. It was not even that someone was at the end of the process and in charge of deciding; it was that the process itself was the culprit. Hence, it was extrahuman and nonpersonal. One could be denied admission by metaphysics.

Process racism as a metamorphosis of institutional racism dominates educational institutions. The reason for this is fairly simple. Faculty groups have more power than ever before as a direct result of the black student and white leftist confrontations with university administrators in the 1960s. In a sense, the students took power away from presidents and gave it to faculties. This has been catastrophic both for blacks in universities and for academic governance. Faculties have traditionally relied on committees for decisions. Committees are by their nature conservative and indecisive. They are excellent forums for argument and information gathering but notoriously poor for decision making and action. Caught in the clutches of faculty affirmative action committees, whether at the department or university level, African Americans were squeezed in the process. The idea was for an institution to give the impression of running while standing still. Faculty committees made this possible by establishing guidelines and criteria that were extensions of their own personal racism.

The new mechanism is now fully developed. All the trappings of vocabularies and apologists have gathered around. Screening committees are "seeking qualified minority and women" candidates. Prior to the process racism stage, universities sought candidates for positions. "Qualified" was never used as extensively for white males as it has become for black and women applicants. By definition, process racism views blacks, Puerto Ricans, and Native Americans as unqualified. Therefore, it becomes necessary to seek "superior," "qualified," or "outstanding" applicants.

In some institutions, personal racism is manifest in the institution's ability to change the process whenever it feels threatened. One academic department at a major university wanted to extend the grade point average for entry into a graduate program from a usual 3.0 (B average) to a 3.5 in response to the large number of African American students who sought entry. Process racism as a manifestation of personal bias is as abhorrent as institutional racism. It is less frontal, however, and much more insidious than institutional racism. Procedures may be established today only to be disestablished tomorrow.

The next round must be the last. It has to strike not at institutional and process racism but at the source: personal racism. Rather than study the victims of racism, it is now time to study the psyches of the perpetrators, including their socialization patterns, lifestyles, and value-belief matrix, and ways to modify racist behavior. These are the challenges of the next few years. Indeed, they are the kinds of challenges that will require new methods for analysis. The dominant research paradigm in the West has been reductionist and consequently fails to discover any more than what is intended and operationalized.

One can go so far as to say that most social science in the West is founded on linear thinking and exalts a reductionist position often while disclaiming to do so. To the prosecution of linear thinking we owe imperialism, racism, exploitation, and the disrespect for other people's culture by Western people. Anthropology, psychology, linguistics, communication, philosophy, and sociology are significantly alike in their linearity. The cause-effect, stimulus-receiver, reward-punishment, sender-receiver, and cost-benefit models are all representative of the straight-line thinking that leads to social and political aggression. This approach is intent on reducing human activity, in whatever discipline, to a single rationally intelligible pattern. Of course, such a position must always clash with the higher creative forces that come from the inner resources of the masses. Whether the political ideology is capitalism or communism, it is clear that the dichotomies—good-evil, beautiful-ugly, workers-bourgeoisie, rich-poor, black-white, Palestinian-Zionist, and literate-illiterate—reflect a strong hierarchical bias in Western thought. The rise of empiricism has clarified the racism of the West by demonstrating the results of prosecuting a linear doctrine.

Empiricism is linearity in method. Nothing is tragic about this linearity unless it is without substance. Mundane operationalism that eliminates significant questions of human existence and moral ethics has to be a concern of good scholarship. The seriousness of the semantic and indeed ethical problem is manifest when the press refers to an African American political independent as a militant while simultaneously calling a white political independent, in the opposite direction, a maverick. Militant seems to be reserved for black public figures who speak in the interest of their people. Whites who speak in the interest of whites may be mavericks but never militants. Such linearity allows a person to operationalize a concept to prove whatever he sets out to prove without really changing much in the understanding of the human condition. Several years ago during the invasion of the Shaba province in Zaire (Congo) by dissident Zairians, the nations of the West were stunned by news reports which said that one hundred whites were massacred and one thousand blacks were killed. One group was massacred; the other just killed. Such reporting damages the credibility of the press because it demonstrates bias. Although the most radical of empiricisms is firsthand experience, the method can be colored by the inherent biases of the observer. All one has to do is to refer to history for the truism of this point.

It is impossible to talk sensibly about racism without understanding historical content. Bartholoméw de Las Casas was perhaps the key historical figure in the development of modern racism. Las Casas was the first Western cleric to publicize the notion of racial superiority, noting the superior mental abilities of Europeans, the lesser abilities of other races, and the physical strength of Africans (Asante and Mattson 1998). As the "Protector of Indians," he saved them from universal enslavement by arguing that the African was more suited to physical labor. Las Casas was a publicist. In the sixteenth century he was a likely candidate for propagandizing his particular faith. A priest of the church, educated for his day, gifted with eloquence, and an adventurer, he was fitted for his peculiar role in the history of racism. Despite Las Casas's religious training and priestly manner, he was not quite convinced of the benefits of religion for Africans. The story of the church has often been parallel to the story of racism. As an instrument for the propagation of racism, it has been unsurpassed. Communication, therefore, served racism in the past, as well as serving it today.

In America and other multiracial informational societies, race plays a determining factor in the political and cultural media that affect the society as a whole. This is both a historical and a contemporary truth. Marxist and neocapitalist interpreters have both failed to understand the essential character of multiracial informational societies. While class is frequently a temporary contradiction based upon material and status, race is a permanent contradiction in such societies. I guess one could demonstrate social class as a determinant of some forms of political communication. A few years ago we had discussions about restricted and elaborated codes. It is provocative to speak in such a way about how people communicate, but in the Western world researchers have found bifurcations in the language of people from different classes. A person may be prevented from relating to the political institutions of a society by language style or accent. I think this is more a function of not being able to articulate political views rather than any particular accent. When Henry Kissinger was secretary of state in the United States, his German accent did not keep him from articulating his thoughts or relating to the American public. There really is no such thing as a restricted code or elaborated code except in the sense that one is perceived to be one or the other by speakers. All codes have both restrictive and elaborative capacities given the area of their provenance. I might claim that a restricted code relies upon descriptive thinking, predictability, emphasis on form rather than content, grammatical simplicity, uniformity of vocabulary, short sentences, scarcity of adjectives and adverbs, and little symbolism. Or I might claim that the elaborated code is relatively unpredictable and abstract; uses instrumental language, complex conceptual hierarchies, accurate grammar and syntax, and complex sentences; is abundant in adjectives and adverbs; and is the verbal mediation of individuated meaning. In either case I am taking an ethnocentric classification scheme and building value-laden ideas and a political communication argument that lacks factual basis.

Governments are complex linguistic constructions. They find their existence in the rules, regulations, covenants, and documents of the society. Events that influence society are either sanctioned or not sanctioned by the communication documents within society. All efforts to make the documents conform to the people or vice versa are definitionally political. Governments therefore are preeminently meant to maintain a sort of equilibrium. The establishment is a fairly accurate label for the linguistic construction that serves a particular people. Its aim is to continue its existence. This is precisely the character of all institutions. In fact, institutions, whether political or cultural, are established to maintain communication documents. They are our societal memory; without them we would hardly know who we were or to what nation we belonged. I do not mean this in any literal repository sense even though that is also true but more profoundly in the institutionalization of communication. Although governments depend upon communication, they are more specifically communication, that is, they are the message.

Race is the critical element that must be understood as at the base of government's internal decisions in the social, political, and cultural spheres. Class socialization may determine one's grammatical structure, but race provides the fuel for alternative political symbolism. As an established order, government normally demands participation or isolation. Mueller would have us believe that individuals in the lower class would not be able to articulate their sentiments and consequently would not share in the government's largesse. Lack of participation equals isolation. If Mueller's analysis of the lower class is correct and African Americans constitute a large percentage of the lower class, then it could be argued that African Americans would not have the ability to articulate their sentiments, grievances, and alternatives. Obviously African Americans have had the ability to generate symbolism and alternatives from a base even though we do not uniformly share the same class. By now we know that to understand political alternatives, language must be used analytically. We must be careful not to rush to apply the lack of analytical use of language to lower economic classes. This would be an obvious attempt to make everything fit. However, the masses of people have frequently articulated alternatives more clearly than is realized. It is one thing to say that a linguistic code acquired from your environment limits your linguistic growth and quite another to say that this means you cannot articulate your political needs. It is not a linguistic code that determines your ability to present political alternatives. One can accept the idea of class-specific variations in speech behavior but not as warrants for a political statement. The principal warrants for political statements remain materialistic: food, shelter, clothing. In the United States African Americans have had little difficulty articulating needs in the most dramatic, symbolic, and expressive manner.

Martin Luther King Jr. led the most dramatic movement since Marcus Garvey in American history. The age of King, 1953–1963, was the height of dramatic intensity in American moral practice. Unlike the controversy surrounding abolition of slavery, the King era involved the mighty forces of the black masses themselves. The Sojourner Truths, Charles Remonds, and Frederick Douglasses of antislavery and abolition operated within a limited sphere and with few blacks; the majority of blacks at the time being chattel slaves in the South (Bennett 1990). Thus Martin Luther King Jr. was the crystallization of the political and social commentary that preceded 1953. He embodied the meaning of civil rights; his clarion call for decency, morality, and equality was a composite of what had gone on before. King is at once separated from and connected to Marcus Garvey, W. E. B. DuBois, and A. Phillip Randolph. His separateness stems from his Southern base. Embodied in his Southern heritage were the seeds of a mass movement. Never before had a black spokesman of such powerful eloquence used the South as the hub of his activities. King was to reorient American history and to shift the civil rights momentum from the South to the nation at large. Education and upbringing prepared King to take over a leadership role in the black church establishment. Emotion, tradition, and reason, however, conspired to make him nontraditional, activist, and dramatic in the interest of the masses of his people. For him it was necessary to never accede to the so-called privilege of the elite while one's people are being exploited. Racism and privilege, as practiced in modern informational nations of the West, are twin clutches of minority intellectuals. As Frantz Fanon understood in relationship to his experiences in Blida—the City of Roses—and in Paris, it is possible for the colonizer to accept the doctor and attempt to separate him from his people although the masses continue to be oppressed (Fanon 1965). Those who cannot speak out against the injustices of the oppressed because they are beneficiaries of racism and privilege have no right to be treated seriously. King denounced race and class and stood with the blacks and poor.

The practical function of any society is to establish mechanisms that will serve human needs. In America, blacks are frequently driven to desperate solutions in order to maintain sanity. Any society that induces desperation in its members is a nonviable society and will eventually be replaced. There can be no prior claims to rationality or logic that must stand in the way of this truth. Neither ethics, culture, worker solidarity, nor pseudonationalism can prevail against the truth. Thus, whether it is persecution in Ireland, Israel, Uganda, South Africa, Russia, or the United States, it must be denounced and done so vehemently.

Unfortunately, a whole generation has grown up without either knowing or understanding the significance of King, Malcolm X, Elijah Muhammad, and one hundred other activist-orators of the 1950's and 60's. Historical discontinuity is the greatest barrier to moral and intellectual advancement in American society. Absence of a historical sense creates culturally and politically impoverished masses.

Perhaps, very unusually in American history, the succeeding generation will be more conservative than the preceding one. Television has paralyzed a whole generation without meaning to do so. If it had meant to do so, the coming generation would have been more aggressive than the present one. But the violent rhetoric of the sixties and the sabotage and bombings of the early seventies were prime-time television news. Television does not educate; it inculcates. The children of the sixties and seventies were inculcated with antiliberal views. This occurred, not because of news commentators' views, but because the children of television (preteens in the late sixties) saw their elders' repulsion of violence as a revulsion against liberal social sentiments. They associated the black and student radicals with violence. Never in the history of the American people had violence so captivated the imagination of the public. Antiviolence became synonymous with antiliberal views. Progressive thinkers were impotent in the face of such startling contradictions. They feared a renunciation of violence would seem a renunciation of social reform. The liberals' rhetorical problem showed the extent of the trap. They could not disentangle themselves from the violence of the sixties because they either believed that violence was redemptive or that to separate out those who were rationally violent and those who were irrationally violent was impossible.

Violence is never redemptive. It merely transfers the burden of proof. Had the liberal thinkers spoken to the need for radical change and had they consolidated their own moral, political, and economic powers, Martin Luther King would never have died. A half of a generation saw the silence of the liberals as an acceptance of violence. The social rights issues were lost in the stampede to make violence the target of public discussion. An adage of the time went, there can be no justice without law and order first. Of course those voicing the adage had never sought justice, neither had they any intention of doing so, even if law and order were established. Those who reflect on the condition of African Americans know that it is only an uneasy peace before the dam breaks again.

NOTES

1. In a series of books after *The Declining Significance of Race*, Wilson sought to soften the argument he had made in the 1979 book. In fact, in *The Bridge over the Racial Divide*, which appeared in 1999, he made it clear that racism should be looked at as a system of racial domination. Seeking to make a case for multiracial political coalitions, Wilson recognizes the nature of racism but still fails to see the need to raise the issue of white racial supremacy as a doctrine of domination apart from coalition politics.

2. In a very important book, *Black Visions: The Roots of Contemporary African American Political Ideologies* (2001), Michael Dawson uses a combination of quantitative and qualitative data to suggest that black political thought has developed black autonomy as the most authentic realization of the black vision.

chapter 7
A NEW ARCHITECTON OF IMAGES

Images are indicting. This is true in war and peace. During the past three hundred years Africans in America have been engaged in a high-stakes contest to prevent the ultimate destruction of our culture. It is not clear that we will be victorious given the powerful rhetoric that is used to mobilize a reconstitution of social norms and values. While images can indict, whether they are photographs and videos of prisoners being abused or black men being brutalized by police on the streets of America's cities, it is rhetoric alone that isolates, integrates, and collectivizes as it constructs reality.

African Americans are victims of a deadly dose of detachment from reality. Our time is consumed by images that undermine our cultural esteem and make us dependent upon the very negative symbols that we have fought against for decades. So what do we do with our time? How is it structured and organized in terms of symbols, images, and motifs? Who controls our leisure and the images that we see during our leisure? What are the measures that can be taken to create the kind of *instrumentalization*, in the sense of devices and measures that would constitute creative constructions of reality, which would bring us to true human liberation?

The record is clear, however, that Africans in the United States or anywhere else cannot fail to use time and the instrumentalization of images wisely to transform economic and political situations. Leisure does not mean idleness. Even those who seem to stand around and wait for others or sit in their cars and wait for the traffic to move or stand in long security lines at the airports are now fully engaged in writing, listening, creating, discussing, or seeing something. This is the process of instrumentalization. What is it that we are seeing, discussing, listening to, or producing? Are we fully conscious of the necessity for serious cultural revitalization through the images that adorn our offices, churches, mosques, and homes? Whether Godot comes or not does not matter if we have organized our own time by using it to assist in our transformation.

Clearly, in the African American community we have been taught that our characters are formed by what happens in our leisure time, that is to say, what we do with the time that we have apart from the dedicated time for work, family, play, and reverence. I can know you more thoroughly by watching how you formulate your leisure. Do you want to dance to the music, make word rhythms, play computer games? Indeed, the idea that we can create our leisure, that is, fabricate what it is that we do with our time, is central to the instrumentalization of image. I do not mean this merely in a John Dewey functionalist or pragmatic sense. It is my belief that there must be something more—for example, we might say that the personality is in the DNA but the character seems to be formed in the interaction with space and time. Thus, instrumentalization carries with it both a pragmatic and a philosophical component. I am eager to see how character, for instance, plays out in the creation of images of people.

The Yoruba word *iwa*, character, suggests that it is the highest form of the person's being because one cannot exceed *iwa*. It is not love that is the greatest thing in the world to an African sensibility, but character. All of the African traditional systems emphasize the superiority of character. Among the Akan people of Ghana, it is thought that neither land, nor money, nor fame, nor intelligence can be greater than character because character, *soban*, is at the core of the family's sense of honor, respect, and destiny.

How much television and what television do you watch? Have you decided to keep images of death and destruction to your psyche and culture out of your house? In Paris, where there are nearly one million African people, there is no African journalist or reporter on television. One of my colleagues, Jean-Philippe Omotunde of Paris, has started a campaign, the first in France, to raise the consciousness of Africans to the deliberate attempt on the part of the French to maintain a lilly-white media in the face of the overwhelming reality of the millions of Africans in the country. No wonder there remain Africans in France who believe that their ancestors were the Gauls!

Metaphor, the architectonic symbol, becomes a productive structuring device with all of the philosophical and mechanistic components intact when we apply it to our lives. In a concrete sense, cultures differ in their metaphorical manifestations. One metaphor might indicate how we treat our opposition, and another might show how we summarize our own cultural aspirations. Almost all of us use either the organizing, sustaining, or productive capacities of metaphors in our lives.

Political struggle is often the battle of metaphors. The reason for this is because each side wants to define itself and to define the other—otherwise there is no reason for battle. If one side chooses a principal metaphor that suggests "civilization," then the other side is thrust into the position of being "uncivilized." But, of course, this works both ways. Once a principal, that is, architectonic metaphor, is chosen, then it must be sustained by rhetorical discourse. Rhetoric's most potent substance is the metaphor.

In the United States the pressing question now is how shall we manage our leisure with the amusements that present themselves to us in ever-increasing abundance? Indeed, often they are amusements that keep us away from power to control our lives and communities. Why is it that the rap musicians who are most popular are often the ones who are the most vile, obscene, and materialistic in ways that deny African culture? Of course, it takes the audience to participate in order for the anti-African messages and images to be successful. Who buys the CDs of such anti-African purveyors of false culture but those individuals who are themselves victims of false images and motif maligning? Clearly both the artist and the consumer are victims because we have not learned much about ourselves and do not know what is in our best interest. Miseducation is the principal problem of contemporary schooling.

Our worlds are kaleidoscopes of action, and we are caught in a matrix reloaded with new issues of leisure, images, and symbols. We are busy trying to keep Zion from failure, and yet all around us there is the failure of African cultural institutions. What elevating spirit will rise in us to keep us from sinking under the weight of too much Spielberg, Schwarzenegger, Walt Disney, and Fantasy Land? Are there no redeeming images based on the best qualities of the African world? Are our moviemakers so devoid of connection to ancestral traditions and values, so lost from the greatest world of symbols, and too weak to interrogate their own histories that they cannot produce images and ideas that conquer the abyss of leisure in modern America?

Modern cities are jolted upward by the quality of economic power creating vast realms of disjointed parts, and we are frequently lost in the midst of them and at a loss to explain our misfortune. Around us are amusements of all sorts—parks, campgrounds, movies, bars, technological games, restaurants, country clubs, swimming pools, bowling alleys, and recreational centers. Urban complexes are defined by the quality of their amusement.

I have a catalog of memories of cities. I can walk along the beautiful Benjamin Franklin Parkway in Philadelphia and feel connected to nature and the city in the most awesome manner, or walk along the glitz of Michigan Avenue in Chicago and wonder about the perfection of things, or contemplate the Egyptian influence on Paris at the Place de la Concorde or on the Avenue des Champs Élysées, or see the memories of Greece on the Unter den Linden in Berlin, or take in the glories that were England's at Piccadilly Circus, or admire the mass of vendors at the grand Kumasi market, or engage the multiplicity of faces on a brisk walk up Fifth Avenue in New York. I am a child of a new engagement with time and space in our cities, yet I realize that there is a steady subversion of Africa in many of the cities of the world or the taking of what is African and the perverting of it so that not even Africans realize that they are the creators of the images. Consider the rather silly debate that has raged in popular circles about whether or not Africans built the pyramids in Africa. We Africans are often robbed of our sense of self, left to feel isolated in the world from our traditions, and sometimes finding in our children the belief that we, the mothers and fathers of human civilization, are barely present in the contemporary world except as cajolers and amusers for others. This is the great travesty of the age.

Cities are implicated in many ways in the generation of images because they reaffirm traditions in all forms of their innovations whether they repeat what they consider to be Greek or French or Tuscan or English. We either like them or not on the basis of what advantages they have fed us if we need to see, hear, or do something. Indeed, our whole social frame of reference is subject to be modified under these circumstances.

Urban life has changed not only how we work and eat but it has changed how we spend our seeing time and how we communicate with each other. Our emphatic need to transform our images or, at least, the images that are used to create community, to ensure identity, and to maintain society, can be used to transform our response to the urban milieu. What are the important symbols—for example, the Washington Monument, the Pyramid at the Louvre, the Obelisk in London—around which Europe builds its contemporary history and what are the bases for communication about these symbols? Africa is again robbed, and our lack of consciousness based on a lack of information and knowledge further degrades us.

Massive arenas and stadiums dot the landscapes, suggesting the worship of the athlete in contemporary life as the large churches in the past suggested the religion of an unseen deity. There is a competitive madness that fuels this instrumentalization. Philadelphia's new stadium must be larger and more modern than Chicago's, and Chicago's has to have more boxes from which the rich can view the game than New York's, and Los Angeles must have the greatest arena of them all because one way in the modern world to state that you have arrived is to build a large stadium. In some cities, your friends will take you to the stadiums as an example of what is actually an image of dynamism in their city. This has happened to me in Baltimore, Rio de Janeiro, Accra, Paris, and Mexico City. The idea is reverence, "This is our new stadium" or "This is where Pele played" or "This stadium has more seats than any other in the country."

Everywhere in industrialized nations people seem to take to *les vacances*, holidays, with great ease. The French, Italians, and Germans seem to be quite at peace with their love of leisure. In Europe, the fact that the retirement age is lower than it is in the United States and the presence of socialist governments mean that the people seem to have more leisure, more time for play, or they take less time to work. In fact, political parties often rise or fall on the basis of how much support they give to leisure time activities. To be against holidays is like being against religion; indeed, the holiday is a religion in some senses. One worships leisure. However, a combination of games, sport, and the inattention to symbols, images, and motifs will condemn Africans to a role of mere performers and create a permanent sense of loss.

Already around the world the autochthons, representing five hundred million people in seventy countries, are trying to regain what they lost. This should be instructive for Africans. Globalization will bring about increasing efforts to force Europeanization, that is, the creation of the images of Europe, on other people. Many of the five thousand languages that represent the autochthon cultures are in danger of being wiped out forever. If one takes the example of the autochthons in the United States, those languages and cultures that are indigenous to the land and different from the national language, we have a large problem with the disappearance of images and motifs. What is a wampum belt? How many people in the United States have ever seen one of the famous historical records of the Iroquois people? Almost nowhere, with the possible exception of isolated areas of the Southwest, do we have a preponderance of autochthons' cultures. What will be the end of Africans in America if we are dissolved by virtue of our inattention to our cultural forms and values? What does it mean to humanity if we are unable to provide an alternative to the culture of death and destruction?

I know that as a product of *cybertime* and *cyberspace* the problems of urban communication for me are complicated by my radical need to see and hear everything everywhere at any time. In previous eras human beings were seemingly content with hearing and seeing what was available to them in human scale. We want to see on the moon and hear voices from Mars and Venus. I am disappointed when we cannot hear voices from Mars. But I am more discouraged on Earth when the voices I hear and the symbols I see are devoid of the African record. Of course, I rejoice in all human achievement, but an achievement is not any less human because it is an African achievement. Because there are few conscious Africans in control of media institutions—papers, television companies, radio stations, book publishing, and magazine publishing—it means that we are always threatened with image and cultural obliteration.

I went to see the movie *Troy*, and the first thing that struck me was how African the symbols were: the absolute first action in the movie was a scene where Achilles used the *assegai*, Chaka's short stabbing spear, to kill a foe after the enemy had launched his long spears. As a student of Africa I exclaimed, "That's right out of the history of the Zulu." My wife said, "Not so loud, you're in the theater." I saw that the costume designer had put the characters in African colors—blue tie-and-dye fabrics like *adire* from Nigeria's Yoruba people, Bamana mudcloth from Mali, and Batakari-type shirts from Dagara and Asante—and I said aloud again, "This is not right!" Ana said to me, "We will have to leave if you keep talking." I protested, "They have stole African ideas and put them in this movie so now if we ever do an African saga they will say that those fabrics and those actions were really Greek." Much of the background music in the movie was also African drumming.

How much should I protest, though, when the idea is the becoming of the American nation and the makers of the movie *Troy* were aiming at diverse audiences and different points of entry for many people? There is something remarkable about the ability of the moviemakers to create a film that has so many traits from the African culture and yet to market it as a Greek classic. My problem, I thought as I left the theater, was not that the movie should not have been made, or made the way it was made, but that almost no one in the audience recognized the history, concepts, decorations, and fashions of African people in the drama. Once again it was possible for Africans to say that European people have taken concepts and ideas that we know are African and have appropriated them without acknowledgment. More important, African Americans, because we have been educated as the whites have been educated, do not know that they are African ideas and symbols. How many schools teach students about the heroics of Chaka, a Zulu military genius of amazing proportions who created the idea of the short stabbing spear so his fighters could demonstrate that they had no fear?

Seeing is actually quite fine, but seeing and hearing are better. I am disappointed when I can hear and not see; hearing is fine, audio is adequate for some purposes, but bring on the video. In this respect the acceleration of change and the expansiveness of our vision are the most critical differences between our time and previous eras. Transistorized minds, computer responses, and personalities that are close-printed symbols suggest the interconnectedness of our communication circuitry. Often short-circuited by political differences and racial animosities, our relationships have made us victims of mechanics. Mechanization has never been civilization despite the ease with which some could argue that position. Indeed, it is frequently the antithesis of civilization.

A principal scientist who uses the most advanced computers to plot the destruction of people may be considered uncivilized in comparison to a peasant with a hoe who welcomes and entertains strangers. Civilization is a state of mind, not a condition of development.

Urban communication, with its diversity of interests, political machinery, diffusion mechanisms, and loss of inner resources, is unlike any communication form prior to this time. All over the globe, from Eritrea to Thailand, from France to Zimbabwe, we are faced with growing urban populations. Human beings running to cities, the vast concrete mausoleums of this epoch, to escape the village and the countryside is the most common form of migration in contemporary times.

Those people, such as the ancient Yoruba, Persians, Palestinians, Egyptians, and Syrians who have always related to cities, are being joined at an ever-increasing rate by all of us. We are, therefore, victims of the same misery and dignity, witnesses to the same phenomena, and seekers for the same way. In reality, the city created leisure. Farmers and hunters have always been in search of tomorrow's bread. But the congregation of factories and institutions in the city made it possible for city dwellers to complete their tasks and go on vacations. Humans could pretend to be vacant in place and mind. Not so for the farmer whose very existence depended on incessant activity.

In previous times a person could travel no farther than he or she could walk, and then no farther than he or she could ride an animal; now we are able to travel anywhere on the planet. There is no city on earth that cannot be reached by car, train, boat, or plane. The line of communication centers consolidates modernity in our world. Such consolidation, however, is at the root of some basic African social problems. Washington, London, Ottawa, Paris, and Barcelona are not Tokyo, Singapore, Hong Kong, Bangkok, and Beijing; and yet in certain respects they are all similar for African people. The reason for this is that Lagos, Nairobi, Cairo, Khartoum, Johannesburg, and Kinshasa share in the same modernity, even with all the actualities of postmodernity, as every other urban community. Certainly there are individual differences and diverse histories to these cities, but at the core we are speaking about a way of organizing urban life.

The challenge is to create images and motifs that will change how we view ourselves and how we are viewed by the rest of the world. This certainly can be done and is daily being done by the incredible achievements of Africans in science, politics, law, art, education, commerce, and spiritual pursuits, but it must be replicated in the motifs of businesses, the remembrances of ancestors, the collective memoir of a people's resistance to death, the enthroning of the best examples of African cultural values, and the celebration of our heroes in every epoch and in every place. This is a requirement for using leisure wisely.

The use of the popular/dominant communication media like TV and computers is essential in order to transform our symbols or images from those provided by colonial education to those that express a positive attitude toward African culture. We have witnessed the powerful primacy of vision in the Western world during the last fifty years. Children are unable to read as well as they did twenty-five years ago. They seem brighter, quicker, and wittier, but while they are quick to speak, they often lack words to express understanding of a topic. Television and other television-influenced media are the key instrumental, that is, mechanical, differences in the learning environment of today's children as compared to children of other generations. Television has become a cultural context as well as a culture transmitter. We live in it and receive messages through it because it is an absorbing, encompassing context, but often more aesthetics than substance.

Ortega y Gasset explains in *The Revolt of the Masses* (1994) that generation is the most dynamic concept in human history because it is purposeful. It establishes the linkage between tradition and innovation. What is for us at this moment innovative, dynamic, and inspiring becomes to the next generation commonplace, static, and uninspiring. Boldness, novelty, and newness cannot last forever; transition makes all things old. Space age exploration, missions to the planets and beyond, joint ventures in space laboratories, the possibility of human cloning, genetic engineering, and panaceas for human illnesses that are presently discussed will be old hat for future generations. Quite frankly, we are always on the verge of the dehumanization of art, culture, and civilization, and the tension we feel with our environment and with other humans is a sign of the inherent possibilities of failure or victory (Gasset 1976).

A few years from now no one will gasp in amazement at routine flights to the moon or the planets. Our contemporary novelties will be the next generation's traditions. Thus the current age is in the process of transition; it seems natural. However, this transition puts us in deeper exposure to our own expanded vision of leisure and social relations. As one who has been interested in the advancement of African science, I am concerned that the continent has not taken up the challenge to make computer literacy the number one educational goal of the continent. In this way it will be possible for African nations to leapfrog over some of the developmental issues and problems that plagued the Western world to get right into the mix with ease.

There is an urgent need for African nations to adopt a full-scale commitment to total computer literacy. No people can be without the tremendous sources of information available to the users of the Internet and not be left behind. It should be a national priority in every African government. Children in the earliest grades should be introduced to the powers of the computer. This is one way to leapfrog into the forefront of contemporary society. African nations do not have to remain second to any other areas of the world with the advent of the computer.

The expensive media—computers equipped for Internet connectivity, television, and radio—are instruments of our changing communication patterns. They affect how we see the world but they also affect how the world sees us. How does Africa want to be seen and viewed by the rest of the world? You can know a great deal about the answer by seeing how African nations use the Internet. Creating in its population a burning desire to be connected to the world is one way Africa can overcome years of colonial education. Communication media is essential to our symbol transformations.

There is also the role of the media in our daily lives. For example, television often dictates when we sleep, when we wake, how we eat, what we eat, when we make love, and when we go to the toilet. In the United States television watchers normally go to bed either after the news or after the talk show or movie. Local water companies report that during commercials on television the water pressure goes down because of simultaneous flushing of toilets. Our eating habits are affected by television, and some families consider the evening news before preparing their meals. More significantly, what we eat has also been influenced by the time we need to see a certain program on television. Television demands more of us and takes more from us than radio.

At one time it was television alone that made us desire to see everywhere, at any time with perfect resolution. If something happens in Lusaka, we expect to see it on television. Los Angeles freeways now project road conditions on an all-weather screen. The quasi-magic relationship among source-message-receiver is constantly being refined. This has produced in some cases a disengagement of source, message, and receiver because either the source becomes incapacitated by too much information or the receiver becomes incapable of handling its own overabundance of information. Decisions are hindered by information overload. How we communicate or not communicate appears to be gaining dominance over how we work or not work in the estimation of human productivity. This is a radical shift in sociological thought because technology destroys our ability to define communication by our work; we can define our work through effective communication. Books on how to communicate, effective listening, speaking out, and contemporary public speaking abound in the bookstores. Television is our principal means of seeing everywhere and this has put a special meaning on a glib facility with words.

An international machine environment threatens to make Mexico City, Harare, Los Angeles, Miami, Lagos, New York, Toronto, São Paulo, Johannesburg, Hong Kong, and Kyoto in the same mold. The same mechanized environment is found in all of these cities, dotted of course with the familiar hotel chains, fast-food companies, and transnational establishments.

Such similarity produces false impressions. A person can drive from Los Angeles to New York and tell people that he's seen America when in fact he has only seen a strip of cement with gas stations and rest areas where you stop and go to the toilet, get some gasoline, and grab something to eat. What does one really see on such a trip? You could actually remain in Los Angeles and have almost the same sensations; the only difference is that you would not have arrived at the same place.

People get on airplanes and fly away to distant lands and have a holiday and get back on the plane and return home without ever knowing where they have been. If you ask them, they say, "I don't know, we just took an airplane." This is the contemporary attitude imposed upon us by technology. A friend of mine once reported how stupid he felt sitting in his car one night around 11:30 P.M. in a small rural town in the Midwest farm area in the United States. This little town had one traffic light, and as he was driving through the town in the middle of a thunderstorm, the light changed to red and he stopped. There were no other cars around, no people on the streets, lightning was flashing, and he was sitting there in his car. All of a sudden he felt extremely stupid because the light was not changing. Soon he began to mumble to himself, "This light is too long, someone ought to do something about it." Finally, in desperation he violated the law and went through the red light. A piece of machinery had him under control. Modern technology influences all of us making us victims of our own creations.

In a drastic reformulation of its role, television can provide an effective statement about contemporary culture. If we are to be spared the phenomenon of rebarbarization that has repeatedly occurred in human history, television will play an important and different role in socializing all of us. A view of ourselves as well as of others with one foot always on the solid rock of introspection that can be provided by television should keep us from judging each other too harshly.

Properly, television sends us messages from ourselves. Its correctness is a function of the audience. In other words, we get from television what we demand of it. But, of course, in the case of African people in the United States, we can never be sure that television is a reflection of us. In fact, most often it is not. This is particularly true in terms of the news reporting but also true in terms of programming. While there has been progress, it has often been difficult to convince the media leaders that they should recognize the African audience. Indeed, television producers often misunderstand what it is the audience is demanding, and they often take black audiences for granted. This is not merely a racial problem; it is profoundly a problem of cultural consciousness. When Robert Johnson was head of Black Entertainment Television, he made it a point to say that he gave the audience what they wanted, although there were many complaints about the programming of that network. Like other television executives, Robert Johnson simply went to the lowest common denominator rather than seeking to discover the values of the most representative audiences. Indeed, from a commercial point of view the company would have made more money, if that were the issue, if it had concentrated on a more nationalist, professional audience capable of purchasing products. Alas, Johnson's lack of consciousness was at the core of his inability to rise above selfish interests to achieve something collective. This remains a continuing problem in the African American community. It is sometimes difficult to find selfless men and women who seek a higher purpose than self-aggrandizement. They have a rent-a-car attitude about public audiences. They either sell us one kind of television program or another depending on what they conceive as our base interest. We accept television's statement about life, love, war, peace, politics, and trade only to our detriment. In this respect, our leisure world is the creation of television so much so that we make our vacations and holidays in places advertised on television and we buy products that we do not need but have seen on television.

Television is accessible as a medium in many more ways than either radio or print. In the urban centers as well as the rural communities of the world, radio and print have penetrated the most isolated places. Alternative newspapers have made print accessible to various outgroups. On a college campus in the United States there may be five or six newspapers representing the views of Mexican Americans, African Americans, gays and lesbians, women, Japanese Americans, and autochthons. The diversity represented by these papers, however, speaks to the inability of the papers controlled by one group to be accessible to these other cultural and social groups. But where radio and newsprint are accessible, they are more discriminating than television. In what is becoming a visual culture, the grammar of television, unlike print, does not require the audience to know how to read. In fact, television says, in effect, "Bring me the tired, the unlearned, and the dumb, and I will make them learned, articulate, and knowledgeable."

One of the most popular programs on US television has been a noncommercially produced show for preschool-age children called *Sesame Street*. The show demonstrates what television can do with young children before they enter school. *Sesame Street* teaches children to read. Unfortunately, it does not teach them how to discriminate between good and bad television shows.

Television differs from radio in that radio only appeals to one of our senses, the sense of hearing. Imagination is necessary for a full appreciation of radio. If a radio drama is being produced and you are attuned to it, you must prepare yourself to imagine what the detectives and bandits look like. These are the realities of radio. On the other hand, television is accessible and nondiscriminatory because one does not need to know how to read in order to see television. Furthermore, the act of hearing and seeing greatly reduces the amount of imagination necessary on the part of the viewer.

Everything I have written points to the fact that television has an architectonic nature. It is a productive, structuring instrument that has become more than a simple machine but an instrument capable of the most complex innuendoes, information dissemination, and processing possibilities. Like a giant generator, television produces hundreds of images, symbols, and motifs, even recirculating older ones, that have an impact on the way we structure our lives. And since African American children tend to watch more television than others, we are more affected by the images that are produced. To the degree that those images degrade us, we participate in our own degradation.

Television has become the central partner in the transmission of the major symbols of modern nations. In the United States the continuing viability of political and cultural symbols from the Anglo-Saxon heritage means that a multiethnic nation is being inundated with monoethnic symbols. In its general portrayal of national life, American television simply echoes the European values and standards of the major ethnic population. At one time, Western culture was presented as if no other cultural or social groups existed in the United States. Although this has been moderated by the presence of images out of the African American, Latino, and Asian communities, we still see an overwhelming dominance of white images out of all proportion to whites in the population. Television has hardly done anything to combat the insidious ethnocentricity that is at the heart of the American social situation. One possibility is that television should serve an organizing function for information dissemination that would restructure societies so that a holistic rather than a dualistic model emerges. Such a service would be remarkable because we become more aware of our inconsistencies and contradictions by what we see on television or other video media.

Symbols represent our attempt to weld a common experience; when large segments attach emotional value to a sign, symbol, or concept, community is established. We might call these widely accepted symbols *principals*. They almost always have broad social and political implications whereas lessers primarily refer to our use of words to transmit our attitudes or receive information from others. Television is a dissemination of both forms of symbols, but it is in its use of the principal symbols, configurations, and images that it carries out its structuring role. In the principal symbols we have the creation of forms, the acceptance of forms, around the modification of forms that reflect a communion of values based upon emotional attitudes.

Symbols are instruments of order and disorder, and a communion of values based on emotions can lead to the tyranny of the powerful or advance the power of tyranny. We now have machines that fabricate opinions, attitudes, and sensibilities, not just material products. Similarly, television not only helps us to shape our outlook but it also creates the minds that will understand that outlook. A revitalization of the uses of television for urban society means that we will have to use its structuring potential for the common interest of society and not for one segment against another. The revitalization of television is the logical solution to the great unresolved problem in early twenty-first-century America, the abiding distrust between blacks and whites in urban centers.

I believe that a continuing protagonist-antagonist conflict will result in further decay of urban relations in the United States unless television, the principal medium of cultural linkages, is used in a productive, structuring fashion. Clearly two distinct patterns of socialization have emerged in American society. White Americans seem to be acculturated toward neutrality and lack of passion; Africans are acculturated toward commitment, passion, and conviction. These two ways of life produce two different types of individuals. On the one hand, whites are geared and guided toward accommodation and adaptation to the established order of power; on the other, blacks and others who are not white are guided toward conflict with that order because it is a racist order, unless they divest themselves of passion and commitment. On job applications when an employer asks about an applicant's ability to adapt to the ideas of others, the African American must think about the questions in terms of the normal interactions with whites. Some employers seek pliable applicants. If the applicant holds to his opinions with conviction and passion, he is not considered capable of "fitting in" to the institution. Most blacks, acculturated toward speaking against exploitation and oppression, are condemned before they prove their skills. These two divergent behavior and communication patterns color most of our interracial attitudes. Television's role in a structuring process is to reorient the society toward common goals.

Indeed television's place in the order of symbols is becoming more relevant each day. We live in a visual culture where the supremacy of the written word is declining at an accelerating rate. It is the urban communities with the cinemas, photographic studios, audiovisual departments, and television stations that will be most affected by the decline of the written word. As print superseded the spoken word, so the visual image will supersede print. Increasingly, the elevation of intellectual, imaginative, and academic standards will depend upon the adjustment of traditional teaching techniques to include more visual elements. When elementary and secondary schoolteachers brought posters and illustrations to their classroom, we were on the verge of this new development. Today we are not on the verge; we are in the movement. The written word is being edged out at such a rapid rate by movies, television, and video equipment that in a few years our children might see words as less important than visual images. One of the problems already surfacing in some places is that children who enter school after looking at fifty hours of television a week for two years find the written word to be boring and dull. They have developed visual abilities that all too often they must abandon in school.

The human brain is a remarkable organ. It weighs only about three or four pounds yet gives us the capacity to think, reason, discriminate, imagine, and sense. We know that all of our human activities are controlled by this dominating end of the body. Verbal and sound skills used in writing and reading are developed in the left side of the brain. The right side of the brain controls visual learning skills. Television has put us in touch with our right side of the brain more than any other instrument. The age of the right brain is here. At one time, the right side of the brain was thought to be mute. Possibly with the rise in visual literacy we will learn even more about a capacity of the human brain.

Exploration of this concept of the visual will also put into a proper perspective my initial concern about children who could talk but did not express understanding. What I am now suggesting as a possible explanation is that the child who does not write or read well may have already moved to a visually oriented approach to learning. The possibility that my explanation is correct frightens me because we are only now developing the rules for visual literacy. Children who are visually oriented may be held back in their schooling because the school system is verbally oriented. In urban environments where children watch lots of television, the verbal literacy test scores are lower than in societies where children still have a verbal orientation toward literacy. It is for this reason that I suggest the use of television to begin the training in visual literacy as an aid to public communication. Where once they did, words no longer suffice in this new orientation, this novel worldview in human history in which humans demand to see. It may be said that we can fly higher than any bird, swim deeper than any shark; now we have got to learn to open our eyes and *see* like human beings.

Televised communications will succeed to color in every nation in the foreseeable future. The use of color programming can help bring about a reformulation, a reformation in how we see ourselves. We need to see everywhere in color. It is no accident that in the United States when the first men landed on the moon, numerous complaints were sent to Houston because the picture transmission was not in color. Those complaints may have been based on a reasonable desire for clearer resolution of the picture. But the only reason the complaints could be called reasonable at all is because people had come to expect color television transmission. The rise of color television as a technological development parallels the reawakening of the colored countries of the world. The desire to see things in their more natural state—to strip away the artificial and the fictitious, and to see black as black, brown as brown, and white as white—came as no surprise to communicationists whose roots were in the study of human uses of communication symbols.

The narrow dimensions of black-and-white television failed to symbolize the realities of the world condition. Television is a powerfully political instrument, and it has the capacity to shape the vision we have of the world. During the black-and-white era, television portrayals were stark, sterile, and matter of fact. Such was the prepostmodernity of the media.

Media institutions have been always the principal agenda setters in society. They establish relationships and values—good and evil, enemies and friends—and shape the general cultural awareness of what is significant and what is not, what is foolish and what is wise. How that agenda is managed from the top of the social-political-religious hierarchy determines our orientations to the messages we receive. Our behavior is determined by our orientations. Media institutions, usually controlled in large urban centers, have been largely unconcerned about information to help us reduce uncertainties. In some cases, however, too much information has caused frustrations. Bombarded and inundated with symbols, contemporary human beings have reacted from too much too quickly. We are often symbol zombies, visual automatons, disembodied persons, dancing to a million messages seemingly all at once. Setting the agenda, the media provides the pablum of racism in just the proper doses of African American invisibility to create false images and feed the society's taste for stereotypes.

One hundred years ago the Bible was the most widely read book in America. It provided the basis for oratorical eloquence in the pulpit and the Congress. It sent steel mill workers in Birmingham and Pittsburgh to their jobs with the Sermon on the Mount on their lips, and it trained several generations in how to read. Despite these impressive credentials, the Bible is not nearly so ubiquitous in the world as it was fifty years ago. Today the most important source of reading information is from periodicals or magazines. The magazine is everywhere. It is impossible to act or to consider acting without considering the magazine. One can act without reference to the magazine, but whether it will be informed action is hard to say, particularly if the action is in the realm of politics, economics, or education. It seems to me that it only takes two months of missed reading the proper materials and watching some key television programs to put a person one year behind in her information reservoir. Soon, the digizine, such as the *FocusedVM* hip hop format DVD series is called, will be the main form of delivering what magazines now give the reading public.

Our American cities are vast tundras. Each in its own way is like all of the others in superstructure, political chicanery, taxes, and communication systems. While there is the appearance of a frozen and encrusted environ technological level in most of these cities, at every sector there is change and movement. In no place is the change more obvious than in the communication systems.

Television, radio, and newspapers in American cities represent the cutting edge of capitalism much as those same communication systems in Marxist societies have represented the cutting edge of that philosophy. Yet the communication systems reflect the policy changes, societal demands, and international realignments that have appeared in recent years often producing their own productive or generative metaphors.

Our cities are also jungles. In them it is often possible to feel lost, disoriented, and confused. This feeling has little to do with the nature of the universe but a lot to do with humans and the construction of our cities—concrete cages with cement blocks here and there and perhaps a little bit of glass if we happened to live in the Sun Belt. Detachment is the rule of the day; we strive for affiliation through the will to communicate. Sometimes we achieve it and pour libations to our ancestors for it.

Our cities are like mountains with ever-present valleys. Human beings are confronted with the slow assimilation of diversity, induced by the practical activity of living in a multifaceted community. We experience a series of highs and lows based in large part on how we react to the diverse communication messages that bombard us. We can exhaust ourselves in fruitless opposition to the environment, seek to modify it, or be assimilated into the flow of ups and downs.

Only in the sense that concessions can be made that do not touch the core of the media industry are we likely to find a path through the entanglement of symbols found in our cities or, for that matter, anywhere else. Things change their meaning in relationship to their posture or stance.

My view consists of seeing media institutions, at least, in the United States, as having a strong commercial core. This core is never touched, can never be touched, and the integrity of the systems remains. Although I would wish a more selfless system, a more ethical response to the needs of society, a more moral approach to racial inequality, I realize what we are up against. We must always struggle to maintain space. Consequently, what the media operators ask is that any concession on the stereotypical images and motifs be offset by no loss in the profits accruing to the media institutions. Thus, they will continue to give audiences the most negative and degrading images until there is a demand that they discontinue this practice. Needless to say, I do not believe there is any inherent nature of the media to humanize our cities, to change itself, indeed to make society better.

Most media operators, black or white, would say that the media should have no social responsibility. I do not accept that this is the aim of a free society, to create institutions that work against the best interests of the society, to be devoid of social responsibility. We can never accept this position or else we can never hope to challenge contemporary barbarism. Is there nothing that is abhorrent to us? Our objective must be to find ways to insure that we will have a new architecton of symbols and images to liberate us from the enslavement of racist and hegemonic symbols.

chapter 8
COMMUNICATION, CULTURE, AND CIVILIZATION

The large cities of the Western world contain people who, as Octavio Paz has written, move mindlessly in an abstract world of machines (Paz 1961). An enormous spiritual burden now rests squarely on the spiritual shoulders of America as the predominant leader of the informational world, and African Americans, as participants, are once again called upon to make the case for a more democratic and egalitarian America. Indeed, the entire globalization project, what the French call *mondialisation*, is wrapped up in the expansion of Western consciousness and the reach for hegemony. It is not at all clear that this push for hegemony hatched by the Pentagon will succeed, but what is certain in the short run is that passions around the world have been fired against the idea of Big Brother. The world is no longer as it was before September 11, 2001; innocence is lost and we are forced to reexamine our own response to other cultures, nations, and societies.

Germany, Japan, France, and Britain have not escaped the dulling of the senses caused by an ever-increasing reliance on material things. And even in Russia, self-reliance has come to mean reliance on tools, instruments, machines, computers, and weapons. There is a machine, a system, that drives this march toward interaction without humans, this drive toward communication instantly without ever engaging another person in the flesh.

Marshall McLuhan's old extensions have stretched people so far that there is hardly any real spiritual essence left (McLuhan 1964). The so-called third world, by virtue of common struggle against exploitation, sees the West as cold, callous, aggressive, and bent on destruction of themselves and the world because they have nothing better to do; in fact, it is openly thought that the West's capacity for warmth, love, and peace is seriously impaired. Alienated from nature and the universe, Western people have lost the sense of who they are apart from what they read about themselves in some manual for love, or transactional analysis, or winning friends, or gaining power, or leaning how to dance, or growing rich, or even how to think. Such absolute dethroning of the inner powers of spirit and soul means that one seldom knows who is speaking or listening these days. The person who smiles may be trying to get a modeling position; the person who has a desk in the center of the room may be looking for a promotion; the person who wears the pin-striped suit may be seeking a sale; and the person who drives a Jaguar may be advertising a commodity. Human beings so devoid of true emotions and so destitute of honest experiences communicate in the most artificial manner. They live lies.

In a devastating sense, modern technology with its corollaries of mechanical smiles and fake handshakes has achieved the creation of human beings as political or social accessories. There is the illusion of beauty, the illusion of action, the illusion of sincerity, and the illusion of happiness. Indeed, Daniel Wegner has convinced us that there is even the illusion of conscious will. Culture in the West has become a victim of the dominant scientific principles of the society (Wegner 2002).

Linearity destroys imagination. There are no deviations, no fringes, no grounds for exploration—only order and law, rules and regulations. Our spirits are dulled as our lives have been dulled. Disconnected and unhooked, people float from place to place without the benefit of the groundedness that comes from inner spiritual resources. It is possible that those resources are so thinly distributed that they cannot be regrouped. Cultural malaise, already present in Western art, now moves in more fundamentally on Western imagination. Aleksander Solzhenitsyn once said that the West had lost its courage. That statement was not true because the West collectively knew it could not lose what it barely had. What the West may have lost was its will to engage other humans as equals. Its involvement in two earth-shattering wars meant that a deep sense of spiritual depletion existed within the West despite the illusions. I do not mean that there were no courageous people in the West. Dietrich Bonhoeffer comes to mind, Malcolm X comes to mind, Mother Teresa comes to mind, but the mass of people had no general feeling of courage, nothing like the self-sufficiency of the Chinese or the union with nature of the mass of Africans (Diop 1978). True courage is the will to exist in harmony with those around you.

The lack of connectedness creates insensitivity to others, harshness, abrasiveness, and arrogance. Indeed, people who have lost all contact with themselves or who have lost footing in their own cultural grounding demonstrate their loss by their public manners. Anthony Appiah tells of his difficulty in accepting the traditional protocols of the Asante people when his Ghanaian father died and the matrilineal mourners refused his English mother a place in the ritual (Appiah 1992). In effect, loose from his African roots and moorings, he exploded out of "his mother's house" to condemn his father's relatives.

Manners are the most direct manifestations of one's political philosophy. Relatedness to others can be determined by our manners. The way we relate to our fellows says more about our communication with our own spiritual selves than anything else. Westerners have typically shown little grace in the presence of difference, and consequently, they have placed technology between them and other people to the limit possible. This points to our inadequacies as human beings.

Lest the point being made here is misunderstood: I am not calling for absolute harmony at all costs. My position is simpler. Pseudosocial science technique has robbed Western man of his mystery. There is even a belief that harmony is the original state of the human race. Western institutions, and those influenced by Western thought, abound with the mythology that virtue is identical with harmony. Social science literature is replete with the contention that discord and conflict are not normal. As normal, we are encouraged by academic and lay admonitions to seek harmony. However, such admonitions must be understood in context. The real danger is that which is fundamentally a conservative view may be passed off as a progressive view. Concord in organizations, social or cultural, demonstrates status quo. Disjunctions suggest that organizations are in a state of productive change. When the United States was racked by demonstrations and rallies against the war in Vietnam, the society was undergoing a significantly productive change. Old values clashed with new, previous generations scored newer ones and vice versa, political allegiances were rearranged, and timely appraisals of ethics and morality were made. Communication between the political sides, among the disparate groups, and with opposing parties was strained but direct. All political questions can be reduced to issues of production and issues of communication. Much of the Vietnam War debate had to do with communication. A whole new country grew up around the language of the war.

The intent of the Johnson administration and later the Nixon administration once the United States had entered the war was to stabilize South Vietnam and to destabilize North Vietnam. In this view, of course, stabilization represented harmony, concord, truth, and good; whereas destabilization represented disharmony, discord, falsehood, and evil. A classic good-evil confrontation existed. Yet the ultimate end of the American war effort was to stabilize the Southeast Asian peninsula in order to protect the Pacific flank of the American armed forces.

Already, the Iraq War of George W. Bush has entered history as a war of communication or the lack of it. The reason given for going to war was the belief, stated as a fact, that Saddam Hussein had weapons of mass destruction that had not been disclosed to the United Nations inspectors. The war was launched in 2003, and immediately the Bush administration attempted to confuse, in the minds of the masses, the invasion of Iraq with the search for Osama bin Laden and terrorists. Soon all of the war rhetoric became a communication quagmire; it was double- and triplespeak of the worst type, repetitive hype of the most simple-minded style, a format of self-righteous mantras that would have caused Duauf, Protagoras, Merikare, Plato, Khunanup, and Aristotle to cringe with professional horror.

Politicians know that by establishing and maintaining the language of warfare it is possible to keep distances between people. Mutual intelligibility supports social cohesion. However, the fact that I understand you does not in itself prevent the emergence of conflict. That is why our language, whether group or personal, betrays our intentions. During the Vietnam War the language of conflict, dormant since the 1940s and 1950s, reappeared in every sector of American society. We witnessed the absolute militaristic determinism of a society dominated by the military-industrial hegemony. Even Sunday school teachers were saying things like, "Well, if you are going to live the Christian life, you've got to make the right shots." There was a lot of impacting on others. Few people ever spoke of audiences anymore; we sought target groups and practiced guerrilla theater. Terms from the Korean War kept coming up in conversation: for example, brainwashing and Charley. Our educators spoke of infiltrating the nonacademic spheres as others spoke of intervention techniques to upgrade education in the secondary schools. When we wanted to be certain of ourselves, we always had to have a critical mass. Police departments in every major city established search-and-rescue or search-and-seize units after the search-and-destroy missions of the Vietnam War. We confronted anyone on any subject. Our talk was bad. Let me be clear about the use of phrases and words inherited from the battlefield. Language simply reflected the political and military climate; it cannot be accused of creating the climate.

Throughout history, military conquest, harmony and disharmony, and culture have been intertwined. The creation of a climate for political debate or destructive warfare occurs in societies with conflicting parties. Civilizations are said to rise and fall on the strength of political and economic climates. The term *civilization* obfuscates the real character of nations.

Civilization as a concept is dysfunctional. No people can ever be defined as without it. Notwithstanding the ethnocentricity of most attempts to define civilization, modern human beings have discovered new categories for societal description more appropriate to advancement. For me, indeed, as it must be for the world, there is only humaneness and inhumaneness in societies. What constitutes one or the other of these human conditions is what really separates societies.

Who is it that intrudes on my right to think in human ways? I mean, what constitutes an intervention in the process of my becoming. As the ancient Africans of Egypt used to say, one becomes and becomes and there is no end to the becoming. Unless, of course, there is human intervention. The quality of humaneness or inhumaneness rises from a society's laws, religion, communication, economics, organization, property, and technology. Unlike the dysfunctional term *civilization*, for instance, *humaneness* is characterized by how well a people live in harmony with each other and nature. To be inhumane is to live poorly in relationship to your fellow human beings and nature. In one sense, inhumanity allows for the title civilization to be given to the most barbarous of societies. Humaneness, on the other hand, could not be so easily dispensed.

Mayan society, during both the classic and the postclassic periods, was an inhumane society, characterized by a high degree of violence, exploitation, and slavery. However, architecturally, Mayan society produced the greatest ceremonial centers of Meso-America. Uxmal, Tikal, Tulman, and Chichen Itza remain today to attest to the technological achievements of the Maya and the Maya-Toltec people. These technological achievements may cause Mayan society to be called "civilized," but such a designation cannot hide the fact that the society was inhumane.

Roman architecture, in its grandest form, represents the triumph of inhumaneness. Delete the constructions in honor of war, warfare, and victories over enemies, and you reduce the legacy of ancient Rome considerably. The Roman achievement in law, architecture, and communication must be understood in the light of what is humane and what is inhumane. For imperial Rome, law was essential not so much for free Roman citizens as it was for Rome's unfree subjects. Rome pioneered law and order for subjected people and gave to the world the legacy of an imperialistic people. Punishment, cruelty, and barbarity, unheard of even by people who had not yet built arches of grandeur or fountains of splendor, abounded in the Roman Empire. Civilization, as it was called by chroniclers, meant technological achievements; it had little to do with humaneness.

The Third Reich of Germany was probably the finest tuned

technological society of the twentieth century. It possessed scientists, universities, and an industrial complex capable of producing almost any technological creation imaginable. Efficient mechanisms were developed for the delivery to the state of any innovation in medicine, engineering, communication, or weaponry. Yet few nations have ever so vainly, so deliberately set about to massacre people because of their race. Technological advancement did not retard or impede racial hatred. It might even be argued that racial hatred gave impetus to the most barbarous of technological inventions. Awesome creations and inventions were spawned by genocide. Germany, of course, was called a civilized nation. It gave Western social thought reason to pause, but not to see the dysfunction of the term *civilization* in contemporary society.

In contemporary times the erstwhile white government of South Africa was often spoken of by white authors as advanced, civilized, and technologically superior. This ethnocentricity leads to a distorted view of society. In a single issue of the *Miami Herald*, December 28, 1977, there were two items that demonstrated the severity of the distortion. D. Thomas wrote that blacks came from all over southern Africa to work in the gold mines of "*the civilized* [italics mine] South African Republic where they earn five times as much money in the gold mines as they could earn anywhere in their own countries at any available work." He continued in a damning admission: "sales of the Krugerrand do help support a *civilization* [italics mine] like ours in the U.S." What more is necessary to show the dysfunctionality of civilization as a useful concept in describing societies. By objective accounts, as objective as we can attain in our world, South Africa, in the apartheid era, rated near the bottom in treatment of the vast majority of its citizens, in welfare, health, education, economic power distribution, domestic stability, and government participation. In the same newspaper, Larry Heinzerling is quoted as calling South Africa "the most economically and technologically advanced country in Africa." The statement itself makes economic and technological progress much too important. This is the classicly distorted view of human societies. Advancement is not merely technological or economic even though these are the most easily measured.

The inherent problems with the Western formulation of civilization are highlighted by some continuing issues of contradiction and decline. Civilization has certainly taken a serious decline in the historical mind of the West. One only has to read Western literature to see that the most cruel and terrible despots were the ones most glorified by Western poets. Roman poets became lackeys to the state; a Caesarism of the first order transformed the mentality of Rome's artists into slaves of the first order. In fact, Persius, Juvenal, and Petronius complained of the decadence of their time. Although Rome had borrowed from Greece, Greece itself never achieved grandness of purpose, singularity of spirit, or the dynamism of culture demonstrated by the Egyptians. The Hellenes depended upon the Egyptians for their inspiration in mythology and literature. A slavish imitation marked the Greek character and gave the Western world its artistic beginnings. Even so representative a work as the Parthenon, which ranks among Greece's noblest achievements, would never have come into existence without the artistic, intellectual, and constructive influence of the sacred temples along the Nile in Luxor and Karnak (Asante 1990; Ani, 1994; Asante and Abarry 1996; Reddings 1950).

In thought, the Greeks were even more dependent upon the Egyptians.[1] As Chancellor Williams explains in *The Destruction of Black Civilization*, the Greeks enriched the world by not a single idea but were content to follow the old lines already established by African priests (Williams 1974; see also James 1956). Thus, one must not think of the ancient Greeks as intellectual leaders but as true imitators. Chancellor Williams is correct when he says that the "Greeks were the first Europeans to know that the most advanced civilization of the ancient world was in Africa" (Williams 1974, p. 315). Thus they went about proclaiming it loudly and boldly as if it was their own creation. Having been influenced by architectural designs, city planning, sculpture, frescoes, science, astronomy, agriculture, and religion from the Land of the Blacks, Greece became the most enlightened of Europe's cultures (Bernal 1987).

Since Diop (1974) established the African origin of civilization, we have begun to recognize the symbolisms, myths, and legends that tie Western roots, through the Greco-Roman world, to black Egypt.

As the mother of the West, as Herodotus understood, the black race through Egypt bequeathed to the whole world the wisdom and knowledge of ten thousand years of uninterrupted civilization from the Upper Nile. The figure of the Sphinx, in all of its blackness, symbolizes the manner in which the African mind stands astride the political, cultural, and moral histories of the world. When foreigners came into Egypt, the civilization was on the decline and remained so during the conquest of Islam in 639–642 CE.

Indeed, the Greeks established schools of philosophical thought based upon Egyptian religion. The schools of Socrates, Plato, Isocrates, and Aristotle reflected a fascination with African civilization. The Greek mind was precisely ready to receive new ideas and concepts. As popularizers, the Greeks would have no rivals in Europe. Unlike the Romans who attacked the contributions from Greece for a considerable period before accepting them, the Greeks were susceptible to the superior cultural legacies of Egypt. In Rome during the year 173 BCE, the proponents of Epicurus's doctrines were expelled from the city; in 161 BCE philosophers and rhetoricians were banished as dangerous persons. Rome saw Hellenism as treacherous for the state; Greece saw Egyptian philosophy as the highest form of human civilization. The flowering of Western culture finds its source in the African seed.

Narcissism thrives in the West. What it has learned from Africa it now claims as its own, shines it, strokes it, and makes the bequest a part of its own repertoire. Almost all principal concepts and images are narcissistic. The Nobel Prize represents the self-compliments of the Western world. It is narcissistic. It is no coincidence that the awards have seldom been made to Africans or Asians who articulate positions that are anti-Western. They remain political awards in the eyes of the rest of the world. The message communicated is that intelligence and creativity are products of the Western mind. Quite interestingly, when the awards have been given to African or Asian people, they have been either the Peace Awards or awards given jointly with a Westerner. Of course, communists, whether white, black, or yellow, seldom count. Those old Soviet-era writers who managed to become anti-Soviet in their writings were accorded their appropriate places in the Western world. They reaffirmed the West's faith in itself. They were the periodic injections the West needs to feel superior. Portrayal of the dread of Soviet prisons (perhaps as horrible or no more horrible than Attica, Soledad, and Parchman's Farm; prisons are inherently evil, ask Martin Sostre, Big Black, or see Cindy Firestone's cinema verité movie *Attica*) could get a Soviet writer one thousand brownie points with the Nobel Prize committee. What was communicated by awarding recognition to the Soviet dissident was the fundamental political necessity in the world: highlight the difference to consolidate the faithful. On the other hand, black American writers are chastised for their protest writings! James Baldwin never came close to receiving the Nobel or the Pulitzer.

Russia participates in similar political uses of prizes and awards. Paul Robeson was granted the Lenin Peace Prize in 1952 under the old Soviet regime. His defense of black human rights and persistent campaign for the dignity of his people in the United States marked him as a candidate for the Lenin Peace Prize. Much like the Russians who had been honored by the Nobel Award prior to the fall of communism, Robeson was an outcast in his native land. The US government refused him permission to travel to Moscow.

In 1977 the Pakistani government instituted what became one of the most significant international prizes given by a non-Western nation. The Quaid-e-Azam Human Rights International Award is usually presented to the person who best exemplifies the fight against racism. Pakistan has signaled to the rest of the world that the international struggle against racism is honorable. The Quaid-e-Azam Award of $50,000 was made to ex–Zambian president Kenneth Kaunda during the struggle for South African freedom. This was seen as an intensification of the international mobilization against racism.

In no more effective way can the Nobel Prize or any prize honor genius than in the affirmation of the human search for freedom. Again the dearth of moral authority and ethical decisions make culture sick and subject to attack. Because linearity allows the Western mind to separate genius from attitude, it follows that intellectuals and scientists who demonstrate superior brains may receive the highest awards and still be antihuman in their behavior. Surely the prize givers would have honored Immanuel Kant for some great intellectual gift although he supported the despotism of Frederick II and defended and advocated the use of slavery. Surely Thomas Jefferson would have been accorded some singular honor because of his political genius although he kept African slaves and sexually abused a fourteen-year-old black girl. For the Western mind, it is possible and indeed necessary to separate these two areas of a person's life. Such dichotomy is difficult to justify to the African mind. In fact, it is seldom found outside of the European American experience. Human beings possess a unity, a oneness with nature and others, and to be worthy means to have all parts operating in agreement with each other. Furthermore, a person who denies the presence of humanity in others is definitionally not qualified for the highest honors of society. Regardless of the genius of a Joseph Goebbels in propaganda, he could never receive honor because of his destructively negative attitudes toward Jewish people. The Western mind can separate skill and intellect from ethics and morality; this is impossible in traditional African thought. But because it is possible in the West to separate business from play and ethics from pragmatics, ideas originally thought to be sacred have a secular application in current politics.

The idea of state sovereignty has been challenged by satellites and raiding parties. Like the Monroe Doctrine, state sovereignty has just about come to its end. Politics is symbolic. The extension of a political idea takes forms very nearly similar to intellectual ideas; in fact, all political ideas are intellectual by nature or by interpretation. Establishment of a communist nation in the Western Hemisphere sealed the door on Monroe's doctrine regarding interference by nations outside of the hemisphere. It extended the possibility or rather made legitimate the claims other nations would attempt to make for freedom from American hegemony. In a similar fashion, the numerous incursions and invasions into smaller nations legitimizes the right of any nation in its own interest to invade the territorial integrity of another. It was a political idea long in coming, but it had always been in the minds of the most aggressive political leaders. The ill-fated Soviet Union's forays into Afghanistan, Hungary, and Czechoslovakia; the American intrusion or, as Nixon put it at the time, "incursion" into Cambodia; the Israeli raid into Uganda; South Africa's raids into Angola and Mozambique and other nations—all these represent historic military examples of satellite forays into other nations' territory. But they are no different from Iraq invading Kuwait; the United States occupying Iraq, Haiti, or Afghanistan; the mercenary whites from South Africa fomenting war in Sierra Leone, Gabon, and other places on the African continent. Clearly, such political action feeds the philosophical position that contends for more military power. There is no end to the cycle. Nations invade or intrude upon other nations' territory at their own national risk. Consequently, there are no examples, except the most brutally miscalculated, where a nation has intruded forthrightly upon the territory of one of equal military might without first declaring war. It is to the advantage, therefore, for the weaker nation to seek to be stronger. Military power is always defined in terms of who has the most likelihood of being invaded or of invading another. It might also be put in this way: Can we invade whatever nation we so please whenever we so please? If the answer is no, then there is conceivable agitation for more military power or at least parity. Parity prevents us from being invaded by others, but parity is never static and is difficult to achieve.

Sovereignty as a state concept has always been fragile. Cultural invasions are almost impossible to stop. History shows that few nations can resist the cultural advances of powerful nations. Thus, state sovereignty is a concept whose time has come for reassessment. Satellite spying is just an exclamation point on a very pointed sentence. Only with a bifurcated mind can a person even conceive of ethics and pragmatics as separate. The cultural consequences of invasion of any kind, especially as it relates to media, are far reaching.

What we are now witnessing is the transformation of our communication of values. New structures are proposed to uphold the translation and interpretation of our values and images. Communication, as a social science and humanities area, has come of age, but in a period of severe questioning of the moral or ethical decisions nations and individuals make. Religion becomes a focal point for many inasmuch as we are determined to find new communicative purposes and channels.

Politics is the secularization of religion; religion the sanctification of nationalism. There is something disarming about politics and religion joining hands. We wish to remain naive, perhaps innocent, and to let politics and religion operate in their separate spheres totally unrelated. But we know that is not the case. The history of the world can be written in the spread of politics and religion. Whether one studies Oduduwa's propagation of Ifa, Muhammad's propagation of Islam, or Paul's propagation of Christianity, one is undertaking a study of the sanctification of a national culture (Levine 1977).

The origin of religion might be found in human beings' need to depend upon the unknown for explanation of the mysteries of life. When humans could not explain gravity, the clouds, the changing tides, the growth of corn, or the flooding Nile, we sought answers outside ourselves. Our vision of the world reflected our uncertainties, our dreams, and our hopes. We are now more secular but nevertheless greatly dependent upon powers to explain mysteries to us. Indeed, politics is the deification of our uncertainties and dreams and the making of our deifications into practical instruments of change and control.

Paulo Freire suggests that politics is nothing more than putting into practice a certain vision of society (Freire 1970). Where our visions differ is where our conflicts begin. Prophets who see the coming to be of different worlds become the vanguards of political clashes. That is why Karl Marx's vision of the world clashes with that of Abraham Lincoln. Communicating a special vision of society means organizing ideas to influence others and propagating those ideas in earnest. The world is full of competing visions. At some point these visions may coincide, but that is more luck than anything else. Delusion becomes possible when we think that our vision is singular and has no competitors. We must broadcast our vision, if we believe it, and it will make its own way in the political sphere. Persuasion is the attempt to influence others to accept your predetermined objective. Politics is preeminently persuasive. In fact, there are no nonpersuasive politics. What this means, of course, is that our particular visions of society compete for the minds of our fellow humans. The clarity of our presentation adds to the acceptability of our visions. We are like captives. Because of the desire to be free, we send our messages to others as loudly and clearly as possible—voices crying, hopefully not in the wilderness, to be heard and, above all, understood. We seek understanding because it is a fact that effective communication cannot exist without it. Our vision becomes our politics. We are all political prophets regardless of what we label ourselves.

The Russian Revolution of 1917 was capable in its righteous anger of overturning the institutions of czarist Russia. However, the church was so root-bound in the old czarist state that the overturning of the state would mean the destruction of the church. Yet it was necessary, as it always seems to be, for the religious needs of the people to be recognized. The revolutionaries replaced the church with the divine state, and it became the one omniscient and omnipresent god. Lenin, in his glory and power, became the prophet of this new god. His photo appeared everywhere and millions visited his mausoleum instead of the shrines of the Christian saints.

When the progressives led by Mikhail Gorbachev and then Boris Yeltsin overturned the Soviet Union to create a new government, they had to make way for the keepers of mystery, the Russian church. They reinstalled the church leaders, reinvented the Russian orthodoxy and captured it for the state, and instituted a mystery surrounding the church in the same ways as the communists had created the mystery around Lenin. The changing of the guards meant that the changing of St. Petersburg to Leningrad and back to St. Petersburg was nothing more than a recognition of revolutionary power.

The Russian example recognized the need for the manipulation of faith in human beings. This is why faith is not condemned by the state. The Soviet attack was directed against the traditional forms of the church faith but not faith itself. In most revolutions the aggressive stance against the old order of necessity involves all of the institutions that seem to participate in the oppressive conditions of the people. The new revolution in Russia claimed as a victim, not faith, but faith in the old communist state; it resurrected faith in the orthodoxy, perfecting a mystery that was once shrouded in secrecy. Hence, the new rulers sought ways to control the minds of the masses through appealing to the superstitions that had been retooled to serve another taskmaster.

The American Revolution saw an attack on the bigwigs of the Church of England but not on faith itself. Rather, the attack was on the forms of faith. It is a pattern that has been repeated ad infinitum by political rulers, using the weaknesses of the masses as a form of political manipulation.

In China, during the 1960s Mao replaced the antistate teachings of Confucius with his own pronouncements. Mao, in turn, became the center of the new state religion. No political state can tolerate religions that seek to deny the state's authority. In Philadelphia the police attacked the MOVE organization in 1985 because of its nontraditional social and religious tenets, and former president Banda's Malawi sought to rid itself of Jehovah's Witnesses, something the new Russian state announced it was doing in 2004.

The history of Christianity is its adaptation to existing political conditions. Where it could not change those conditions, it succumbed to them. While denouncing the state as the "realm of Satan," the church acquired the same ambition for political power. Thus the church guarded the power concepts of the Caesars and made its bed with political states. The seat of the bishop of Rome in the very heart of the world empire gave him from the beginning a dominant role in mass leadership. Even after the decline of the empire, Rome remained the heart of the Western world, dominating its political ideas, organizing its communications, putting a rein on the northern barbarians' unused power, and developing the papacy as the religious spokesman of the West. It was easy for Christianity now to move from an antislave to a state-affirming religion—it was the state.

Propagation of the state and the church took a sensitive understanding of human persuasion. Compulsion tends to separate, to drive wedges, to create tension, and to produce estrangement. The church in its search for converts adapted, adjusted, and comprehended the feelings of human beings in the political estate. Nevertheless, it encouraged social ties, political coalitions, marriage bonds, and economic unions in an effort to establish permanence of power based upon need and goodwill.

The Indian example is instructive. National integration is a symbolic task. A nation of ethnic diversity overlaid by Hinduism, India finds itself entrapped by its own richly endowed past. It is possible for a Brahmin to pity the Harajins, children of God, who call themselves Dalits, until he cannot pity anymore, but he does not readily renounce his own special place in the Hindu hierarchy of castes. The Dalits, the oppressed, on the other hand, do not wish pity from the Brahmin; where there is consciousness, they seek liberation and freedom.

Mahatma Gandhi became India's premier spiritual force of the twentieth century because he renounced privilege. There could have been no greater symbolic act in a cast-ridden society. What Gandhi did was to thrust his own spirit into the Indian worldview in such a way that it was persuasive. His inducement to India, however, appeared as a result of his activities against the colonialists. An activist politician and spiritual leader, he translated his vision at a multiplicity of levels. Demonstrations against South African racism, protests against British oppression, and agitation against Hindu conservatism made him the consummate symbol of liberation. The effectiveness of Gandhi partly resides in his utilization of India's past, its Hindu heritage, and its masses. He found his arguments in his society. They were only new in their application, not in their essence. Successful national integration is yet to be achieved in India, but Gandhi suggested in his person the kind of message that must be communicated.

In Gandhi, India found both a political and a religious prophet. The secular and spiritual vision was united in him, and thus he was preeminently the symbol he sought for all in his nation. His vision was his politics; his politics his vision. The implementation of his vision was an attempt to demonstrate his politics. Gandhi became the symbol for Martin Luther King's demonstrative use of communication. In King, the world had a visionary and activist capable of highlighting the contradictions in a democratic society in a nonviolent manner. In King, therefore, America had its closest symbol of unity, of human consciousness, and of peace and love. No other American leader could be said to have possessed so much moral power.

NOTE

1. The debt owed to the ancient Egyptians by the Greeks has caused lots of controversy in modern times. This was not the case in antiquity. In fact, Herodotus, writing in Book II of *Histories*, claims that much of the Greek culture was taken from Egypt. In recent times, Martin Bernal (1987) and George G. M. James (1956) have argued that African contributions to Greek society were often downplayed in the Western academic tradition. Both books have sought to reassert the primacy of Egypt in the ancient world. Furthermore, *Egypt v. Greece in the American Academy*, edited by M. Asante and Ama Mazama (2003), underscored the position that Mary Lefkowitz's (1997) *Not Out of Africa* was badly flawed in its arguments against an African contribution to Greece.

chapter 9
RHETORIC AND MYTH

Technological society has murdered the traditional myth; science is no longer merely *theoria*—it is profoundly practical in ways that destroy the traditional myth and render us utterly dependent upon technological gadgetry that literally boggles the mind. Only in the most passionate rhetoric of African culture do we still find the pathos that accompanies the old-fashioned *mythos* into the twenty-first century. This happens in defiance of sterile media. It happens despite the great rush to the Internet because there are those who still understand that even with the computer, those who will be evil will be evil still and those who will be good will be good anyway. These are not obsolete thoughts or behaviors; they are profoundly connected to human society in a contemporary sense. Because technology introduces machines that destroy mystery, it also maims the transcendence of the human spirit, and therefore we must create new channels for myth making based in the act of being human. Acting out the last rounds of his own Ragnarok, technological man seeks to reduce all myths. We live, of course, with the constant background danger of nuclear proliferation, belligerence, preemptive strikes, and the possibility of nuclear holocaust—dangers that have enthroned anxiety in every level of conscious minds. We are reminded by the Bosnias, Liberias, and Rwandas of this era of the danger of mass-killing weapons in the hands of those who would provoke the end of myth. Myth in African thought may be a way to discover the values of a spiritual, traditional, even mystical rhetoric confronting a techno-logical, linear world.

The proper question is probably not what is myth but rather what is a myth? There are as many definitions as there are people writing on myth. Some have contended that a myth is a nonhistorical tradi-tional story. In conventional thinking, a myth is normally considered a story or tale of a traditional nature that has functional value for a society.

Mythos, the Greek word from which we derive myth, actually meant "utterance." When *mythos* was connected to *logos*, we were able to achieve *myth-logia*, mythology, the study of myth or analytical utterance. When it was added to *philo*, we were able to imagine *philomythy*, the lover of myth.

The Africa American has always understood that it is in myth that we find the precise essence of symbolic life in contemporary society. No longer are we victims, if that is what it was, of an alien environment threatening to subdue us; we are, as the continental Africans would teach us, and as we once knew, one with the environment. We have leaped from the environment, the same substance; the cells of the human bodies are of the same essence as the cells of trees and plants. We are quite honestly not humans separated from other matter, but, more correctly as the physicists now understand, of the same nature. Within this context, myth is important as an organizing principle in the area of human discourse.

What is it that humans speak of in their most serious conversa-tions if it is not life or death? And how many ways can we approach these subjects? Between the beginning of consciousness and the unknown is a great amount of human philosophical discussion and activity about the prior-to-consciousness and the after-consciousness; rhetoric is therefore the discussion of life and death, consciousness and unconsciousness, being and nonbeing. To act philosophically is to act mythologically.

Rhetoric becomes mythological action when it considers the prior-to and the after-consciousness, even while occurring in consciousness. These analytical utterances or rather utterances with imbedded messages can be found in many contemporary speeches of African Americans. Amiri Baraka's idea of "epic memory" exercises itself in the oratory of a Jesse Jackson, Benjamin Hooks, Fannie Lou Hamer, Maulana Karenga, or Louis Farrakhan as it did in Malcolm X, Martin Luther King, and Elijah Muhammad (Baraka 1963).

Myth becomes in the language of the African American speaker an explanation for the human condition and an answer to the question of existence in a racist society. Creation myths of the sort found in traditional African and European cultures are rare in the African American cultural experience if we take the beginning, again, (1619) as a point of departure. What is more real is that myth is connected to life.

When we examine the nature of myth in African American discourse, we see that it is about larger-than-life heroes and heroines. The African American myth is the highest order of folk tales. The stories have either a basis in history or anonymous time, but in all cases they are of triumphs and victories, even if they are considered in the suffering myth genre. Out of the African American folktale emerges the possibility of a new function, a new meaning for myth.

A significant function of the African American myth in discourse is the demonstration of control over circumstance as opposed to control over nature (Wilmore 1972; Harding 1981). It is the heroine's or hero's mission, sometimes messianic in nature, to surmount any obstacle in the cause of peace, love, or devotion to family. African American myths are set in the inexact past, unless, of course, they are historic, legendary myths, such as Harriet Tubman. In such cases they are set in specific times and places although they may possess anonymous origins. If we use Stagolee, John Henry, Harriet Tubman, Shine, and John Jasper as examples of some traditional African American myths, then we can see how myth also functions as a protoscience. It provides solutions to crises in the collective life of the people. In this way it is not aetiological, that is, merely offering causes for conditions and circumstances, but rather poignantly eschatological.

What we notice when we examine African American myths is that they possess a kind of epistemological maturity unlike the ancient myth, which is a sort of backward-looking explanation of reality. The idea of hope and possibility rises on the shoulders of an imaginative mythology that sees the future as brighter than the present. Ultimately, such a myth conception must break open toward the future as reality.

There are, nonetheless, some disturbing aspects to the use of myths in African American discourse. The fact that myth functions means only that it is recognized as having certain positive capabilities. On a stylistic level, the managing of myths in discourse could lead to a renewed emphasis on style in oratory and quite correctly introduce another uniquely African American element on the platform. Among the attributes of contemporary African American myth in discourse is the pervasive-suffering genre found even in the most victorious myths. Perhaps this is because victory is often based upon suffering or is it the continuing drama of a slavery memory? How to turn the suffering genre into a positive victorious consciousness occupies the thinking of a whole Afrocentric literary school of thought. This is the literary and political project of the Nigerian author Chinweizu, who has advanced the idea of cultural consciousness as an assault on political and cultural weakness (Chinweizu 1987).[1]

I recognize that the psychology of oppression gives birth to the complex mental confusion besetting the African American. On the other hand, some have analyzed the extent of the cultural malady that afflicts a whole generation of thinkers and artists trapped by European cultural domination. A crucible, formed by an accident of history, is responsible for the suffering genre prevailing in our discourse.

People believe that suffering brings redemption. In fact, it is the peculiarly African American emphasis in the Christian myth that gives it the potency it possesses in contemporary society. There is the myth of the suffering Christ who brings redemption to the world, a myth that to me simply reflects Western civilization dumping its concepts of good and bad guys onto a psychologically hobbled black population. Black essayists and orators have frequently allied themselves or the masses with this suffering Christ who would save humanity. In the rhetoric of Booker T. Washington one could see the myth of suffering redemption at work when Washington spoke of a divine purpose for a suffering people. Various purveyors of myths declared that, like

Jesus Christ, the African race was going through the "valley of the shadow of death" to rise again at the new dawn having saved the world through its substantive creative experience of pain.[2]

New myths are emerging in art forms such as dance and painting. We are seeing in the choreography of Kariamu Welsh the Afrocentric *mfundalai* artistic style that links the past, present, and future. Her work is not a renunciation of suffering existentially; it is rather an acceptance of victory historically. Every art form that employs a holistic concept extends our knowledge of myth. David Hammons has shown in his "blight theme" at the Hartsfield International Airport in Atlanta that technological ideas are also susceptible to new myth. Our rhetoric must become fully committed to history. This means opening ourselves and our peers to all of the creative possibilities.

The mother-earth myth is similar in pervasiveness to the suffering type. It simply reduces everything to the motif of caring. The African mother is often depicted as the universal mother figure. Thus the African American myth of the suckling mother is a multimammarian who gives milk to all equally. Our speakers speak of "the brotherhood of man and the fatherhood of God" and move on to aptly illustrate that if God will not take care of others, then our mothers will mop the sweat off the brow of all. Notwithstanding the mother symbol, the suckling genre is not purely a female symbol. Malcolm X understood as much when he said that the slave would often ask the master "are we alright?" In Marcel Ophuls's film *The Memory of Justice*, he showed how some of the victims could believe that they had been guilty of some great wrong or otherwise why were they being so brutally punished. The suckling myth establishes the African American as the moral protector of the world—somehow we will purge the world of its sins through our own suffering. In his autobiography, Malcolm X (1965) confronted this demon of the suckling myth—this protector of all others, except one's self—in his own life and sought to eliminate it in the lives of other blacks.

The hero myths that occupy significant places in the African American mythology are John Henry, Stagolee, Shine, John Jasper, Harriet Tubman, and a host of religiously related myths such as the story of Job. They are hero or heroine myths, as in the case of Harriet Tubman, because they extend the ordinary to the superhuman or supernatural. Job, a Hebrew story, becomes quite exceptionally an African American myth of a suffering hero. The personal drama of Job, who was tried multidimensionally, reminds the African American of the ways we have met our own struggles. The individuality of Job's suffering brings home to each of us our particular interface with the uncertainties of life.

Of course, there are myths that speak to the strength of the African American. John Henry is the strong, powerful steel driver who is capable of drilling a tunnel through a mountain quicker and cleaner than power-driven drills. His ability to use muscle power and physical stamina to overcome the mountain is indicative of the African American emphasis on strength. Use of the John Henry myth is usually confined to instances of physical confrontation or maintenance of philosophical positions. There are instances when the John Henry myth shares some of the characteristics of the Stagolee myth; this is true mainly as each myth regards physical prowess.

Stagolee is the prototype bad man in the sense that no one threatens Stagolee, not even the devil. He is known for his supranatural skill at surviving the worst possible personal tragedy and emerging victoriously. The myth's persistence within the African American community is testimony to its appealing communication characteristics. Stagolee, unlike John Henry, does not represent the protestant ethic. John Henry is the good man working hard to achieve victory through blood and sweat. Stagolee is his opposite who will achieve victory by any means necessary. Both myths are authentic within the context of the African American experience.

It is rare for an essayist or an orator to call among the names of John Henry and Stagolee in discourse because the myths are so embedded in the culture that their use is almost impossible to avoid. The real mythical essence of these heroes occurs with regularity in the discourse of the African American orator. It is to Stagolee that Robert C. Weaver, the late secretary of housing and urban development in the United States, referred when he said in a speech given before the Challenge to Democracy of the Fund for the Republic Symposium, on June 13, 1963, that "Negroes who are constantly confronted or threatened by discrimination and inequality articulate a sense of outrage. Many react with hostility, sometimes translating their feelings into antisocial actions." Weaver's use of the Stagolee complex was perfect for his description of conditions to a largely white audience, although it did not explain anything about the will of blacks to change the conditions. It was wild, outrageous, hostile, and antisocial behavior that occurred in response to what was a more calculated wild, hostile, outrageous discrimination. Weaver knew the Stagolee myth so deeply in his soul that he was even able to frame his mouth to say that in some parts of the community "a separate culture with deviant values develops" (Smith [Asante] and Robb 1971, 131). Stagolee is the myth that allows the African American to act against evil with violence—to shoot, cut, maim, or kill if that is necessary to restore a sense of human dignity. When any speaker or writer uses the appeal to Stagolee, directly or indirectly, she is addressing one of the principal hero myths of the community. A classic use of the myth was in Malcolm X's "black revolution" speech given before a packed crowd at the Militant Labor Forum in New York City. Malcolm said that "you've got 22,000,000 black people in this country today, 1964, who are fed up with taxation without representation, who are ready to do the same thing your forefathers did to bring about independence . . ." (Smith [Asante] and Robb 1971, 240). Much of Malcolm X's image as a dynamic orator came from his embodiment of the Stagolee myth in his oratory and in his person.

Harriet Tubman is a legendary historical mythical character whose symbolic presence infuses every conscious act by blacks in America. During the nineteenth century, she made nineteen trips to the South to rescue a total of three hundred persons from slavery, becoming by her heroic deeds the strongest mythical character in African American history. It is from Harriet Tubman that we get the numerous "Moseses" who arise to deliver the people from bondage to salvation. She is not a Messiah in the sense of either Moses of the Old Testament or Jesus of the New; she is rather the spirit-mother protecting, suckling, and leading her children. The Harriet Tubman myth manifests itself in how blacks relate the stories of the Bible to everyday realities. Those stories are not real because of the lives of

Moses and Jesus; they are real because the experience of Harriet Tubman lives within the heart of every African American person. That is why people find it difficult to accept the appellation "the Moses of her people" for her. She was more than Moses; she was a signifier for life and love, performing not out of duty to her people but out of love for them. This is the myth that is found in much of the language of Martin Luther King Jr. In the eulogy to Dr. King, Benjamin Mays, himself a celebrated orator, said King "was acting on an inner urge that drove him on, more courageous than those who advocate violence as a way out, for they carry weapons of destruction for defence" (Smith [Asante] and Robb 1971, 298). Not in his nonviolence was King in keeping with Harriet Tubman but in the "inner urge" to deliver the people. According to the Tubman myth, she once told a reluctant slave with a gun pointed to his head, "I'll see you buried and in your grave before I'll see you a slave."

Myth in its Afrocentric reinterpretation may be used to elevate and sustain the creative and productive forces of black Americans. A communicative experience, deriving from our own symbology, will add to the human capacity to speak clearly, directly, and with propriety about the immensity of the crises in intercultural communication that we now share with white Americans. An Ogunic[3] thrust into the flesh of creative myth is always made in search of a communicative frame of mind that will lead to positive human interactions.

Beyond specific uses of myth in communication, an element of futurism has catapulted us into the arena of communication as myth. Phutotonics offers the possibility of unhinging myths from the past. In that way, we become witnesses in the great drama of the future now. Lasers already exist with the capability of targeting a single cell. Holography presents us with the present as future. Our myths become ourselves, making and reshaping environment. Holography is not merely magic but the enthroning of myth. We therefore are now in the drama rather than in the audience, and our potential for unhinging myths from the past rings like the truest of possibilities for those who are committed to some element of mystery.

NOTES

1. Chinweizu has written two books dealing with the mental and cultural dislocation of Africans, *The West and the Rest of Us* (1975) and *Decolonizing the African Mind* (1987). In a similar way, Ngugi wa Thiong'o, the novelist and essayist, has written *Decolonizing the Mind*.

2. Such reliance on an acquired myth has made it difficult for African Americans to overcome mental dislocation and to find grounds for cultural advancement. Nevertheless, there are those who would argue that all myths are acquired, it is just that some myths are acquired from outside of the culture.

3. Ogun, a Yoruba form, introduces energy into the creative process as the blacksmith must be aware of the exact moment of creation of that which is transformed.

chapter 10
PRESS POLITICS IN A RACIST SOCIETY

Just a couple of years prior to the release of Nelson Mandela from prison in South Africa in 1991, Percy Qoboza, former editor of the *World*, a paper sponsored by the *Rand Daily Mail*, was at Harvard. There someone asked him what role would the press play in the liberation struggle? He answered that "it will play the same role as the *shabeens*, people will become drunk." Indeed, at that time with the cancellation of press rights in South Africa the racist regime had heightened its internal strife and created enemies among the white elite as well as the African masses. The ground was being laid for a national orgy.

Chenhamo Chimutengwende, a former minister of communication in Zimbabwe and a keen political observer, had written *South Africa: The Press and the Politics of Liberation*, a provocative and profound book on the subject of the press in southern Africa back in the 1980s. Chimutengwende's brilliant analysis of the press situation in South Africa spoke to the inherent faults of a racist society. He challenged the reader with his perceptive insight into the core of a controlled press that dictated the nature of the political discourse that people could engage in as well as predicted the punishment for those who did not toe the line.

The information scandal trials of the Muldergate period attested to the fact that the external efforts at news management were as seriously flawed as the internal efforts. Muldergate, as it was called, was the funneling of money and purchasing of propaganda, among other things, in South Africa. Recipients of "Muldergate" money included the Unification Church of the Reverend Sun Myung Moon, who got about $4.5 million in exchange for a substantial South African interest in the church-owned *Washington Times* newspaper. Following his retirement as prime minister of South Africa in 1978, John Vorster was elected to the honorary position of president of the old apartheid regime, the Republic of South Africa. His tenure in that office, however, was short-lived. In what came to be known as the Muldergate scandal, so-named after Dr. Connie Mulder, the cabinet minister at the heart of it, Vorster was implicated in the use of a secret slush fund to buy the loyalty of the *Citizen*, the only major English language newspaper that was favorable to the conservative National Party. A commission of inquiry concluded in 1979 that Vorster knew all about the corruption and had tolerated it. He resigned from the presidency in disgrace. He died a broken and defeated man in 1983, at the age of sixty-six.

Chimutengwende could see this in his analysis and was able to identify the strategies used by the South African press to defeat reality in the minds of the people. In fact, it was possible for South Africans to see the decline of the society and be told by the press that the society was flourishing and then believe the lie that it was prospering because the media moguls and the politicians were in a conspiracy of denial.

Not long ago, on August 28, 2003, forty years after Martin Luther King Jr. gave his memorable address at the Lincoln Memorial, I walked out of my back door and looked to the southwestern sky and saw Mars, thirty-five thousand miles closer than it had been to Earth in sixty-thousand years. For the majority of those of us who saw the red planet, this was a media event. We had been told that it was coming. What if the media had not told us anything about the coming of the planet? It is the same with the South African media and the end of the apartheid regime. They never told the whites that the end of apartheid was near; some believed until the day Mandela walked out of prison that the regime would last for a thousand years.

The Boer press in South Africa operated in several distinct ways internally. It (1) sought to minimize internal disorders, (2) elevated and mythified Boer culture, (3) disunited Africans, and (4) asserted white supremacy in every sector. Under the white minority regime, what was clear was that race in South Africa was stronger than economics. From Verwoerd to Vorster to Botha to de Klerk the aim was the same: the *use of the information agencies of the country to distort reality to maintain racial domination.* Much like Robert C. Smith's profound understanding of the nature of racism in the post–civil rights era, as indicated in his book (1995), Chimutengwende's earlier analysis of a situation in South Africa shows that the ability of the ruling elite or establishment to change in chameleonic fashion is what constitutes the challenge to the oppressed.

With twenty-eight million hungry—for liberty—black faces staring officials in the eyes, the white government would have dropped from fatigue were it not for the United States and other Western governments that propped it up. Successive American administrations found ways to get around the boycott of South Africa. The United States was in a spiral of lies and illusions about South Africa. The work and words of the white journalist Donald Woods of the South African *Daily Dispatch* demonstrated the difficulty experienced by whites who wanted to unravel the heinous crimes against the people, especially in the case of Steven Biko (Woods 1978). When interrogators Goosen, Snyman, Beneke, Coetzee, Marx, Fouche, Siebert, Wilken, Nieuwoudt, and Fischer beat and stomped the life out of Bantu Steve Biko, a cover-up of immense proportions, even for South Africa, was put into effect. I recite here the names so that they will be remembered in history as vile and obscene names of vile and obscene men. James Kruger, as minister of police at the time, began to lobby against the remaining press rights in South Africa when he saw the overwhelming disbelief of not only the international public but his own racist public.

In March 2004 my wife and I visited the grave of Bantu Steve Biko in the Garden of Remembrance in Ginsberg, on the outskirts of King

William's Town, just as I had visited the grave of James Byrd, the African American who was killed in Jasper, Texas, in an effort to get close to the madness that was never translated to us by the press as madness. I wanted to understand why an innocent man would be hijacked on the road from Cape Town to Port Elizabeth in South Africa and then killed by those who did not like his consciousness of history, politics, and justice. My friend Dr. Xolela Mangcu, the executive director of the Steve Biko Foundation, explained that Biko had grown up in Ginsberg, a black township outside of King William's Town, an enclave reserved for whites. He had seen the inequality, the injustice, and the brutality whites regularly imposed on the black population of Ginsberg. He was not alone in his resentment of the impositions, the beatings, the passbooks that blacks had to carry whenever they traveled, and the hardships, nearly slavery, that were supported by the government. So he started teaching the people that they were humans and should not allow any other humans to humiliate them because they were the equals of anyone. It is this seditious teaching that the South African government and its press could not support because truth undermined the political order.

Those newspapers that supported the government—particularly those of the Orange Free State, the bastion of white truculence— were rewarded with government advertisement contracts. Strategies were employed in the press that reflected the government's cynical view of black agency. They sought to pit black against black. Of course, the classic example occurred in Soweto during the last major ethnic uprising before the liberation of the country. The Boer press headlined the attack on some of the people by Zulu youngsters who turned out not to have been Zulu but tools of the white police. Such newspaper rhetoric was not given in the best interest of informing the people but inciting them to riot against each other. Boer journalists looked for every opportunity to show blacks in a negative light, even to each other. Such negative portrayals deepened the contradictions in the racist society because the political conscious leaders of the African community saw through these journalistic tricks and resolved to continue their search for a united front. A South African leader told me that the press's attempt to cast aspersions between groups would backfire because the literate blacks have developed an unstoppable consciousness.

Finally, most of the journalistic enterprise of South Africa was in support of white supremacy. The banning of editors from time to time had little to do with the overall philosophy of the papers but more with the specific violations of certain government rules. The words of the fascist leaders were quoted verbatim on any question or issue that may have been controversial. Thus, the effect was to make the word of the party the fact when it was nothing more than a view and at best an opinion. Nationalist Party members took on a certain papal infallibility when speaking on subjects of state. It appeared that the voice of the *verligte*, or purified, would push the apartheid press to some strange political gymnastics in an effort to maintain power. Fortunately, however, blacks in South Africa had crossed their own political and social Zambezi, thanks to the spirits of Mandela, Soubukwe, and Biko. Times like the white racists Hendrik Verwoerd and Balthazar Vorster had seen would be no more and the time of Peter Botha and C. W. de Klerk soon disappeared in the quickening fire of African nationalism.

The Boer press in cooperation with the government tried to destabilize the black community through support of the racist homeland policies. The Boer press was also gravely concerned about Boer culture. They were preoccupied with their lack of culture and respectability and could not understand that their racist philosophy had made them political and social outcasts. Living in the midst of large nations whose histories went back hundreds if not thousands of years and at the same time in competition with the English who claimed superiority over the Boers—an amalgamation of Dutch, French, and German stock—the Boers sought to exalt their culture, politics, and religious ideas. One of the points of tension with Africans was the Boer insistence on using their language as the medium of instruction. This position was roundly attacked by every respectable African leader. Not only did the English people reject it but the Africans saw Xhosa and Zulu as more significant than the Boer language, which they called Afrikaans.

Afrikaans may be thought of as really a creolized Dutch, or more appropriately what happened to Dutch when it came into contact with the more dominant languages of the environment, Xhosa and Zulu. New words and ideas were picked up from the context and became a part of the language. In conjunction with the elevation of the Boer culture, the press emphasized Boer political ideas. The threat of the English-speaking minority was ever present in the Boer heart. The Boers' reaction toward the English was always a tribal reaction or ethnic reaction.

I spoke with Donald Woods, the famous South African journalist mentioned earlier, on this subject, and he admitted that the constraints on all journalists in South Africa were such that not even the English editors dared to speak out against certain policies of the fascist regime. This same opinion had been conveyed to me in Harare by Allister Sparks in 1982.

Distortion through minimizing was a policy pursued by the Boer press to contain the people's outrage. One only had to look at the most vitriolic of the papers such as the *Capetown Die Burger*, which made a practice of writing headlines showing blacks in a negative light. To a large extent it was *Die Burger*'s headline "Blood and Bodies Called for by Steve Biko" that helped to incense the whites in South Africa while at the same time it sought in the article to minimize the danger of any social disturbances.

In my view, the whites in South Africa knew that they were in the most precarious position of whites anywhere in Africa. Like a mighty river, the phalanx of the people's will rose up, and no guns, no technology, no American sophisticated computers, no passbooks—nothing was able to stop their rise.

Under the white regime and during the apartheid era in that crazy country, they considered black consciousness a major crime and the expression of anger against white rule as terrorism. A meaningful translation of this consciousness and anger was accomplished by the collective will of the people in the election of Nelson Mandela. But we all know that liberation of a people is both an art and a science. In South Africa the final liberation of the masses will be the orchestrated work of the developed news network among the people whose determined efforts will have to be vindicated by ultimate political, economic, and social equality.

I am a firm believer that the traditional modes of communication will augment the electronic means of communication in order to keep the people mobilized. These traditionally developed modes of communication include (1) friendship circles, (2) working circles, (3) travelers' circles, and (4) professional circles. Thus, when an event occurs, the word of that event will be spread first among the specific members of the circle who first learned about it and then to all subsequent circles. There are few, if any, blacks who live in South African cities without access to one of the circles. Friendship circles are the peer groups and other affiliated and filial groupings. Working circles represent the people who labor in given areas and on specific jobs, whereas travelers' circles are comprised of people who move around the country. Professional circles are the people who occupy semiexecutive positions that bring them in close contact with whites. These circles represent the communication network that people have always trusted because they were the mechanisms that got them through when they could not trust the white media. Thus, as during the days of apartheid, the masses will continue to be educated for liberation through the legitimate social and political channels of the townships and rural areas. South African liberation cannot be maintained merely because we wish it to be so; it must be fought for everyday in the halls of government and in the hearts of the people. A new architecton built on justice, equality, and harmony will have to be established in the myths of the nation for it to survive as a multicultural society.

chapter 11

HABERMAS AND THE TYRANNY OF REASON WITHOUT PASSION

In many ways Jürgen Habermas has come to represent the best and the worst in the Western search for truth and understanding in communication. He is at once engaging in his defense of rationality and at the same time frightening in his commitment to the most awesome demons of transcendental reason.

Situated in the florid context of twentieth-century critical theory, Habermas emerged as a leading social thinker in modern Europe during the latter part of the century, perhaps bringing together many of the ideas of his mentors from the early critical school in Frankfurt. Max Horkheimer, Theodore Adorno, Herbert Marcuse, and Erich Fromm were important influences in the early writings of Habermas. In fact, in 1962 he wrote *Strukturwandel der Öffentlichkeit* (*Structural Transformation of the Public Sphere*), a historical work that inquired into the nature of the public realm itself, that is, how is it created and how does it disintegrate—all questions of serious concern to any student of communication as those interests had been for his teachers. For Habermas, the public sphere must remain a place where differences of opinion can be settled by rational arguments, not by appeals to customs and established doctrines. This position is problematical, since so much of modern European history has been complicated by the irrationality of ethnic and regional conflicts and wars.

The world's most devastating attacks on rationality have been offered by the military warlords of Europe, although Asia and Africa have not been without their recent political, social, and economic insanities. We are struck by the fact that a sort of linear thinking, a by-any-means necessary rationalism, was used to measure out the most severe and brutal punishment in the Bosnia war. In Africa, the raging wars of power and greed that have engulfed Congo, Rwanda, Sierra Leone, and Liberia brought out the meanest elements of humanity. Nothing escapes the rational line of thinking that believes that "might makes right" in the world. In Afghanistan the Taliban may be out of power, but they are a serious threat to any government that does not compromise to win the peace. Israelis regularly bulldoze the houses of Palestinians and Palestinians regularly create fear with bombs in Israel. The results of these wars and acts of violence are simply the last sum of a severe history of brutality across the world at the top end of the century.

The public sphere in the West found its source in the public debates, cafe society, political forums, and discussions groups that were the vanguard of progressive attitudes. Of course, what Habermas seeks to establish in this early work is that the public was really the bour-geoisie in the capitalist state and, therefore, its interests were always served. This being the case, it was impossible to have free speech and discursive will formation or transformation because the role of the public, even the bourgeois public, would eventually be restricted to serve the ends of capitalism. Accordingly, public relations work and public opinion research, and perhaps opinion poll surveys, would replace discursive will and attitude formation. He saw these develop-ments as the logical consequences of a society deeply committed to the capitalist ideology. In many ways he has been right. I think, however, that in highly industrialized, informationalized multicultural societies, one cannot forget the difficulty of speaking of the public as if it is one public. There are many publics in places like the United States, France, and England. There may be one audience in Japan or Poland, but this is hardly true for the United States, France, and England. It is probably not true for most of North America and Europe. The idea that the bourgeois public is unified and everywhere the same is a fiction.

Habermas is keen to point out the ineffectual basis of capitalist society in regard to maintaining the public sphere in much the same way as I have tried to do in *The Afrocentric Idea* (Asante 1998). He understands that the role of technology and science in the West is to make discussion impossible and to create instead a manageable system totally reliant upon technocratic rather than discursive means. Thus, in *Toward a Rational Society* he argues that capitalist society is oriented toward the "solution of technical problems" not the realization of practical goals. Technocratic consciousness replaces public discussion.

The implication of this for communication is far-reaching. Indeed, when the Somali people were outfitted with guns and patrolled the streets and roads of that country, they were given the name "technicals" essentially for the reason that they were capable of providing solutions to problems of safety. The end of that logic is seen in the utter destruction of the values and morality of the Somali society.

To engage this issue of technics, Habermas tells us that it is necessary to see another type of action not another type of science, as Herbert Marcuse would have us accept. Indeed, Habermas sees the same problem as Marcuse but argues that the development of science occurs in purposive rational action; therefore, instead of alternative science, Habermas sees communication action or interaction as the key type of action. It is in the removal of barriers to communication that one gets the conditions necessary for discussion of practical, hence, political, issues. Arguing that Aristotle, in the Greek tradition, expounded the notion of politics not as technics but as pedagogy, Habermas seeks to show how the cultivation of character is central to and indistinguishable from moral pedagogy. Although he contended that science and technology in conjunction with the positivist tradition undermined the original idea of political action by bringing to the forefront the notion of technical solutions, he is convinced in his own works that communication action or interaction is the answer to overcoming this emphasis on technics. Furthermore, he believes that reflection can be captured as an intellectual experience and thus lead to better interaction. In *Knowledge and Human Interests* he tries to demonstrate how one could reflect on the conditions of the possible by showing that various scientists used different approaches to achieve their ends because there was no one road to science. In effect, Habermas challenges the positivists who eliminated reflection—at least, in the Kantian sense—and replaced it with manipulation of data and the embellishment of method.

The Afrocentric critique owes a considerable debt to Habermas for opening the way toward appreciation of disciplines that seek to revive cultural legacies by analysis of the past in ways that the positivists cannot appreciate. The "empirical-analytic" method does not elucidate interests or legacies in historical or cultural texts or artifacts in ways that eliminate obstacles to communication. One could probably agree with Paul Feyerabend that the events and results that constitute the sciences have no common structure and the imposition of a form of abstract commonality serves no real ends. I examine Habermas's dependence on reason, even if it is a reason that finds its base in opposition to Marxism's instrumental control of nature, and discover in my examination that his symbolic system of culture might hold the same difficulties for me as any other system that establishes an abstract commonality. What is it to know anyway? How do we know? Who is to say that the root doctor in southern Georgia who treated my grandfather did not know? Or that the whites who brought their children to my grandfather Plenty Smith for him to spit in their eyes to cure them of disease did not know something themselves?

Although I have raised questions about the nature of Habermas's enterprise, I recognize that his differentiation between sensory experience and communicative experience constitutes two distinct object-spheres, for example, natural and social sciences in the Western context. Habermas sees one of these as the observation of the natural world and the other as the understanding of culture and history. It is, therefore, in this context that he is most critical of the work of Marcuse, believing, and rightly so, that Marcuse sees the rationality of science as a historically derived and transitory structure. To this position, Habermas argues that scientific knowledge cannot be treated as simply a historical project because we cannot conceive of any alternative objectifications. The assault on Marcuse's position is carried out with all of the technical efficiency found in the analytic empirical tradition. Habermas insists that scientific objectivity is totally unlike what one might find in the discussion of symbolic relativity, say, in historical or cultural studies. Thus he distinguishes between what he calls symbolic interaction and purposive rational action.

This means, however, that the two projects are projections of work and language, that is, projects of the human species as a whole and not of an individual epoch, a specific class, or a surpassable situation. The idea of a New Science will not stand up to logical scrutiny any more than that of a New Technology, if indeed science is to remain the meaning of a modernity inherently oriented toward possible technical control. This is precisely the point of Marimba Ani's argument in *Yurugu*. She is convinced that the Western orientation to science is built upon a bifurcation of the human into mind and spirit. Ani contends that the European thinkers have distorted the way humans acquire information (Ani 1994). What is the humane substitute for this technical function and who do we serve anyway if not humanity? The domains of instrumentality and symbolism could both be central to the human epoch, regardless of culture or class, if we accept that Habermas had a clue.

Of course, as I said at the beginning, I find much in Habermas that is engaging and correct, particularly his rejection of a historicism and his attempt to provide a modified transcendental argument for objectivity. However, I find his emphasis on the bifurcation of the object-spheres into instrumental and symbolic to be another step in the Western dichotomizing of the universe—that is, it's not an improvement or "advance," but the reverse. While I appreciate the great difficulty the transcendental argument has in both positing what the conditions of arguments ought to be and yet remaining beyond the boundary of analysis itself, it represents the fundamental heart of the problem of achieving knowledge in the West.

Afrocentricity prefers to view the human experience in organic terms in which the dichotomies, if they exist, are not oppositional but appositional. Therefore, all aspects of the world experience, spiritual and nonspiritual, must be seen as adding to our knowledge. Why should it be that more information is worse than less information? Why is it that we believe the simpler the principles, the more advanced the thought or the closer to nature something is, when, in fact, life is very complicated.

I am willing to acknowledge that in our society rationality means agreeing with the group interest, the culture's interest, because every idea, Afrocentricity, for example, that challenges the majority group is not looked at rationally. In fact, Afrocentricity is called "wrong-headed" even by some black writers. Setting my position in this frame, it is now possible to see why I have spoken of the tyranny of reason. After all, in another light, Habermas continues the Western rational argument in another manner. We view Habermas as laboring in the same vineyard as those he has criticized; his complaint, in effect, is that their systems leave the Western world too exposed. However, the point I want to make is that Habermas is not concerned or interested in the way the world is viewed by Native Americans, Chinese, or Africans. His project seeks to establish communication based on understanding by following Georg Wilhelm Friedrich Hegel's fundamental Eurocentric position.

The goal of coming to an understanding *(Verständigung)* is to bring about an agreement *(Einverständnis)* that terminates in the intersubjective mutuality of reciprocal understanding, shared knowledge, mutual trust, and accord with one another. Agreement is based on recognition of the corresponding validity claims of comprehensibility, truth, truthfulness, and rightness.

One has to consider the possibility that there are facts which exist in every culture and which are not necessarily accepted as important in Western culture. The Asante in the central region of Ghana know the names of numerous trees and herbs, their utility in medicine, and their value in society; these are facts, but they are not necessarily facts that are considered important by the Western botanist at Temple University. Therefore, knowledge is not simply the number of facts or the precision of facts but what facts are considered important. Habermas understands the danger of his position, and others have asked whether his position "represents instead a thinly distinguished Eurocentrism." Furthermore, Rudiger Bubner claims that "the universality of the structures Habermas singles out cannot be established inductively: for it is quite clear that they are not characteristic of communication in all cultures and in all historical epochs, nor even of all communication in advanced industrial societies" (1982b). But here, Habermas seems to anticipate the dangers of Eurocentrism and writes that when one pursues research into universals, "one must be aware of the dangers that lie in seizing upon historically limited and rather variable capabilities for cognition, communication, and action, and stylizing them as universal competencies; or in reconstructing what is actually a universal pretheoretical knowledge from a culturally and historically distorted perspective so that the reconstructive proposals are caught up in provincialism. It goes without saying that one must allow for such possibilities of error" (1971).

Actually, the Afrocentric idea is to put the observer in the proper location to observe phenomena centrally rather than from a cultural periphery. Habermas's division of action into two principal parts serves to frustrate the centrality of the observer; indeed, the observer must question whether the object-sphere is technological or interactive. A number of authors have pointed to Habermas's critique of Marcuse's notion of the double function of scientific-technological progress as having validity. I accept the validity in Habermas's position, which is of course Marcuse's as well, that there is a new reality brought on by technology's relationships to power. However, Habermas contends that this new reality does not create a force of production and of domination. This is not credible given the historical realities. Habermas's inability to see the interconnectedness of technology and domination or his refusal to recognize what it means for expression is perhaps his most disappointing failure. Indeed, he takes the position that science and technology are neutral forces. Of course, there are no neutral forces in human society—all forces assume relationships to human interaction. What is called neutral is by definition in support or defense of the status quo and in opposition to change. Thus to argue that science and technology become tools of domination only when they are used by humans in such and such a manner is to ignore the predominant ideology of technological presence itself. The mere presence of tanks in the streets of Baghdad is a symbol of power, perhaps even a message of domination.

More dominating, however, are the definitions appended to the technological power present in an arena of war. When it was revealed that there were "civilian security men" in Iraq supporting the American and coalition forces in carrying out their responsibilities, some Americans were shocked. How could thirty different security groups be involved in the war in Iraq in April 2004, many of them paying their people ten thousand a month on government contracts? These were mercenaries, clear and simple, just like the South African mercenaries who had been captured and arrested in Zimbabwe a month earlier. But in the context of the American-led coalition forces, the "private security men" who do the same jobs as rogue hired guns from South Africa are called protectors of democracy and free enterprise because they do their dangerous work for American enterprise and government entities. The subtleties of power language betray a cesspool of definitional domination.

Although I understand Habermas's need to reinterpret Max Weber in order to solve this technology dilemma, Weber did not fully comprehend the problem as it relates to a society such as present-day America. Nevertheless, Habermas tries to tackle this problem posed by Marcuse.

There is work, and there is interaction in Habermas's view. Work is seen as purposive, rational, instrumental action, while interaction is viewed as communicative action. This is the point put at its simplest without questions as to what happens when people are forced to work against their wills or how do we decide that work is purposive. According to Habermas, work is governed by technical rules, while interaction is governed by social norms. Habermas proposes that one can distinguish between institutions on the basis of the type of action and type of rules that predominate in the institutions. For example, the family is interactive and the state economy is rational, purposive. The university, he would argue, is rational, and in most cases he would be wrong, particularly if he considered the nature of racism at work in the administrative and arbitrary workings of a university.

One can no longer in the West write as if the West is monolithic or monoethnic; this is what I accuse many Western scholars of doing. Habermas does not see, or if he sees, does not show, how this bifurcation plays out in a pluralistic, multiethnic society. Eurocentric writers often remind me of those who would see Japan as a model for the United States without taking into account the fact that Japan is essentially homogeneous and the United States is heterogeneous. Nevertheless, the implications of this development are severe. At the least it means that interactive space is being limited. Communication will find its semiotics more and more in the world of technology so that interactive video, faces, computer disks, and audio disks will be the tools in the assault on human interaction—thus, undermining the communication situation.

In this sense, capitalism, as Weber understood—with its market pressures and emphasis on efficiency and productivity—has assisted in the rationalization of human contact. Our language, as I said in *The Afrocentric Idea* (1998), is imprisoned by the technological imperatives of the system, yet we are not totally enslaved. There is still the confrontation with the "system" each time we are successful in getting into contact with someone behind the computer to discuss our phone bill or mortgage or hospital bill. But science would grab even that space from us. The driving force in the Europeanization of consciousness is technological rationalization. The tyranny of reason is the tyranny of losing a human place in which democratic discussion and debate is narrowed to mean nothing more than striking the keys to choose the best options given a certain set of circumstances. Human communication cannot mean merely the increasing accumulation of technical understandings and no appreciation of social norms and moral values. To stifle human interaction in this process is to propose the creation of automatons who will wander mindlessly in the abstract reality of steel and cement of the Houstons and Los Angeleses of tomorrow with nothing better in their brains than being more efficient than the next person.

chapter 12
LITERATURE AND CRITICISM

The principal question that must be answered by the critic of the writer is, what is the purpose of writing itself? Why write? Why am I writing? Does it make any difference, and if it does—I presume at least for the moment that it does—then what is the quality or the nature of the difference that is being made? If it is true as I suppose it is and have argued that it is in previous books that the African writer has different purposes, if that writer is serious, from other writers, what then is the burden of history on African writers? I mean by African writers, of course, Africans on the continent but also in South and North America and in the Caribbean. How does that writer establish a sense of space and what constitutes the uniqueness of the space carved out by the African writer, whether in the continent or in the diaspora given our peculiar history because of European colonization and the European slave trade?

A writer from Burkina Faso or Chad or Nigeria must deal with the constantly nagging issues of the elimination of the rituals of society. How can you really write if around you all the structures of identity are falling into the trash bin of history? What does it really matter about the American stock market if you are not able to pass to your children the values that were passed to your parents and you cannot give those same values to your children? There has to be, it seems to me, a compact with the present to insure the future; otherwise, the African writer would simply be writing in isolation.

I am convinced that these issues must be dealt with if we are to make any sense out of what the literary critics are saying and certainly what the writers are writing. At the moment it seems to me that both are operating in a rather vast and relatively uncharted field with little or no direction. Simply put, neither the African American critics, the critics of the critics, nor the writers have been properly located. If, in the end, there is location, then we have a better sense of where people are mentally and intellectually, and we know what gives rise to writing in the first place.[1]

Let me be clear, I locate myself within the frames of the historical experiences of African people as a part of human history (Williams 1974; Quarles 1964; Reddings 1950; Moore, Saunders, and Moore 1995). I am not unaware of the necessity for the theorist or critic to be located. You must have a vantage point that is not moving all the time; it must give you a relatively easy perspective from which to view the facts.

Location is the principal metaphor of an Africalogical analysis (Asante 1998). My aim is to set a proper focus on the condition of writing. It is a condition much more than it is an art; art forms having certain peculiar meanings within the European worldview. This is a point I will examine further in the text. However, for the moment, location carries with it the concept of place, of stand, of position, of terms; and to be centrally located within one's cultural and historical context is to know what particular terms and frames are necessary for negotiating the condition. The critic must know these terms and either place herself or himself in these terms or outside of these terms. In placing oneself outside of one's historical and cultural terms, however, one relinquishes the appropriate vantage point from which to view reality. This does not mean that you cannot have a view; it simply means that your view is from the margins, the fringes. You can also see from the margins, but it does not give you a central sighting. Perhaps the vision is blurred by mediations that interfere with your own perceptions and comprehensions of what you see.

Now, the African American writing anything—criticism, poetry, fiction, social essays, or drama—cannot get away from a certain influence of the historical experiences. Even the African American writer Frank Yerby found that it was necessary, at least on occasion, to come home to what he knew as an experience in his background. But this is another story. It is a story of an African trying desperately to find acceptance outside of his own circle. But why should this be necessary? What is the fundamental audience of any European writer, of any Asian writer? What is the situation that demands that an African writer seek to find himself or herself in the circle of Europeans? This does not happen with the Asian context, for example. That is, African writers are not trying to impress Asian critics or Asian audiences, but the writing for European audiences, even more so than for African audiences, is problematic. The *asili*, the seed, of the problem is in the location of the African writer. Where the writer locates herself or himself is chiefly responsible for the confusion that inheres around the question of audience. As Houston Baker has pointed out in *Afro-American Poetics* (1988), there is something to be said for the way we create. All human beings create out of the materials that are available to them. This is information that is remarkable and can be remarked upon.

It may be true that the condition of writing in the African American experience does not suffer from the quality of location as much as I think it does, but it is definitely true that criticism of that condition most often starts at the wrong place. There are certain folk proverbs that make sense, you cannot use an oppressor's language, tropes, metaphors, and figures in the same way as the oppressor and ever think that you can liberate yourself. What this proverb means is deeper than lexical items, and it is deeper than grammar; it is essentially a point made in connection with terms—terminology in the sense of being located on the same ground, using the same weapons if you take a military posture.

We must be grounded in our own situation and must speak to the hard facts of our historical experiences. Only writing that demonstrates the insight to see in a Romare Bearden painting or an Elizabeth Catlett sculpture some of the possible frames of our experiences, some of the genius of every condition that is entailed in the literary process, can provide us with hope for liberation.

I am able to move toward liberation because I reject rejection when it is rooted in playing fields that do not take into consideration the historical experiences of the African people. It is simply not an issue and should not be an issue. I am all that I need to be in my literary life within the framework of my own culture. This would be so if my ethnic group comprised one hundred thousand people and I spoke for and to them out of the centrality of that experience. This is all that I can do. This is all that a writer should be required to do. We cannot expect and should not expect the white American writer to speak for us—they cannot speak for us, and they are not us and do not share our particular experience in this country. They can speak only for themselves, and that they should. They should advocate, criticize, provoke, initiate, and create tragedy and comedy out of that experience. When they write scripts or novels that have us in them, they always write from their experiences, and consequently Africans often say of white writers' books or scripts, they were all right except for the part where they showed the black person.

This is because the special history of the white writer—be that writer Joseph Conrad or William Faulkner, and be that writer considered great and outstanding by the European critics or Afro-European critics—is essentially antagonistic toward African life and experience. Now this is so whether it is admitted by critics or not. That is the condition of the European cultural context and environment out of which we write. Is it possible for that context to change? Of course it is. In fact, change is predictable, but the issue is not really change but change to the best location from which to view African phenomena. Now that is another question.

Signs and significations occur with some locatable content. They are not to be understood apart from what the writer intends. As I write this essay, I am fully aware, that is, conscious, that I am writing for an audience that will evaluate, judge, and criticize or praise me by the significance that I make. I have no doubt that I could, if I wanted to, make some inexplicable statements that would mystify my meanings. The writer has control over significations to the extent he or she uses that control to empower the reader or to disarm the reader.

African writers who have become known to the world outside of

Africa have usually worked within the context of the signs and significations of Europe. Yet one must know that there are more writers in
Africa writing in indigenous languages than are writing in European
languages. What does this mean to the American or to the European?
What does this say about our store of knowledge of African writers
and writings? If we do not understand that in Yoruba, Ibo, Shona,
Zulu, Swahili, Gikuyu, Hausa, Wolof, Lingala, and one thousand
other languages there are African writers, we are totally out of touch
with human reality. And suppose, as must be the case, that some of
those writers are as skilled as Wole Soyinka, Ngugi wa Thiong'o, and
Chinua Achebe but can write only in their own language. Since translation of African writers into European languages has not occurred at
the rate it should, we are left with the writers who speak to us in English, French, Portuguese, Arabic, or Spanish. Even here, however,
the point is that whatever the writers write in these foreign tongues is
locatable by virtue of the themes and subjects chosen for the works.

I recognize that the ambiguity of location in literature can present
some problems, but this is normally taken care of by establishing what
the compositional framework is for the work. This may be difficult to
establish at first reading, but in the end all of us who write leave a
pretty good trail of our whereabouts. In his presenting of the invisible
man, Ralph Ellison takes us to places that we had not been before,
although most people in 1952 could have imagined what he was
talking about; they simply could not locate him without establishing
the compositional framework.

In the end, it is the cultural condition of the writer that determines
what his or her composition will purport to tell. Culture is not sub-
servient to either economics or politics but is the soul of both. The
manner in which the writer conveys a thought, structures a sentence,
and decides on the solution to a problem is grounded in the culture
that is derived from the society. Culture is a complex concept, and in
some circles the argument is made that economics dictates culture;
however, it seems to me that culture precedes economics and gives us
the particular response to literary subjects. To understand what a
writer writes, then, one must analyze the cultural components of that
writer's society.

But therein is the problem for a people who have been subjected to such cultural bombardment backed up by force. What now are the cultural components of such a society? We know that certain elements in the circle of memory, the location of principal mythoforms of a culture, constitute the critical determinants of how a people perform in the midst of circumstances. This is no mysticism; it is the reality of how we have come to know ourselves. The percussive element, for example, in our music is heard and felt whether we are in Chicago or Philadelphia, Atlanta or New Orleans. We could be Baptists or Episcopalians, Jews or Muslims, and yet the percussive elements stir something deep within us. This is the circle of memory.

For the African American, language is the real substance of relationships. There are few examples where language does not play the dominant role in the relationships between people. The structure of the language contains all of the elements found in the circle of memory: myths walk the syntax, and soul is invested with sentences and vice versa. Thus, the writer, to be located properly, must find his or her resources from the recesses of the people's memory. As a writer, I am a reflection of my people, of their sufferings, their joys, their victories, and their myths. Without them, I am nothing and could have no particular reason to speak or to write. The African American writer can never be outside of the circle of memory and remain relevant. To be outside of the circle of memory means that you might misunderstand some very important messages that are fundamental to appreciating the culture or revealing it.

I remember hearing a white movie critic comment on seeing Spike Lee's *School Daze* and *Do the Right Thing* that he could identify with nothing in the movies. The reason he could not was that the movies came from the most inner sanctum of the circle of memory. The most illiterate African American living in the United States would have understood them, while the white movie and literary critic could find nothing in them that would give him a clue.

Spike Lee is inside the circle of memory. Radio Rahim is my big brother. Tina is my sister. I know the street in Brooklyn where Sal's pizza shop is located. My old man is the Mayor of the block. Mother Sister has given me many readings, and I have respected the mysticism of her presence. I have stood on the spot where the police killed Radio Rahim. I am the stutterer with the photos of Malcolm and Martin.

There is more here, however. What Spike Lee brings to us is not just the memory of our places, but of our past. Beyond memory he shows us the possibilities and gives us the options, that is, the source of his power with nonblack audiences. They are able to see in his genius the intellectual themes that govern social life in these United States. Thus, he performs a central service for the literary field by showing that to create Afrocentrically does not mean to create negatively but rather to create from a centered position as an African person. This is our only imperative. What I mean is that the genre and focus of our works always give way to the inevitability of personal aesthetic choices after the imperative of centeredness. A movie is not a book; it is not even a play—and therefore how we view it must be as a movie. Spike Lee's work is central to an appreciation of this artistic mode.

The Afrocentric writer structures both the internal and the external world; they are essentially the same worlds. The difference lies mainly in the way both worlds relate to the investiture of cultural vision—that is, whether or not there is actual difference in vision. Perhaps the only way that the writer can structure both is to see them as one. Of course, this runs us right up against the Parmenidean inheritance of Western philosophy that infuses difference with qualitative value. Ancient Kemetic thinkers—Seti, Kete, Ptahhotep, Duauf, and Kagemni participated in the same vision of reality as that of the Afrocentric writer, hundreds of years before Heraclitus introduced that concept into the Greek world. It is not enough to say of the Afrocentric writer that he or she is outside of or inside of a language; one must say that the writer embodies language and its various manifestations in structure as poetry, drama, fiction, or essays.

At this moment of writing I am totally what I write even as I write with Coltrane playing in the background on WRTI-Philadelphia. The way the lamp to the left of my monitor throws light on me is a part of the entire moment of my creativity. I abandon myself to myself, but in doing that I do not lose my culture that is also part and parcel of what I do and am doing. Instead of trying to listen to every beat and every melody of the music or instead of trying to feel the light on me, I discover important attitudes and ways of being in tune with the rhythms of culture by just being myself. I cannot be outside of my culture, although I can refuse to accept it, ignore it as a factor in my life, and derogate it in my writings. But this is to be out of synchrony with self. One must find intellectual peace in the traditions and attitudes of one's existence. You cannot be out of existence. There again the African worldview has always articulated that perspective. Religion, art, literature, science, agriculture, iron making, and philosophy are inseparable, just as inseparable as I am from my culture of which I cannot and will not ordinarily be divested.

NOTE

1. If we say it is through inspiration that we are motivated to write, then it seems to me that we must realize that it is not something outside of us, but something that we make, manufacture, structure, and create as an architecton.

chapter 13
AFROCENTRICITY, SEXISM, AND *MAAT*

I t is a truism that the more one learns the more one finds that the limits of knowledge are farther and farther away. Such seems to be the case with the interrelationship of the issues of gender and race in the twenty-first century. There has been an explosion of postmodern works on sexuality and gender since the writings of Michel Foucault.[1] A considerable energy has gone into the assertion of a new identity for many people with the corollary that there is new confusion about the question of gender, sexuality, sexism, and Afrocentricity.

I approach these issues in the context of the transformation of human society and the movement toward a condition of *Maat*: harmony, order, reciprocity, truth, justice, righteousness, and balance. As an Afrocentrist, my perspective is based on the readings of the classical texts of African culture as well as more contemporary observations. Of course all of my readings are mediated by the circumstances and contexts of contemporary society. In ancient Kemet (Egypt), one of the major ethical documents was the *Book of the Coming Forth by Day and the Going Forth by Night*, or the *Book of the Dead*. When one examines the forty-two negative confessions or declarations of innocence, one thing becomes immediately clear: the Kemetic people had strong feelings about certain human behaviors. Everything was not acceptable; there were boundaries to human behavior in the interest of human community. For example, for a man to be judged righteous, he had to declare that he "had not lain with another man." There is a contrast between this and the Greek classic *Symposium*, written by Plato, where homosexuality is recommended as a desirable state.

Since Kemet resonates as the classical civilization from which cultures as widely separated as the Peul, Wolof, Mbochi, Igbo, Yoruba, and Akan draw correspondences, it is important that we gain a clear conception of what the ancient Africans of Kemet thought about the questions of gender and sexuality. This will give us a starting point from which to refer. Otherwise we have no useful way to approach the subject of Afrocentricity, sexism, and *Maat*.

Ancient Kemet was based upon the foundation of *Maat*. The key to this idea was the heroic attempt to hold back chaos and to retain a sense of balance in human society. For a man to lay with another man was considered a violation of one of the forty-two Declarations of Innocence. This prohibition was rooted in the Kemetic ideal of the divine trinity. Historically, the idea of Ausar, Auset, and Heru as the ideal family found its source in the earlier deities such as Amen, Mut, and Khonsu. Wherever the African turned, there was the example of the deities operating in their sphere as models for humans.

All African moral teaching is derived from classical sources and rooted in a strong belief that a man should provide for his family and that a woman should raise the children. There is nothing like the abandonment of the family because family is central to the African concept of being. How a society defines itself—that is, its core characteristics and objectives—has a lot to do with how that society approaches the questions of gender and sexuality. Clearly, if you believe that sexuality is for human reproduction, then you will value fertility, perhaps even create rituals and ceremonies to demonstrate the important place fertility holds in your society. This is what the early Africans established because of the idea of family being constituted by a father, a mother, and a child.

Many people confuse the discourses around equality of women, the overthrow of patriarchy, gender and sex, and the assertion of mutuality as the basis for all human relations. By gender, I mean the properties that distinguish organisms on the basis of their reproductive roles. Although I understand that gender roles are created through socialization, all societies create socialization processes based upon what they see as their objectives. In every society, of course, gender roles may be deconstructed and redefined. One of the processes going on in the Western world now is a redefinition of the masculine and feminine gender roles with the aim of creating more equitable distributions of social and economic power. How this plays out in terms of responsibilities and expectations of women and men will help to determine society's objectives.

We know that gender is not the same as sex. Indeed, sex refers to biological differences between men and women, while gender refers to the various social roles that define women and men in cultural contexts. As I have pointed out, the traditional African social roles for women and men are different from those roles in the Western world. Therefore it is difficult for one culture to impose its will on another society by dint of might. One could appreciate or not appreciate another culture's way of defining gender, but one cannot assume that the Western way is absolutely the only way, or necessarily, the right way. This smacks of cultural and social imperialism.

One thing is clear for the Afrocentrist and that is that the role of women in the world economy is not only central but in most societies an absolute necessity for any semblance of human living. Women do most of the work in the world, whether in agricultural societies or information-based ones. The crude assaults on women such as wife beating, mental degradation, killing of girl children, forced sterilizations, and violent physical and psychological abuse are most often the results of actions by men. This is an antiwoman environment. This is the context in which all attempts at transformation must begin.

Increasingly, the legitimacy of authority in societies will depend upon the degree to which they demonstrate that they are antisexist and antiracist. In fact, it is true that the character of industrialist society tends to enthrone antifeminine attitudes. I predict that the informational society will quickly obliterate paternalism for a more African idea of complementarity (See Hudson-Weems 2003). This idea is one of female equality, female partnership with males, and female roles and responsibilities based on choice and adaptive reactions to environment and need. There is no natural warring of the sexes in the historical African context. Where paternalism or patrilinealism appears as a dominant and oppressive system in Africa, it is the result of extra-African influences, not the indigenous forces of Africa. No area of the world has had as many female leaders as Africa, and no people have ever been so sensitive to the roles of men and women as Africans. This is because it has never been viewed as a problem area.

Despite the fact that in a society such as the United States where energy expended on the question of inequity has increased since the 1990s, many women have remained victims of economic and social degradation. I believe that the new informational society will not enshrine a sexist or racist hierarchy. Since the gender hierarchy in the West—where there was a clean division between what men did and what women did—is in serious question, I do not see any reason for the lingering around of sexist hierarchy. Race, I suspect, as Hudson-Weems believes, will be harder to handle (Hudson-Weems 2003).

Afrocentricity, as a novel perspective in the intellectual life of the West, holds that human values must be not merely neutral in regards to sexism but aggressively antisexist. Essentially, the centric perspective holds that all experience is culturally grounded but that one is most centered psychologically when experience is viewed from one's own culture. This is particularly true when you speak of African culture and experience; not to be centered means that you have marginal experience. The same holds for the Afrocentric view of women—the centrality of women in this view is a fundamental necessity for both the corrective and the aggressive antisexist, antiracist project.

Afrocentricity is not the opposite of Eurocentricity, which is often an ethnocentric view based on ethnic colonization and the degrading of others by imposing its white male patriarchal dominance as universal. Afrocentricity does not argue a mere geographical term but an axiological and epistemological foundation useful as a theory and method for humanistic interpretation of phenomena. In this regard it is a central perspective in the postsexist construction of reality. Nevertheless, it is a critique of the liberal elitist ideology that pursues the language of antisexism while simultaneously asserting that some things are natural—meaning, for instance, the exploitation and subjugation of women.

To demonstrate that society can be transformed by Afrocentric logic, it is necessary to lay out what constitutes the fundamental constituents of Afrocentricity and to show how those constituents seek to unravel the tightly constructed "reign of vernacular gender" as well as the more "archaic regime of economic sex." In reality, the entire question of gender and sex has become trapped in a Eurocentric enterprise since the sixteenth century. This is to say that the relative position and experience of Europe, in its particularity, has become identified as the universal position and experience of the world. This is not only arrogant and pathetic but also the cause of more misery than other ideologies.

Afrocentrism proposes emphasis on four levels of inquiry: cosmological, axiological, epistemological, and aesthetics—and the infusion of the truly human, meaning the full scope of the human experience, into any analytical process. These levels represent relationships to the cosmos, to value, to knowledge, and to the beautiful (Asante 1990).

There are three approaches to these levels of inquiry: functional, categorical, and etymological. We must seek congruence in each of these areas in order to effect an Afrocentric reality. What I mean is that Afrocentrism centers women while at the same time centering the African people. One cannot truly be liberated as a woman until pejorative language about Africans, Native Americans, Asians, or any other people is eradicated. How can one be centered and grounded vis-à-vis males and at the same time hold anti-African and/or anti-Hispanic views? The emancipatory process must be one that seeks a wholistic human liberation, beginning, of course, from one's own center as female or male. One must not be merely oriented; one must be located. This is the key to Afrocentricity. The objective conditions of women have changed in dramatic ways, but the relative status of women has not changed so much. Gender itself is another issue—in essentially a different way. What I mean is that gender as a cognitive division appears to be more fundamental than any other division in the sense that boys and girls grow into their respective genders early on—in effect, where the objective conditions of women may have changed the question of gender and particularly the value of the feminine remains fundamentally unchanged. Actually, identification in gender is one of the first things a child recognizes. This means that a child develops preferences for a particular gender at an early age, and the process of demonstrating the equal value of genders must start almost immediately.

African American expression in drama, poetry, and fiction has generally followed the path of the valorization of the masculine gender, while African American women have frequently and effectively appealed to antiracist arguments to attack sexism in African males. After all, African American males do participate in the currency of male domination, though certainly not at the same power level as white males. It is a regime that must be overturned. The white feminists, to be serious in overturning patriarchal dominance, must seek more than a share in the regime. The truth is that black patriarchal dominance and white female racism must be added to white patriarchy for assault.

I posit Afrocentricity as a path to humanizing society in such a fashion as to call into question the continuing exploitation of women. It is a gender issue precisely because humanism is considered a "feminine" quality when, in fact, it is strictly nongender. To banish sexism, to regain ecological balance in the earth, to reduce race prejudice, and to establish peace it is necessary to implement a humanizing force in all sectors of society.

This must be done in such a way as to lead to an acceptance of gender value, and not simply by paying lip service to women's issues. There is a widening gap between myths that are pursued and the material realities that exist. Institutions are run by men, and men do not often live up to the mission of their institutions when it comes to equality for women. The gender gap, in terms of authorization, still exists and must be challenged on every front. The story of Nzingha, queen of Angola, is instructive. Hunters whispered in the forest that she would never be queen, but she was already entering the third year of her reign. The transformation can truly take place aesthetically and dramatically. A shift of attitudes about gender will necessarily bring about a dramatic transformation in an institution. It is happening and will happen even more in the next century throughout the world. Women in the United States make only 60 percent of what men who work make; this is so despite the fact that one hundred years ago the ratio of women's pay to men's was the same as now. Yet women constitute nearly 46 percent of the US workforce. More women are working and yet women are held in the same virtual economic prison, and this is the condition that must be transformed. I am speaking about a set of protocols, not simply an orientation but a location that makes possible the human by protecting all equally. The proper perspective on any condition, including gender, can be determined by discovering the totality of one's cultural location (Blackshire-Belay 1992). Afrocentrists of whatever gender have always advanced radical transformation in centering as the key to liberty.

To insist that this new perspective might emerge from a thorough examination of an African worldview is not to valorize this worldview beyond others but rather to suggest that the ascriptive world of race, sex, and gender reality created by patriarchic Europeans may not be best suited to deal with these issues.

I raise these issues because in an Afrocentric sense I have contended that power determines the condition for the interpretation of reality and that the creation of reality is controlled by power, making it possible for changes and transformation to occur to accommodate new politics. The inherent right of women to be treated equally and fairly or African Americans or Native Americans to be equally and fairly treated existed before our regulation or legislation. Power dictated the realities (Forbes 1993).

I am reminded of the fact that in 1808 after the glorious revolution of the Haitians all people, Africans, Europeans, and those defined as mulattoes—those whose ancestry could be traced to Africans and Europeans—were made by executive decree, blacks. Similarly, in Zimbabwe, after the Second Chimurenga War, there was no longer any racial distinctions recognized by the government, though by habit and customs the society lagged behind the decrees of the government. Yet I am convinced that in time the Nile of power will have its way.

We do have the concrete biological realities of estrogen, testosterone, and melanin with the possibility of making us distinct and different. However, gender seems to be another question, where femininity and masculinity represent attributes and choices. But in making this distinction and drawing these lines of argument, I am raising the issue of what Maryse Conde has called the colonized gender. The problematic of the colonized gender, like the colonized race, is fundamental to an understanding of the current social project. Gender is a social construction and represents, perhaps, a spectrum, although we normally make the assignation in a duality of feminine and masculine, as opposites.

Now what I would like to do at this point is to discuss a set of philosophical issues that might provide openings for further consideration of transformation of image. Think for a minute of yourself twelve thousand years ago in northern Europe. If I ask you what do you need in order to be here next year, what you absolutely had to have in order to be alive next year at the same time, you would say food. The highest value of the society, therefore, becomes the acquisition of that object—the getting of food. But look at this situation. Since you cannot plant between September and May, you only have three months in which to prepare to get food—that is, as a food gatherer. June, July, and August are the months in which you will have to make haste. Since women are likely to be employed in sowing and reaping, they are also likely to know a lot about herbs, roots, and plants for medicinal value—what can cure various ailments, what teas are good for which sicknesses, and which foods to avoid.

Women with such knowledge could be considered dangerous, and that is why in the West the notion of woman as witch took hold as an attack on women for possessing such powerful knowledge. Nathaniel Hawthorne and Arthur Miller have dealt with this in *The Scarlet Letter* and *The Crucible*. Of course, along with this went the idea of woman as the keeper of time, particularly lunchtime and the number of days in the cycle. There was the beginning of the month; there was the end of the month. Thus, measurement becomes the standard of knowing, one knows through counting. The logic of such a situation is clear, either one does something or one does not, either one is feminine or masculine, male or female, black or white, and so forth. Indeed, opposites are dichotomous and often antagonistic in such cases.

What this means, of course, is that if males impose force on females, say to force them out of the shelter in the middle of February, the females are essentially on their own. To maintain her shelter a woman might decide to remain indoors under such a situation but in effect become a slave to male interests for protection and shelter. The idea behind the rule of thumb was that a man could beat a woman with a rod no bigger than the thumb. She became by virtue of the conditions of this axiology an object—property—because the highest value was in the acquisition of the object.

Take the African back twelve odd years ago—if I say to you gather seven stalks of bananas and keep them from September to May, do you do that? Did Africans do that? No, because bananas grew all year round. Women and men had equal access to herbs. A man forced a woman out on her own. Could she get her own yams, cassavas, and bananas? Yes, if you are a woman who is in such a situation, you can do it yourself. Take the African value, for example. The highest value is in the interpersonal relationship between individuals. (One knows through the symbolic, through imagery, through intuition, through rhythm.) Women find their support for equity maintained in the traditions. Thus, a father will take out a loan to send a daughter to college but will rarely do so to send a boy to college as a way of maintaining equity. Actually, in the culture the father and mother speaking to the daughter about education and their sacrifice for education will say, "I'm doing this for you so that if anything happens, you can take care of yourself." Time implications exist where you have twelve months instead of three months. Behavior in relationship to time is different.

Thus, the African woman is not a Joan of Arc waiting to be burned but an Nzingha who goes to fight the Portuguese, and when she speaks to the Portuguese in her role as military queen and is refused a seat, her soldiers compete for the opportunity to have her sit on their backs. This is the tradition of leadership and nobility and character of Harriet Tubman and Fannie Lou Hamer. Men have always recognized the authority of those women, like men, who exercised leadership. It was no different under Hatshepsut, Sobeknefru, Amanitore, Nanny, Yaa Asantewaa, or Tubman.

I have discussed this at length to explain that transformations, whether in dramatic works or others, can come about only when writers are taught to interpret all of the nuances of culture in the process of our humanization. Afrocentricity establishes itself as a leading perspective in that direction.

The attack on the feminine gender is often subtle, but it is equally as insidious as an attack on people because of race. Race is often commonplace in its class dimension as capitalism, in its culture dimension as Western, and in its religious dimension as Christianity. I argue as an African in America that class, like gender, aggravates the race question—race relations is important because it encompasses a discussion of the various other dimensions—the battlefront is everywhere. To attack women and more pointedly to attack the feminine gender as being emotional, generous, flexible, and resilient is to attack a very major part of our humanity. A male who believes in peace, sentiment, nurturing, and family should not be attacked by gender terrorists either. We are all victims in this society of the elevation of masculine ideas and the denigration of things feminine. But that is not all; we are also prone to exaggeration and hyperbole.

The judge who set bail for the captain of the Exxon ship that spilled oil in the ocean off of Alaska in the 1980s is reported to have said, "This is the biggest environmental tragedy made by man since the bombing of Hiroshima." In this generic use of "man" he includes Africans, Asians, and Hispanics and others—indeed, he would argue that he includes women, yet the fundamental truth is that "man" is a euphemism for patriarchal European man. We are all called upon to share in the tragedies that result from misguided greed. I want no part of it. African cultural perspectives may have led us to different tragedies but certainly not the pollution of the oceans and the atmosphere, and the killing of all the animals. The unity of the living, dead, unborn, and of all the animal kingdoms keeps that away from Africans.

Power results from force that makes it possible for you to create situations, define reality, and have others respond to your creations as if they are your own. Afrocentricity seeks to provide a method for disengaging from such reality traps. One disengages by delinking and reconfirming. One of the greatest hindrances to disengaging is that often the doctors, those of us who teach and research, need the same brain transplants as our patients, those for whom we write and lecture.

We are caught in a most inhospitable situation created by an ego-centric culture that has stacked enough nuclear weapons to destroy the world more than two hundred times. The United States alone has more than twenty thousand nuclear bombs and thousands of biological and chemical weapons. In the past few years our nation has campaigned to control weapons of mass destruction in other nations, but it is our country that has the most weapons of mass destruction. How shall our politicians be reined in? What can we do to make the world safe for human relationships? How do we make others feel safe that our nation has not become a civilization of clashes? What do you do with the bombs?

There is a worship of fire, perhaps epic memory of ice and fire, the awesome nature of its beauty—on the Manhattan Project the scientist who made it and saw it tested said, "How beautiful," "How secure I feel," "It is a perfect instrument of war." All of these expressions are normally used in connection with deity—the bomb had become god for its creators. The destruction of the military and infrastructure of Iraq in 2003 was accomplished with what became known as "shock and awe" intelligent bombs. Of course, bombs are meant to destroy, not just buildings and bridges, but humans as well. And now we must still guard against any type of phallocratic madness played out by newly minted renegades with their rockets pointed at each other's people in an effort to settle who has the most power and whose rockets are the biggest. But if we think we have the bomb under control, shouldn't we go after the handgun, the deadliest weapon of this era? How do we bury the hatchets of our past without a very real sense of courage in the present? The transformation to image occurs when we transform ourselves and see relationships, not as objects to be possessed or destroyed, but to be built, nourished, nurtured, and protected.

NOTE

1. Obviously there was discourse on sexuality and gender before Michel Foucault, but we might safely say that with Foucault's penetrating monographs we were able to have a more open discussion on the nature of human sexuality.

chapter 14

NARRATIVITY AND THE RHETORIC OF IDENTITY

THE POSITION OF THEORY

In his important book *Introduction to Black Studies* (2002), one of the most important creative thinkers of the century Maulana Karenga has placed the study of African and African American studies in a radical tradition, emphasizing the ability of the field to bring about a human response to the most pressing issues of contemporary society.[1] Karenga, the creator of Kwanzaa and many other positive concepts in the African American community, has privileged the idea of cultural reconstruction in his philosophy. His book, a significant contribution to the organization of the field of black studies, is in the same mold as his other cultural projects.

It is a broad work, grounded in the intellectual work of engaging organic intellectuals who believed in the ability of the cultural masses to reveal the inadequacies and the strengths of rational thought. Thus, Karenga has challenged the ethical and moral philosophers of the day with a new ethic that has its origins in the best practices of African human values.

Africans have always asked questions about life, literature, nature, religion, and humanity. It is the nature of humans to ask questions when confronted with difficult issues and then to search for answers.

Unfortunately, in this age of human history it is necessary to emphasize that this search for solutions is not a European idea; it is a profoundly human process.

When the first human in Africa came to the bank of a river, she or
he had to decide how to cross it. This is not a unique process in our
human thinking. Now, how we decide to cross it, what motifs we use
to decorate our craft or our bridge, and what rituals will be performed, and to what deity, are all cultural issues. But one thing is
clear: the crossing of rivers is a common human problem. Afrocentrists are like the traditional African doctors, trying to protect the
society against evil forces by analyzing conditions, determining possibilities, and suggesting effective ways of managing our quest for
answers. In this capacity the Afrocentrist seeks to identify disorientation and dislocations in an effort to show social, economic, or political strategies for recentering. No person is permanently dislocated or
disoriented if provided with the proper information for new consciousness.

Afrocentricity, therefore, is not to be understood as Africanity.
"How one approaches these concepts in large measure determines the
efficacy of a challenge to hierarchy. The substance of one term is not
that of the other, and the consequences of one can create problems for
the other. In other words, one idea, Afrocentricity, seeks agency and
action, and the other, Africanity, broadcasts identity and being"
(Asante 1998, 19). Afrocentricity is a way of approaching data, an orientation to data, based on the agency of African people. In the tradition of the communication scholars who seek to discover how people
invest themselves of culture as a way of being communicative in the
world, the Afrocentrist is interested in centeredness as opposed to
marginality, being as opposed to nonbeing, and an active instead of a
passive role for African culture and ideas in the world.

In this regard the Afrocentrist is a scientist—that is, she gathers
facts, verifies data, and subjects her interpretations to rigorous tests if
she is studying human behavior. On the other hand, if the Afrocentrist is examining text, history, or events, he seeks to gain insight into
these phenomena by making unambiguous statements about them.
The Afrocentrist does this by distinguishing between the language of

centeredness and the less precise language of decenteredness in relation to culture. The way Afrocentric scholars have constructed a
response to the intellectual and cultural decenteredness of so many
writers of African descent is through what I have called the use of *sentinel statements* as clues to marginalization and decenteredness. In this
manner Afrocentricity also becomes a critical tool for determining
how closely related a given communication text or address is to the
actual historical or existential reality of African people. This means, of
course, that it becomes a critical tool.

Sentinel statements—those statements that signal a text's location
during the earliest parts of an analysis—are used as standards by which
the Afrocentrist views an entire text. For example, if you are reading a
text and as soon as the author introduces his theme he makes a statement such as "Harvard is my home," you have a fairly good sentinel
statement by which to evaluate the remaining part of the text. This does
not mean that the person has abandoned Africa or his cultural grounds
yet; it merely means that the potentiality for abandonment appears
early in the text. Since it is possible that there is textual confusion
throughout the document, it might be that the author comes around at
last.

Follow my explanation of this phenomenon in order to move
toward a deeper appreciation of how theory assists us in social
analysis. Theory is important because it directs us to the proper questions to ask and the methods to use to acquire data that can be interpreted in a way that makes cultural, psychological, and literary liberation more certain. Liberation, for the African American, is to be free
from the unwarranted assertion of white racial domination in our
minds and lives. Of course, anything done to us without our permission is a measure that takes away our freedom. In communication this
means that our paths are complicated often by the unwieldy use of
concepts, symbols, arguments, and opinions that hound our intellectual discussions. It is as if Jews were left with only the concepts and
ideas of Nazi Germany for their own explanations of self and community. The limitation of such language imprisonment is profoundly
demonstrated when we are unable to break through to the essence of
our own cultural realities. Theory, particularly Afrocentric theory,

drives us closer to explaining how conceptual distance from our own centers leaves us on the margins of the European reality.

There are expectations that come from theory. We learn to accept that if an Afrocentrist follows the protocols of the theory—that is, is able to examine the text, observe the phenomena, apply the assumptions, and gather the data—certain results will happen. For instance, we could expect that the information is either supportive or nonsupportive of the Afrocentric theory. To that end, it might be necessary to rethink the theory. Afrocentricity is open ended; it is not a closed system. Of course, since it is a paradigm and a paradigm can support several theories, that is, several nonconflicting theories, it might be said to constitute a galaxy of theories. Such a platform for social theories is necessary to deal with the different issues confronted by Africans in the Americas since the enslavement. The platform also supports theories that seek to explain the social and cultural conditions on the African continent.

I do not have space to demonstrate this principle ad infinitum, so let me establish a framework, a historical framework, for the analysis of narrative.

The history of all past discussions of race in Europe and America has been nothing more than the attenuation of the conditions of white dominance. Whether we have talked about race, racism, or race relations, we have done nothing more than to play on the shifting conditions of white domination of other races. In fact, the discussions or antidiscussions of race, such as those by Cornel West, bell hooks, and Paul Gilroy, have been about shifting authority. Most of the time those discussions have been accusatory of black people, whether by saying that we suffer some form of nihilism or by telling us how we ought not be African (West 1992; Gilroy 2000).

It is easy to see how this array of intellectual confusion can create double vision. These writers say racism is deeply embedded in Western culture, and then they say there is no race because it is only a social construct, and then they say the only real racists, that is, people who talk about race, are black people, who should stop talking about it as if it exists. And anyway, they say, we are certainly not Africans or if we are, we are so committed to other cultures that we have little to call our own. This brings me to a discussion of a narrative of location or dislocation because this is a narrative that is supposed to deal with our sojourn in America and our liberation from enslavement (Ball 1970).

Eddie Glaude has written an odd book titled *Exodus!* It is an ambitious work that seeks to demonstrate that the biblical image of the Jewish exodus was appropriated by African Americans to give an account of "the circumstances of their lives," and serving as "a regulative ideal to guide action and to define the nation, it ensured retribution for the continued suffering of God's people" (Glaude 2000, 10).

Glaude's premise is based on a flimsy foundation. The idea that African Americans looked to the Jewish story as a way out of suffering and pain is apocryphal. It is a sentinel statement, a hint of problems that will appear later. Not to engage the trope of Egypt with all its contradictions in the African mind is an enormous omission. How did African writers manage a factual black Egypt if they saw white America as Egypt also?

Glaude erroneously seeks to show Jewish history as a model for the Black Nationalist idea. Black and Jewish histories stand on their own merits. I have noted elsewhere[2] that the peculiar experiences of African people in America and the peculiar experiences of Jewish people in Germany reflect parallel ways of acquiring character, of dealing with death and destruction, of seeking to repair broken and mangled relationships. It is not necessary for me to claim the Jewish experience nor for Jews to claim the African experience; both histories have been ritualized in the context of our own historical experience.

Glaude misses these realities, and he also dismisses three principal arguments for nationalism: self-liberation, racial solidarity owing to our condition, and unity of moral community. Thus, freedom, unity, and ethics, the key components of the Black Nationalist thrust, are set aside as insignificant. The central problem is that Glaude's thesis rests upon the belief that Africans utilized the Jewish exodus trope as a principal method of organizing themselves and creating a national identity. He believes that the basis of African survival during the enslavement may rest in this trope.

The problem is, however, that there was no early Christian public among Africans in colonial America. Glaude conveniently forgets 175 years of African history (1619–1791) during which time Africans were not flocking to white Christian churches or any churches. In fact, it is quite interesting that Glaude does what others have done when they cannot deal with African history from the earliest times in America: they start discussing Christianity in the "early nineteenth century." This does not present a difficulty for me; they are right to do this if they are discussing Christianity, but they often do it without knowing why they are skipping the seventeenth and eighteenth centuries. Or they do not tell the readers why they are skipping the true story of the image of a nation.

When Africans arrived in 1619 to the English colony of Virginia, they would be looking at more than 150 years before there was anything like a standing church among them. The African Baptists and the African Methodists were not founded until the late eighteenth century. They were essentially churches of the free blacks. What about our enslaved ancestors? Whose church housed them and gave them sustenance and made them understand the Jewish exodus? There was no such movement. Indeed not more than 15 percent of the African population was Christian at the end of the Civil War. Yet there was a definite belief in certain African concepts and ideas that gave rise to group feelings of solidarity and expressions of freedom. In 1822 Denmark Vesey was ably assisted by Gullah Jack, an African priest, who held power over the masses because of his spirituality, eloquence, and ability to demonstrate the presence of God. So it was not so much the black church that gave us our nationalism, but rather nationalism was used by the Christian church to advance its own mission. Missionaries who flooded the South sought to save the souls of the newly emancipated Africans in a variety of churches. It was probably not before 1900 that the majority of Africans could be called Christians. Thus, there is no evidence that the "church stood not only as the institutional organization of the community's resources and a kind of ideological and cultural common ground for everyday interaction or association among antebellum blacks" (21).

Glaude argues without evidence that the "analogy with the Jews of the Old Testament occupied the religious and political imagination of antebellum blacks" (Glaude 2000, 29). No, it did not! It occupied the minds of a few blacks in the North who were influenced by whites, who heard the myth, and who believed it. There were nearly four and a half million Africans by the end of the Civil War. Glaude concentrates on a Northern leadership class, but such a class barely existed. The South was where the overwhelming majority of Africans lived. Who led them "between 1777 and 1818"? (Glaude 2000, 28).

Yet it was only in the North during the late eighteenth and early nineteenth centuries where Africans were free to have churches. Africans had been led by men calling themselves preachers during the nineteenth century in slave revolts, but neither Gabriel Prosser, Denmark Vesey, nor Nat Turner was formally an African Methodist or African Baptist. The former was organized in 1793 and the latter in 1805. So what were the Africans doing before this time since our presence was nearly two hundred years old by the time of the African Baptist?

Another issue that lurks in the background of this discussion is the compromising role of the church among Africans, that is, the church as a dissuader of nationalist ideas. More often than not, the church was an extension of the white denominations in the North. Even in its reach to express a desire to have a public space, the black church during this period was often a space to deal with "the irreligious and uncivilized of the race" (Glaude 2000, 26).

If you seek to engage a master, you must meet him in the arena, not throw stones from outside the walls. Not once did Glaude engage the philosopher Maulana Karenga's ideas in his discussion of ritual in regard to Kwanzaa. Particularly distasteful, however, is Glaude's comment that Maulana Karenga envisioned Kwanzaa "as a vehicle for the proliferation of certain political ideas" (Glaude 2000, 88). Unable to deal with the philosophical underpinnings of Kwanzaa as an expression of Africans celebrating themselves, Glaude is constrained to say that sometimes those who practice Kwanzaa are empowered to act regardless of the creator's intent.

In discussing William Whipper's position on the American Moral Reform Society, Glaude admits that Sam Cornish's view of Whipper was that he was "vague, mild, indefinite, and confused," but in an odd, dislocated way Glaude seems to continue Whipper's awkward position. Glaude seeks to find in Whipper a place to stand, but there is no *stasis*—no primordial mound not even for a college professor—here. The ground is shaky. Whipper had argued against all-black institutions because this reinforced prejudice against blacks. Glaude derides the historian Sterling Stuckey's position on Whipper, seeking to resurrect him in the public's mind (Stuckey 1987). But why should an all-black institution create resentment except in a society already geared against Africans? Does an all-white or all-Japanese organization create such a problem? Glaude is not finished with his rehabilitation of Whipper; he writes, "the fact remains, however, that Whipper never advocated the rejection of all things African in his people's culture. He simply rejected the use of racial language by all Americans" (Glaude 2000, 137). This is the highest form of doublespeak. Glaude's resurrection of Whipper is akin to his attempted resurrection of Judge Clarence Thomas. In a racist society, how can you speak of your culture without racial language if you are black?

In the epilogue, the author tries to use nation-language but wishes to avoid being seen as a nationalist. How does any nation exist? Does a nation exist apart from land? Was not modern Israel a nation before it occupied land? Is Palestine a nation now even without its own capital? What does nation have to do with white people? These are questions that are never answered directly in this book because Glaude seeks to make one more incorrect indictment of nationalism, claiming that it "is predicated on definitions of sameness and otherness grounded in nature" (Glaude, 2000 163). Black nationalist tradition has always found its source in the will of African people to act in their own interests and to oppose those interests—white or black, capitalist or Marxist, integrationist or reactionary—that seek to demean, undermine, destroy, or stifle freedom; in this way it becomes the most revolutionary ideology in a racist society. This is a position not "grounded in nature" but rather one rooted in historical and cultural experiences.

MANTHIA DIAWARA, *IN SEARCH OF AFRICA*

This is another problematic work. It is organized around four situations: Sartre and African Modernism, Richard Wright and Modern Africa, Malcolm X: Conversionists versus Culturalists, and Homeboy Cosmopolitanism. The idea is to loosely follow Sartre's organization in *Situations*. This is the first mistake for an African writer. Rather than seek a pattern from his own traditional discourse methodology, he abandons it for something that he obviously believes is better, is more intellectual, is superior as a technique. Thus, although Diawara is writing about Africa, his book has the feel of a quilt rather than a kente cloth—it is *pieced* rather than woven. One gets this experience even though the editing of the project tries hard to make the seams invisible. It is the quality of Diawara's gift with conversation and his ability to self-reveal, in the Western mode, that holds the attention of the reader. As an African reader, you wonder what is the meaning of this self-display?

Source

The principal myth in Manthia Diawara's work revolves around exile and modernism. Diawara has spent most of his life outside of the community of his birth. In a sense, the story he tells in the book is one not just of uprootedness but of unrootedness, fluidity, fleeting moments, disconnections, and historical discontinuities. Diawara finds in his childhood experiences with an African playmate, Sidime Laye, the only groundedness to his own life. Laye's story is both a compass and ballast for us to locate and center Diawara. When they were young in Guinea, Diawara and Laye were inseparable as friends, enjoying the possibilities of the revolution as envisioned by President Sékou Touré, the legendary African leader who defied De Gaulle and claimed independence for Guinea. Laye was the brightest, most charismatic, and most likely to succeed of Diawara's compatriots. In the end they would both tire of Sékou Touré for different reasons.

Diawara's father, a Malian, was accused of working against the Guinean revolution, and the family was forced to leave Guinea along with many others soon after independence. Sidime Laye's family had stayed, and instead of being "a big person" in the government, as Diawara had predicted when young, Sidime Laye had become an accomplished sculptor. On the other hand, Diawara had become "modern," the cosmopolite; in other words, he was the person he had thought Sidime would become. Sidime, when Diawara found him, was creating ritual masks—in effect, he had become a keeper of tradition.

I have serious arguments with the point of view, that is, place of view, in most of this book despite my appreciation of Diawara's masterful narrative style in his various vignettes. *In Search of Africa* is one more book in a growing line—Kwame Appiah's *In My Father's House*, Keith Richburg's *Out of America*, Henry Louis Gates's *Colored People*—of works that might be seen as *une révélation complexée*, that is, as personally complexed by cultural questions.

What is revealed in this type of work is a postmodern diversion that criticizes all forms of cultural definition except the European notion of individualism. Diawara's adoption of this technique causes him to engage in the denial of Africa in its historical context. Africa is a mode of thought, albeit fleeting, in the Western mind, and Diawara has become identified with that particular moment. Thus, Diawara, an intelligent man, demonstrates the tension in his own insights into Africa. He searches for Africa and, I believe, he finds it, but because he is blinded by the concepts of the West, he cannot recognize the object itself. It remains invisible even as he handles it, discusses it with writers, and comments on it. Yet he does not embrace it because for him to embrace Africa as seen by Williams Sassine and Sidime Laye is to embrace essentialism, and for Diawara there is nothing more antimodernist than essentialism. He says of Salif Keita, he "is modern because he defies the dictates of clan and caste" (96). But, of course, it is not essentialism that is problematic, but *immutabilism*.

Joel Kotkin's book *Tribes* (1994) explained precisely how the British, Jewish, Japanese, Hindu, and Chinese people were prepared for the postmodern world by virtue of their strong sense of ethnic and cultural identity. Why should rebellion against ethnicity or cultural heritage necessarily be a mark of modernity? Rebellion against ethnic triumphalism and ethnic dominance is much more a key to modernity than the simple appreciation of one's ancestors. Opposition to racism, anti-Semitism, and anti-Africanism are far more telling about our belief and acceptance of modernity than our denial of ancestral cultures.

I believe that what lurks underneath Diawara's *In Search of Africa* is the fear of inferiority, or perhaps, the fear of being left behind Europe. The aim, therefore, is to recast African history in the light of European intellectual traditions. This is a lethal form of racism, a new form to be sure, but also the latest manifestation of the old form. The African narrative is valid within its own context and on the basis of our own historical experiences.

One of the reasons the Afrocentrists have claimed that Kemet must be the foundation of any rewriting of African history—any true understanding of the African personality and any spark for creating a new fire of civilization—is to advance a consistent view of an African origin. This allows us to avoid the default position of seeking Europe or remaining indebted to Europe as a junior partner (Asante and Abarry 1996). We can and we must stand on Africa's own legs. This does not mean that the discourse on Kemet is the only discourse of the Afrocentrists. Clearly it is not. We must be engaged in the contemporary world, must examine the social and economic plight of African people today, and must question all forms of oppression. But we must do this on the terms of our own agency.

Refining the Search

In a similar vein, Diawara turns the tables he turned on Senghor and Negritude on Afrocentricity by stating that Senghor's speech at the 1956 Paris conference "is one of the founding texts of Afrocentric philosophy and art criticism" (Diawara 1998, 62). This speech is not only twenty-three years before the birth of the Afrocentric movement with the publication of my book *Afrocentricity*, but Diawara's statement suggests that he is unaware of the Afrocentric critique of Negritude. Senghor would have never conceded to call himself an Afrocentrist, but he called himself a proponent of Negritude. These are two different perspectives. Senghor remained firmly a Eurocentrist in most of his practical and intellectual life. Diawara's mistake is common for those who are dislocated; they assume that when we say Afrocentric, we mean anything about Africa. Thus, Senghor, giving one of the first speeches on African art by an African, is called an Afrocentrist.

Diawara's Dilemma

I see the "separation anxiety" Diawara speaks of manifesting itself in his approach to African culture; while he claims that Africans wanting to identify as Westerners are exhibiting separation anxiety, his approach to his own origins and evolution suggest his inability to cope with his own place. One can gain a country, but culture is far more lasting and no one can divest one's self of culture—either you accept your own or you claim another.

It is unfortunate that Diawara has continued to use the Afrocentrists as a whipping boy, without referent or reference, in trying to defend a certain cultural position. One must ask why he would write that "Afrocentrists define their Negritude by resorting to the binary Euro-modernisms, which freeze black and white, good and evil, sedentary and nomadic, sun people and ice people into an eternal antagonism" (Diawara 1998, 10), without any authority for such statement except to pander to reactionary postures on African agency. Furthermore, Afrocentricity is not Negritude, and there is no such thing as "the Afrocentrist's Negritude."

Clearly Afrocentricity argues that African people, concepts, and ideas must be viewed from a subject rather than an object position (Asante 1998). The aim is agency, not division. But Diawara is unfamiliar with the hundreds of articles and books on the subject of Afrocentricity and therefore does not write confidently about Afrocentric theory or philosophy.

There are a number of words that hint at Diawara's path to Africa—for example, "ethnophilosophy" and "tribes." It is not from a sense of antagonism that the Afrocentrists say that to use "ethnophilosophy " for Africa and "philosophy" for Europe is to impose Europe over Africa—or to use "tribes" when speaking of Mandinka, Yoruba, and Akan while using "ethnic groups" when speaking of Serbians, Croatians, and Albanians is to buy into a European construction that parades as essential. Such constructions are responsible for maintaining the structures of white racism, hierarchy, and dominance in thought and practice.

Diawara admits what his friend Laye would never admit that he suffers from "identity fatigue" (Diawara 1998, 13) This condition exists because he has a unique situation in the Sartrean sense. He has followed a nomadic path not really able to connect with Africa since his childhood. He is like Richard Wright missing from Mississippi, exiled on the Left Bank. And so Diawara was vulnerable when he traveled to Africa though he tried everything not to show his vulnerability in Africa. He spoke Mandinka so that the taxi driver would not take advantage of him (17). He spoke the Susu language so that others would not take him for a stranger, and yet he felt like a stranger. The disconnect was not produced by Africans; it was induced by deliberate divestiture. What if he had embraced Africa?

AFRICA AND MODERNITY

In the 1990s Africa was already in the modern world as defined by Westerners. In fact, Africa may have been the first explicit area of modernity's expression in the individualism of white missionaries—the quite outrageous indiscipline and unattached actions of the merchant-hunters and the white renegade criminals of the African interior, acting as if they were God's agents on the earth. They were without kin, community, constraints, and often without principles. They were thoroughly modern. When Karl Peters of the German occupation of East Africa took his revolver and shot dead the members of the royal courts of villages to demonstrate the power of European technology, he was most definitely acting out of the modern mold. No moral restrictions or spiritual taboos or communal restraints could have stopped his senseless assault on the people of the German East African Colony.

Thus, I am puzzled by Diawara's idea of modernity, the idea that Africa had to "catch up with the modern world" (11). In one area it was pre-eminently a modern venue—that is, in terms of white behavior in Africa—but in the moral area, Africa had nothing to learn from Europe. The eminent Akan scholar Kofi Asare Opoku has reminded me that Akan traditions like those of most African people are based on observation, long years of natural observation. He says that Africans had to have been the first to try individualism at the very dawn of human existence, and they quickly abandoned it. Maternal and paternal affections did not just happen but evolved over the years. Africa's philosophers have emphasized communalism, collectivity, and cooperation not because they are unfamiliar with individualism but because in thousands of years they have seen the value of the collective idea. Indeed, the collective idea is, in Africa's eyes, the more progressive one. Two proverbs make this point:

Hama, hama kyere ketebo—one string joined to another can bind the leopard.

Atwe abien boro evi—two small antelopes beat a big one.

Diawara's modernity or rather his desire for Africa to seek modernity is actually a search, not for modernity, but for Westernization. He writes, "The independence movements brought it (Africa) back into history, and devised various structural strategies for catching up with the industrialized countries" (57). Africa was never out of history, and the self-consciousness of African people was never at stake for them; Diawara is describing a Western problem. It is like Mungo Park being cited for "discovering" the Niger River.

Is this modernity as expressed by the West what Diawara seeks for Africa? Is it technological warfare, personal alienation, sexism, apartheid, racist murders, street gangs, and individuals fending for themselves against the aggressive powers of state institutions and petty criminals? The state in this modern world breaks down community to create individual problems. Group identity is degraded and community is called backward. Democracy is labeled the modern electoral system of government and all other systems are condemned.

While democracy is more convenient, efficient, and precise than consensus, it is not a better system of representation. It might even be worse where the majority dominates the minority.

AFROCENTRICITY AND AFRO-PESSIMISM

In many ways Williams Sassine says the truest and most provocative things in the book, and it is to Diawara's credit as a writer that he is so fair to an author who is at odds with his own position. Sassine is quoted as saying, "Afro-Pessimism is a style which resists the tendency to use pessimism and blackness as a way of putting down black people. It's like the Afro-hairdos or Afrocentricity, you know."

What one detects in the questioning of this philosophy by Diawara is *une révélation complexée*. He asks Sassine: "Don't you think your kind of literature is a false resistance to modernization?" To which Sassine responded, "Clichés!" In the end Diawara comments, "The Afrocentrists proceed by investing in the past as the only site for identity formation and for the continent's renaissance into a scientific, political and economic empire" (55).

There are many problems with Diawara's perception of Africa, Afrocentricity, and identity formation. The central issue of the Afrocentrists, like the Afro-Pessimists of Sassine's type, has never been "identity formation" for the sake of some mythical empire; it has rather been about an investment in African agency. African is a self-selected category like European or Asian or Arab. It does not have to be created or fabricated—it exists. Those who are African in this sense seek their agency based appropriately on the best wisdom from the past. Furthermore, all renaissances are based on the past as inspirations, motivations, and stimulants for contemporary creativity. To the degree that Africa lacks a functional past it will never be anything but a dark imitation of the French, the English, and the German cultures.

This brings me to another issue that is not only found in Diawara's type of "put down" but has been seen in the writings of the English African scholar Kwame Appiah's works. Diawara seeks to warn us of the Afrocentrist's motivation to posit a "black anterior superiority" as a way to deflate the fear of inferiority (55). There is no truth in this position as far as I have read Afrocentric works. It is historical and scientific fact that modern humans originated in Africa. No superiority is either suggested or possible by the statement of this fact.

NEW DEFINITIONS

What goes for modernity as Diawara sees it? Individualism, universal education, and women's emancipation (96). Africa is firmly in the grip of an approach to society that claims essentially that to be human one must be human in the midst of community. As the !Kung say, "You cannot dance alone." To say this does not mean that there is nothing personal in terms of history, latitudes, and possessions. Individualism and personalism are two separate ideas—one is the human, detached and fluid; the other, the human, attached and centered.

Diawara assumes that schooling will bring modernity. Schooling is not education, and in Africa where there has been nontraditional schooling—institutions brought by the Christians or the Muslims—we have seen imitation and duplication, not innovation and tradition. The Akan people who created kente cloth never attended the Rhode Island School of Art or the London School of Design. Yet their creations rival those of the most trained students of the West.

Women's emancipation, as Samora Machel said, can never be an act of charity; it is a fundamental necessity of any mature society. But to assume or to assert that Africa is behind other cultures in regard to this issue is false. Women in some European countries just received the right to vote, for example, within the past thirty years. Few African nations have been born where women lacked the vote, and even in the past the rights of African women were protected by tradition more than in Western societies. What is the source of this cry for women's liberation in Africa? It is mainly the issue of polygamy and sexual inequalities. These are not small matters; nevertheless, it is only recently that European women have shared equal rights with men while in Africa women roles in society have protected them from the common abuses of individualism. The numerous communal taboos and rules against bad treatment of women are often forgotten in any analysis of women issues in Africa, a continent that remains the one with the most women rulers in history.

RICHARD WRIGHT AND AFRICA

Diawara's reading of Richard Wright's appearance at the 1996 conference at Paris, like his interactions with Sidime Laye and Williams Sassine, is cast in the same light as his own reading of his exile. Wright clearly did not understand nor appreciate the complexities of African history and could not have addressed the issues raised by Nkrumah with a simple American vision of modernity. The idea of Africa was too involved in the history of colonizations and abuse to be adequately assessed by an African American who still saw himself as an American Negro. Those who regard themselves as Africans are Africans. Nkrumah said, "We regard West Indians as our brothers." Identity is only complicated in an oppressive, racist, heterogeneous industrialized nation. That is why I cannot believe and Diawara does not give proof that "Wright was even more disappointed with Nkrumah . . . than with colonial force for surrendering the weapon of individual freedom to religious and political power" (71). If Wright was so disappointed, it was because he, like so many of us on this side of the ocean, did not understand the intricate and revolutionary ideas inherent in the African traditions themselves.

The assault by African American and Continental African writers on Africa is relentless, persistent—and as long as Continental Africans refuse to examine the content of their cultures rather than fall into a blind Westernization, Africa will not be able to find itself, let alone be visible for others. The mistake in this book is that Diawara searches for Africa with the same lenses as the Europeans. The Africa he finds will not be the one the masses of Africans understand. This is the situation of a decentered people; and Wright's predicament is no better than what he found in Africa. Diawara is, as John Henrik Clarke once lamented of an African scholar, "betrayed by his education."

Laced with contradictions, the book is a tour de force of unnecessary compromise. What is the meaning of a passage that has Richard Wright wishing that "Africa could be the new place of hope, given that Europe and America had betrayed the traditional hopes of Westerners" when Diawara has just spent considerable space speaking of how Wright wanted Africa to adopt European ideals? What is definite is that Africa could never be the place of hope running after sectarian wars, racism, destruction, sexism, and the pollution of the earth's atmosphere and waters. Africa must not reject modernization, but it must find its path out of its own tradition even if that means a cultural reassessment of the principles of the ancient cultures. In fact, the modern history of Africa has been a mad rush to emulate Europe in wars, ethnic cleansing, and official injustices. Africa has not been itself.

I wish Diawara had explored how both Wright and James Baldwin in so many ways were beguiled by the French notion of culture and saw their differences with Continental Africans through their own experiences of Western oppression. Had he done this, it would have been exceedingly clear that there was no "resurgence of Africanism" among African Americans (73). There has never been a period devoid of the African energy. During the time of the giants Wright and Baldwin, the African energy was as strong as it had ever been in America's African community. This is to be expected; these were African people.

Why would Diawara titillate his Western readers by repeating Wright's unfortunate comment on "fifty women, young and old, nude to the waist, their elongated breasts flopping loosely and grotesquely in the sun" (74)? Wright is obviously unable to process what he saw except through his Western lenses. Modernity had destroyed his ability to grasp the dancing forms of the human body—to appreciate true freedom. Yet he may have approved of pale bodies in all sizes and ages, flopping about in the nude on the banks of a Wisconsin river or some other nudist camp at the beach!

INNOVATION AND TRADITION

Innovation must always derive from tradition to lead to stability. If you do not rely upon your own traditions, you will find others with which to establish your innovations. Yet there is nothing easier or more consistent than the elasticity within one's own culture. Diawara is critical of Africans who "renounce modernity to engage in still-celebrated medieval performances" while not being able to see how Western forms, not celebrated, such as medieval caps and gowns in university commencement exercises, reflect the Westerners continuation of tradition. We do not say that these Westerners renounce modernity because they do not. Neither does the African who is attached to traditions renounce modernity.

Diawara spends considerable time with the traditional Mande story of Sundiata. He rightly discusses Djibril Tamsir Niane's philosophical and literary contributions to Africa and the world. In his analysis of *Sundiata*, as written by Niane, he criticizes the worship of the hero, although this valorization in Africa never reaches the point of Europe's valorization of Alexander, Napoleon, and Joan of Arc. Indeed, the religions of Jesus and Muhammad are the ultimate expressions of hero worship. Out of Niane's *Sundiata*, new plays, movies, values, and ideas have emerged to suggest that it will always be a loved tradition bringing forth innovation.

Because he does not accept the value of tradition, Diawara cannot truly appreciate African American culture. It would have been useful, for example, for Diawara to read Amiri Baraka's classic text *Blues People* as an illustration of what a writer could do with culture (Baraka 1963). In one sense Baraka's appreciation of African American culture was in direct contrast to the more recent interpretation of African culture by Diawara. What is one to make of the road we have traveled in African letters since the beginning of the Black Arts movement in the 1960s?

African American culture in the twentieth century is a degradation in Diawara's conceptualization. He sees the elements of deviance as the central tenets of African American culture because he does not see its resiliency. For example, "Detroit Red sinks to the bottom, and the narrator with him as if black culture has died with them," (123). From this passage he goes into a discussion of Billie Holiday's drug addiction. African American culture is not pathological. In fact, the true repositories of modernity have been black institutions.

This is why I cannot understand Diawara's misunderstanding of Malcolm X, as when he recalls that Malcolm X "identifies with law-breakers" (130). The implication is that the petty criminals are cultural interpreters. No one would permit someone to say that the French petty criminals are cultural ambassadors. Manthia Diawara can only allow this of Africa because he does not appreciate the traditional cultures of African Americans, derived from creative resistance. The spirituals, blues, jazz, and gospel traditions predate hip-hop. The linkage is real, and you cannot fully understand the war music of the young generation without understanding the resistance in the spirituals. Tradition generates innovation. Take Diawara's statement in the Homeboy Cosmopolitan that "the same transformative energy at play in Sidime Laye's work is found in hip-hop, a transnational cultural form that started with young African Americans (237). But is the "Duga" a transnational form or a Mande form that is now played by other people? In reality, hip-hop is an African American cultural form that has become transnational (Walker 1997).

My critical locating of Diawara as a leading exponent of *une révélation complexée* is based on his approach to Africa. In a cogent and telling passage he writes that the cementing of a relationship between modern technology and European man guarantees that "any participation in the technological revolution must necessarily import European culture" (148). This is a strong statement but one that is inaccurate. The problem with his insight at this level is that he has distorted the idea of technology to mean only Western technology. Culture is not just things, objects, and materials; culture can exist if nothing material is produced. Technology, also, is not European. I sense that this is a search undertaken by Diawara while looking over his shoulder.

To say *In Search of Africa* is complicated is a way of saying it has a confusing rhetorical structure. More important, there is no guiding philosophy and in that regard the writing is considerably postmodern.

The writer engages Africa in a provocative, almost combative, manner. Immediately it becomes clear that he does not distinguish Africanity, customs and traditions, from Afrocentricity, self-consciousness, and this leads to a major problem. Diawara demonstrates a truism that being born in Africa gives no special advantage from which to discuss the continent and convinces me that as far as Africa is concerned, it is possible to see and not see at the same time. The aim of Africa should not be to catch up to Europe but to be Africa.

Now we return to the initial problem of this essay: how does the theorist interested in language and communication determine the nature of dislocation in a text? What is demonstrated by both the Glaude and the Diawara texts is something all too normal in a racially hierarchical society: the search for a way to reduce marginalization by compromising Africanness. This cannot be the answer to the problem of dislocation because the only way to return from the margins of history, literature, culture, economics, or any other sector or sphere of life is to reassert a centered place within one's own experiences. So any determination of dislocation must begin with the place where the writer stands culturally at the moment of writing. When this is done, it is easy, by virtue of sentinel statements, to see both the extent and the depth of the problem that must be confronted to reestablish a centered place.

NOTES

1. Karenga placed the definitive founding of the field of black studies in the decades of the 1960s through 1990s. He advanced the notion that the professional organizations of the discipline, the Afrocentric initiative, the black women's studies movement, the multicultural studies movement, and the classical African studies movement were critical to the development of the tradition of intellectual activism. See Maulana Karenga (1990, 40–64).

2. I included this in a presentation to the Children of Jewish Holocaust Survivors Association in Philadelphia in April 2004.

chapter 15
REPARATIONS, REASONS, AND RHETORIC

Advancing reparations is fundamentally a rhetorical issue within the context of a reluctant public. In effect, my aim throughout this book has been to demonstrate how communication functions to create alternative visions of race and identity, thereby constructing a new social architecton. There is nothing either in America's history or in its documents that argues against reparations for victims who have been wronged. In fact, America, of all countries, is the most adamant in its support of reparations. I do not know whether this is because the crimes committed against native peoples have been more obscene than those in any other country or because there is something in the national ethos that suggests an aspiration toward fairness. Whatever the reason for the behavior, the American nation has paid reparations as compensation for wrongs on many occasions. This is as it should be in a nation that prides itself on fairplay. France is one of the few European nations to declare the enslavement of Africans "a crime against humanity," but it has not paid reparations. What is necessary, it seems to me, in the United States, is for the American nation, through the very American practice of compensating victims, to pay for the crimes of the fathers.

Richard America (1993) understood very early in the debate on reparations, as seen in his book *Paying the Social Debt: What White*

America Owes Black America, that reparation for Europe's enslavement of Africans in the United States was a credible idea. Randall Robinson's persuasive work, a decade later, *The Debt: What America Owes to Blacks* (2000) and Raymond Winbush's *Should America Pay?* (2002) have become the standards for discourse on the subject. These are not the legal briefs, nor yet the grand philosophical arguments that will be made by lawyers and others, but they do represent the voices of the masses. This is the voice that has always interested me because I am convinced that until the masses of Africans sense the urgency of the call for reparations, we will not gain the moral strength necessary for the final push.

Reparations as a form of payment for crimes committed against the Iraqi prisoners at Abu Ghraib prison in Iraq were called for by the American secretary of defense, Donald Rumsfeld, in 2004. There had been reports of sexual brutality, gross physical assaults, and humiliation in the prison, and when photographs of Iraqis in various positions of nudity with American guards in a celebratory mode were broadcast around the world, there was immediate outrage. One of the first suggestions made by Donald Rumsfeld before a congressional hearing in May 2004 was that reparations be paid to the victims and their families.

What African Americans have been saying for years is that the culture of the nation—indeed, in our case, the laws of the nation—for a very long time assaulted the entire African community with a vicious antihuman and antimoral position. It is not simply a problem of abnormality, but a more profound problem of cultural ethics. While racist arguments have become increasingly sophisticated, as in the case of the work by Vincent Sarich and Frank Miele, *Race: The Reality of Human Differences* (2004)—the intent is the same as the more overt racism that led to the enslavement of Africans and the extermination of the Native Americans and the holocaust of the Jews. If one accepts the idea that Nordics are superior to Alpines, or that Aryans are superior to Mediterraneans, or that whites are superior to blacks, then it follows in this line of thinking that one group is more entitled than another group to life, liberty, and the pursuit of happiness. Indeed, it may even be possible to speak of the elimination of the less endowed groups. This is the basis of the immorality of the idea of racial superiority.

James Allen's *Without Sanctuary* (2000) started a new discussion in the nation about what kind of people are Americans. The genocide of the natives, the dispossession of the Mexicans, the enslavement of Africans, and the racial hostility against Jews, Chinese, and Japanese have been enough to cause us to wonder what America would have been like had schoolchildren been properly educated to the brutal past of the nation.

Leon Litwack's descriptions in the foreword of Allen's book brought me to tears, perhaps because being from Georgia I remembered in my soul the events of that state's sorry history of white racial animosity. Litwack writes in the foreword about the lynching of blacks as one would write about any passion: "Thousands of black men and women met the same fate. Varying only in degrees of torture and brutality, these execution rituals were acted out in every part of the South. Sometimes in small groups, sometimes in massive numbers, whites combined the roles of judge, jury, and executioner. Newspaper reporters dutifully reported the events under such lurid headlines as 'Colored Man Roasted Alive,' describing in graphic detail the slow and methodical agony and death of the victim and devising a vocabulary that would befit the occasion" (Allen 2000). Don't we need a major psychological evaluation of a nation that finds its happiness in the masochistic and sadistic assault on people's sexuality and humanity?

What then are we to make of Sarich and Miele's insistence on highlighting what they falsely see as racial differences? The impetus for distinction, particularly negative distinction of Africans, is not dead in the United States. We are still confronted by a school of thought that would promote the notion of racial superiority despite all of the work that has been done in science and scholarship. Perhaps, Kwame Ture's often-repeated advice when he was a student leader in the 1960s is important here. In the fire of his eloquent rhetoric, as Ture, who was then called Stokely Carmichael, was describing a concept or giving an analysis of an idea, he would say, "All definitions tend to be autobiographical." To some degree, when we read those who are writing to defend racial differences, we know that they are simply attempting to support an autobiographical position.

My view is simply that racism and all forms of oppression, homophobia, and religious bias are progressively eclipsed to the degree that we institute in our personal and national life the idea of mutuality. But herein is the problem because those who hold power seldom give it up voluntarily. To hold power is to hold power over something or someone, and in the case of race relations, it is a fact in American society that whites hold both power and privilege over black people. Therefore, arriving at mutuality demands two forces: *internal* and *external.* Since racism is an oppressive system and its intent is to remain oppressive, the natural reaction to it on the part of its victims is to resist, agitate, confront, combat, and go to war. This is an external force. On the other hand, the internal force—that is, the self-seeking moral idea—is generated from within. Both forces meet resistance from the obdurate forces against change, indeed, against any form of mutuality. Those forces believe that to give up anything is to be seen as less, to be seen as giving up the rightful place of those who are entitled by race to maintain their oppressive control. We are here in the realm of the human inane.

Helen Stummer, the prize-winning photographer, has perfected a photographic argument against racism over the years. She has been determined to demonstrate that the cleavage between African Americans and whites is a result of ignorance. And although Andrew Hacker captured the pain of the relationship between blacks and whites in this country in *Two Nations* (1992), by showing how whites gain and maintain privilege, it has been Stummer's campaign to publicize how that privilege leads to the degradation of black life. Stummer documents the conditions of black life at the hands of land owners, police, and government agencies and then confronts the perpetrators with their crimes against the humanity of African people. Not only has this tactic been successful in changing some of the conditions, but it has also empowered African Americans who live in some of the poorest inner-city areas of the Northeast to take up their own fight. What I have not seen on a large scale in American society are whites who, like Helen Stummer, are willing to dedicate themselves to correcting the wrongs of white racial domination. White people in America join all types of organizations and have relationships with many institutions that articulate ideas against pollution, animal cruelty, environmental issues, and so forth, but when it comes to racial oppression, there are fewer organizations.

A CARDINAL VIRTUE

Western liberal democracies have long contended that equality under the law was one of the cardinal virtues of modern society. The egalitarian idea is probably derived, in part, from the concept of mutuality and is underscored by the commonly accepted notion that you should treat others as you wish them to treat you. Until reparations are granted to African people, the concept of mutuality will be nothing more than an empty political idea. To have meaning and to become real, mutuality must be based on the principle of human equality. Numerous authors have discussed the difficulty whites in America have had with the idea of black equality (Dawson 2001; Feagin 2000; Hacker 1992).

Definitions of human equality, mutuality, and reparations provide historical accounts of the image of Africans and demonstrate that the earliest African arguments against racism, enslavement, discrimination, and segregation were based on the idea of equality. Of course, the great difficulty in securing reparations for Africans may be attributed to the general contrary attitude among the majority of whites in American society. This contrary attitude is derived from the doctrine of white superiority, which denies black equality. Ultimately, nothing can be achieved in human relationships without mutuality based on the idea of human equality. Thus, the call for reparations is simultaneously a call for the relinquishing of the doctrine of white superiority.

I am affirming the position first taken by Maulana Karenga, who argued that it was difficult for us to raise "a definitive African way" of addressing our own issues because of the "holocaust of enslavement, the savagery of imperialism, colonialism, and racism" (Karenga 2003, 158). But the call for our own involvement in self-definition must not excuse whites of their own role to play in the dismantling of the false edifice of racial superiority.

Human equality refers to a correspondence in quality, quantity, value, or ability between various ethnic and cultural groups. Indeed, the synonyms of fairness, justice, and impartiality have often been used to suggest the concept of equality. The doctrine of human equality, often referred to as egalitarianism, pertains to a correspondence in quality and value of all people. *Mutuality* is the quality of reciprocity, that is, the condition where all parties in a relationship benefit. *Reparations* are payments to victims and their descendants for past crimes against humanity. These concepts interact on the larger discourse stage to establish a general environment for discussing the issue of reparations and human equality. My aim, therefore, is to use these concepts to advance the discourse in a way that will underscore mutual benefits for the society. Of course, we confront the most massive problem of all when we engage the issue of how numerous whites have viewed Africans in American society.

CAPTURE AND ENTRAPMENT

Africans did not appear in massive numbers in the Americas because of some need to escape religious persecutions, political harassment, or social ostracism. Our arrival in the Americas in mass was due to capture and entrapment on the coast of Africa. The ideological warrants that caused Europeans to enter the African continent with the objective of securing free labor had already become factors in the way Europeans structured their thoughts about Africans by the sixteenth century. I shall not repeat them here because they are well established in the literature on reparations.

The initial entry into the African continent by Europeans was through trade and religious missions. Soon, however, the expansionist and triumphalist attitude of Europe sent thousands of ships, over a period of three hundred years, to stalk the shores of Africa for human beings. Sailors from the streets of Liverpool, Nantes, Amsterdam, London, and Lisbon became slave raiders intent on securing for themselves material gain. They became the capitalists of the Americas with their involvement in the horrible raids into Africa. In this sense, they aggrandized themselves while undermining the wealth accumulation and labor formation of Africa, further adding to the debt owed in any reparations. Not only was our labor stolen, but our potential to amass wealth was seriously interdicted by the capture and entrapment of our people. Moreover, Africa lost possession of its ability to use all of its resources to generate development and happiness for its people.

Europe cannot place at the door of Africans, as several historians have attempted, the burden of the enslavement of West Africans. This burden belongs solely to Europe. While it is true that there were some Africans who worked with the Europeans, the overwhelming fact is that Europeans were engaged in raiding, conquering, and pillaging the villages of the coast and interior for Africans who could be driven in coffles to the slave factories on the coast. Thus, some Africans kings, for reasons of religion or military advantage, participated with the Europeans in the capture of other Africans. The use of Africans as guides and interpreters was common and constant in the sordid business of the slave trade.[1]

THE IMAGE OF THE AFRICAN IN THE WHITE MIND

During the fourteenth century Africa was not simply equal in development to Europe, but according to some experts, superior in technical development to Europe in its civilization. The civilizations of Ghana, Mali, and Songhay had no peer in Europe during the time they flourished in West Africa. Known for their emphasis on justice, peace, and fair play, the African civilizations established themselves as citadels of enlightenment. When the Dutch visited the West Coast of Africa, they found the city of Benin greater than the city of Amsterdam.

It would take the voyages of Christopher Columbus to the Americas to introduce a new frontier for European expansion and a radical new interpretation of the African world. Expansion in the Americas brought with it the demand for labor, and Europe quickly turned this necessity into a need for slave labor. Although Irish, English, and Native Americans were used for indentured work, Africans became in the English colony of America the first people to be placed in perpetual servitude.

Along with the new policy of perpetual servitude, whites created new theories about African people and civilizations. Perhaps because of the cognitive dissonance created by enslaving Africans and claiming Christianity, whites had to reconstruct their own images of Africans as well as state their objectives in religious tones. For example, Africans were seen variously as subhuman, heathen, primitive, non-Christian, and anti-Christ. These views of Africans constituted justifications for enslavement. If Africans were subhumans, then no harm was done by holding them in bondage in perpetuity. If Africans were heathen, then enslavement gave them the best possibility of becoming Christian. If they were primitive, then they needed the civilizing influence of white Christianity. If they were anti-Christ, they could be punished, abused, and mistreated with no sense of guilt. These lines of argument were significant for the white Christians whom David Walker called in 1829 "the most brutal" people on the face of the earth in his pamphlet *An Appeal to the Colored Citizens of the World*, published in Boston.

EARLY AFRICAN ARGUMENTS BASED ON EQUALITY

Prior to 1800 Africans in both the North and the South argued for the equal treatment of all human beings. Indeed, the 1793 epidemic of yellow fever that hit Philadelphia nearly destroyed the city. Only the courage of Africans in the face of the calamity helped to save the city from utter disaster. Nevertheless, Absalom Jones and Richard Allen had to respond to the scurrilous lies and gossips of the white community about the role of the Africans in the epidemic. Since a solicitation had gone forth from the city leaders for the Africans to come forward and assist the distressed, perishing, and sick, on account of the belief that blacks could not get yellow fever, the black community responded with great generosity. Of course, we know now that the assertion that Africans could not contract yellow fever was wrong and demonstrated the racist attitude of whites toward blacks in the eighteenth century. Yet hundreds of Africans participated in the saving of the whites by washing, burning, and burying the dead, and assisting men, women, and children who lay dying in their houses.

When the crisis had abated, a white writer claimed that the Africans had really extorted the white sick by charging them large sums of money to look after them. To this report, Jones and Allen responded with a poignant pamphlet in which they claimed that they rendered essential services to the white population in the face of the greatest dangers and did not seek to aggrandize themselves on the account of the whites' illness and fear of yellow fever. In fact, many blacks succumbed to the disease after helping whites by burying the dead, burying the beds, and caring for the desperately ill. Jones and Allen pointedly argued that Africans were not any worse than whites. They said, "[T]hat there were some few black people guilty of plundering the distressed, we acknowledge, but in that they only are pointed out, and made mention of, we esteem partial and injurious, we know as many whites who were guilty of it, but this is looked over, while the blacks are held up to censure—Is it a greater crime for a black to pilfer, than for a white to privateer?" (Jones and Allen 1794, 7).

The issue confronting the two most important black men in Philadelphia in the 1790s, one that would further propel them to establish separate black institutions, had to do with equality. The problem existed in the minds of whites who had articulated a false and racist view that blacks could not get yellow fever—a view that caused many blacks to rush to assist whites in the face of their own threat of death. When the crisis had subsided, the whites then argued that blacks had taken advantage of whites who were ill. They neglected to mention that whites had also taken advantage of whites. This set up the argument of Jones and Allen regarding the unequal treatment of blacks and whites. Thus, for more than two hundred years this same argument has been made by blacks: whites tend to treat blacks negatively different.

Whatever action taken by Africans to free themselves from captivity, segregation, and discrimination, it has always been due to the belief in human equality. Indeed, the National Coalition of Blacks for Reparations (N'COBRA) advanced the idea of equal justice and became a national force when under the leadership of Ron Daniels and Asiba Tupahache, presidential and vice presidential candidates in 1992, reparations was one of the key political planks.

Africans have not sought to articulate or practice some notion of black superiority over whites and others, but rather to advance the idea of equality. Take the slave revolts of Denmark Vesey and Nat Turner and the example is clear. Vesey in 1822 developed a plan to liberate his fellows from bondage. Perhaps in the history of American slavery there was never a more serious and involved scheme for freedom. Vesey was betrayed by some of his own comrades who quaked at the idea that blacks were equal to whites and could free themselves from bondage. Henry Highland Garnet was correct to observe, however, that his name would be honored alongside that of Toussaint L'Ouverture, the hero of Haiti (Garnet 1843, 69). Nat Turner's revolt succeeded in freeing several hundred Africans for a brief time. His revolt in August of 1831 was a violent uprising against the brutality of the slave masters. His name is recorded in the book of nobility because, as a patriot, he loved justice and equality so much he was willing to sacrifice his own life for the eventual liberation of his fellows. His revolutionary ambition was for an end to the constant exploitation of black labor and the utter destitution of the black masses.

The exploits of Sengbe aboard the *Amistad* (1839) and Madison Washington on the brig *Creole* (1841) must live in history as attacks on the structure of inequality. Both Sengbe and Madison believed in the equality of the African and launched their takeovers on the belief that slavery was unjust to them as human beings.

Into the nineteenth and twentieth centuries Africans have argued the same issues regarding equality and justice. If there have been champions for human rights and civil liberties in the United States, then Africans have been at the forefront of those battles. Thus, the warrant for reparations finds its source in the rhetoric and argument for human equality.

DISCRIMINATION AS AN ANTIEQUALITY ACTION

The US government has a record of reparations. It apologized to indigenous Hawaiians for the overthrow of a sovereign nation and the decimation of the Hawaiian people and their culture. Even the Methodist Church apologized to Native Americans in Wyoming for the 1865 massacre of Native Americans at the hands of a Methodist preacher. The US government paid reparations to Japanese kidnapped in Latin American nations and placed in concentration camps during World War II; and the Southern Baptists apologized for their support of the enslavement of Africans.

Whatever else is a part of the answer to the question about antiequality—that is, the belief that blacks do not deserve the same treatment as whites or as any other group—the mark of the enslavement constitutes the one single and all-powerful symbol of inequality in the United States. Thus, even where there are racist actions, discrimination, and prejudices against Asians or Latinos, those behaviors on the part of whites rarely take the venomous attitudes and viciousness heaped upon Africans. There is something deeper at work in the discrimination against blacks. Thus, the history of the relationship between blacks and whites has been laced with the discourse of inequality.

Discrimination has been the cornerstone of the white reaction to Africans since the initial entry of blacks into the English colonies. This reaction, that is, discrimination toward blacks, was based on the belief that blacks were not equal to whites. Thus, almost at the beginning of the Africans presence in North America, we find discriminatory actions. Consistent with white opinion from the pulpit to the halls of Congress, the popular sentiment in the United States was that Africans were not equal to whites in any form or fashion. Blacks were inferior to whites in the rhetoric of the leading white thinkers in America. Indeed, differential treatment based on individual characteristics is different from those based on ethnic and cultural categorization. Thus, racial discrimination is often made on the basis of natural categories with no relation to individual capacities or capabilities and includes the following:

- unequal recognition before the law
- inequality of personal security
- inequality in freedom of movement and residence

- inequality in protection of freedom of thought, conscience, and religion
- inequality in the right of peaceful association
- inequality in treatment of those born out of wedlock
- inequality in the regulation of and treatment of ownership
- inequality in the protection of authorship
- inequality of opportunity for education or the development of ability
- inequality of opportunity for sharing the benefits of culture
- inequality in services rendered in health, facilities, and housing
- inequality in the right to nationality
- inequality in the right to participate in government
- inequality in access to public office

TOWARD AN AFROCENTRIC IDEA IN HUMAN EQUALITY

Africans did not see themselves as inferior to Europeans when they met as merchants and traders on the West Coast of Africa. Nothing in the history of Africa had ever conveyed to Africans the idea of inferiority that would result in unequal treatment. Historically, Africa is the original home of humans, the seat of civilization, and the repository of an enormous store of human wisdom. Actually the concept of *Maat*, central to the ancient Egyptian notion of human interaction, political harmony, and the creation of community (Karenga 1994), is the antithesis of any notion of human superiority. Consequently, it would be uncommon for Africans to accept the idea of inferiority to whites. This idea was Europe's idea, created out of the Christian notion of non-Christians as heathens and therefore inferior to the white Christians. Thus, in the sixteenth century not only were Africans cast as the inferior other, so were Jews.

Self-delusion created in the European the need to project on Africans the idea of blackness as inferior. While it is true that many Africans accepted this projection as a part of their own reality, becoming, as it were, inferior to whites in their own minds, most

Africans never succumbed to this arrogant idea. Yet the prosecution of it as a doctrine of white racial supremacy, articulated at the highest levels of European institutions, became the principal task of the supporters of the enslavement and the practices of segregation.

REPAIRING THE BROKEN RELATIONSHIP

One of the keys to reparations is the repairing of broken relationships, but this can only occur with the participation of both parties. Since the relationship between human beings was damaged with the doctrine of the inequality of the races, it is only logical that those who prosecuted that doctrine, lived by its edicts, supported its tenets, and practiced its philosophy must seek to repair the broken relationship caused by their injustice. In 1989 Congressman John Conyers of Michigan took the leadership in introducing HR 40 to the House in an effort to galvanize public opinion in support of the Commission to Study Reparations Proposals for African Americans. He sought to bring attention to the inhumanity of slavery, establish a commission to study slavery and its impact on freed people, analyze the impact of slavery on contemporary African Americans, and recommend to Congress appropriate remedies (Brooks 1999, 367). Such a reasonable legislative packet has found stiff resistance in the US Congress.

We are confronted by a paradox in the contemporary reparations debate. Postmodern authors have pretty much established the fact that race is a trivial term and that it has almost no physical or biological legitimacy. It is also true that one cannot ascribe to the term race any common intellectual or moral characteristics that would have much meaning in today's understanding of science and morality. Yet at the same time we recognize that there are some biomedical values to the DNA clusters found in continental geographic groupings of humans. Certain diseases, responses to medicines, and biomedical markers seem to relate to these DNA groupings based on continental and geographic areas. This is not to argue for some psychological value to these groupings but rather to admit that differences do exist. Of course, one cannot make any good case for differential or inequitable actions toward individuals on the basis of skin pigmentation or hair texture. Nevertheless, as we have shown already, racism remains a prime structural trait of American society and impinges on everything that has to do with reparations.

At the core of the discussion on reparations is the fact that whites enslaved black people. This is the fact of history. They did not enslave Asians in the United States; they enslaved Africans. They did not enslave Europeans, but Africans. One only has to follow the discussions of the Group of Eminent Persons (GEP)—a cadre of influential people of African descent set up by the International Conference on Reparations held in Lagos, Nigeria, in 1990—to understand the fundamental issue for African people. Reparations, inter alia, is simply the final step in decolonization and antiracism.

Dudley Thompson, Ali Mazrui, and Olusegun Obasanjo were among the key figures in the Second Conference for Reparations held in 1993 in Nigeria where the Abuja Proclamation was issued. It stated, "Emphatically convinced that what matters is not the guilt but the responsibility of those states whose economic evolution once depended on slave labor and colonialism and whose forebears participated either in selling and buying Africans, or in owning them, or in colonizing them; convinced that the pursuit of reparations by the African people on the continent and in the Diaspora will be a learning experience in self-discovery and in uniting political and psychological experiences; [this proclamation] calls upon the international community to recognize that there is a unique and unprecedented moral debt of compensation to the Africans as the most humiliated and exploited people of the last four centuries of modern history" (Robinson 2000, 200). The Group of Eminent Persons understood that Europe was responsible for the enslavement and exploitation of Africans. This was the act for which Europe had to assume guilt, but the GEP argued that they sought responsibility from Europe more than guilt. Yet it has been difficult to move the European nations toward greater passion for African reparations because the original rhetoric and logic of enslavement was based upon a view that Africans were inferior and whites were superior. If Africans are not considered "human" or "equal" to other humans, the rhetoric goes, then reparations are not necessary. This was the only way to support their position on the enslavement of Africans. Herein is the problem of inequality. Racism is not simply a complex of meanings but rather a series of actions that underscore the belief that one group of people deserve privilege over another group.

To be in support of reparations means that one understands that the struggle is against an edifice of false ideas erected on the foundation of white racial superiority. Our aim must be to dismantle the columns that support this edifice by insuring that the institutional, ritual, and social practices that contribute to white privilege, and therefore a practice of treating Africans inequitably, are unable to function in a just society. It is impossible to overlook the relationship between power, definition, institution, ideology, and the sustaining of inequality. Thus, that relationship must be severely critiqued as it relates to the evolution of the discourse on reparations.

There is a danger in assuming that race does not exist and therefore racism does not exist and therefore there is no reasonable way to discuss reparations based on race. The danger is that everything is interpreted as a matter of ideology, where we are concerned only with perceptions of class based on material or economic conditions, when in fact it was the enslavement and subsequent deprivation of economic and material resources that affected the life chances of Africans as Africans, not as representatives of a particular economic class. In this sense, one could argue that whites deserve reparations as well, particularly if they have the same perceptions and beliefs as Africans. I am, of course, extending this argument to suggest the pitfalls that await the discourse on reparations in the simplest of terms. I do not believe that the historical experiences of black people can be counted merely as inappropriate or inadequate representations of the human experience. I believe that the enslavement in many ways was a defining historical moment for the African and European worlds. It created the chasm, established the terms, and set the agenda that we are now questioning. We cannot wish it away nor can it be defined out of existence since it remains grounded in the lived human reality. We know that racism is largely responsible for the unequal distribution of resources, power, education, and privilege in American society. But how is it produced in American society or how was it produced?

The unequal distribution of justice in American society is a result of the ideological meanings, rhetorics, laws, and relationships between the material and educational conditions in the society. Black people were not only deprived but also unequally dispossessed of labor and the fruits of labor, and the dispossession is the basis for a demand for reparations. Recognizing and supporting reparations for descendants of enslaved Africans places the nation on the road to a just recompense for a prolonged assault on the legitimate human rights of African people. Human equality is itself the most provocative statement in support of reparations. What one would wish for oneself one must also wish for others, and therein is the profound basis for reparations.

REFERENCES

Allen, James. 2000. *Without Sanctuary*. New York: Twin Palms.

America, Richard. 1993. *Paying the Social Debt: What White America Owes Black America*. Westport, CT: Praeger.

Ani, Marimba. 1994. *Yurugu: An Africa-Centered Analysis of European Thought and Behavior*. Trenton, NJ: Africa World Press.

Appiah, Kwame. 1992. *In My Father's House*. New York: Oxford University Press.

Aptheker, Herbert. 1963. *American Negro Slave Revolts*. New York: International Publishers.

Asante, Molefi Kete. 1990. *Kemet, Afrocentricity, and Knowledge*. Trenton, NJ: Africa World Press.

———. 1993. *Classical Africa*. Maywood, NJ: Peoples Publishing Group.

———. 1998. *The Afrocentric Idea*. 2nd ed. Philadelphia: Temple University Press.

———. 2003a. *Afrocentricity*. Chicago: African American Images, 2003.

———. 2003b. *Erasing Racism: The Survival of the American Nation*. Amherst, NY: Prometheus Books.

Asante, Molefi Kete, and Abu Abarry, eds. 1996. *The African Intellectual Heritage*. Philadelphia: Temple University Press.

Asante, Molefi Kete, and Mark Mattson. 1998. *African American Atlas*. New York: Simon & Schuster.

———, eds. 2003. *Egypt v. Greece in the American Academy*. Chicago: African American Images.

Baker, Houston. 1988. *Afro-American Poetics*. Madison: University of Wisconsin Press.

Baldwin, James. 1964. *The Fire Next Time*. New York: Dial.

Ball, Charles. 1970. *Fifty Years in Chains*. New York: Dover.

Banks, James A. 1981. *Multiethnic Education: Theory and Practice*. 2nd ed. Boston: Allyn & Bacon.

Baraka, Amiri (Leroy Jones). 1963. *Blues People*. New York: William Morrow.

Bell, Derrick. 1992. *Faces at the Bottom of the Well: The Permanence of Racism*. New York: Basic Books.

Bennett, Lerone. 1990. *Before the Mayflower*. Chicago: Johnson Publishing Company.

Bernal, Martin. 1987. *Black Athena: Afroasiatic Roots of Classical Greece*. New Brunswick, NJ: Rutgers University Press.

Blackshire-Belay, C. Aisha, ed. 1992. *Language and Literature in the African American Imagination*. Westport, CT: Greenwood Press.

Blassingame, John. 1972. *The Slave Community: Plantation Life in the Antebellum South*. New York: Oxford University Press.

Brawley, Benjamin. 1937. *The Negro Genius*. New York: Dodd Mead & Company.

Broderick, Francis L. 1959. *W. E. B. DuBois, Negro Leader in a Time of Crisis*. Stanford: Stanford University Press.

Brooks, Roy. 1999. *When Sorry Isn't Enough: The Controversy over Apologies and Reparations for Human Injustice*. New York: New York University Press.

Bubner, Rudiger. 1982. "Habermas's Concept of Critical Theory." In *Habermas: Critical Debates*, ed. John B. Thompson and David Held. London: Macmillan.

Carmichael, Stokeley, and Charles Hamilton. 1967. *Black Power*. New York: Random House.

Chimutengwende, Chenhamo. 1978. *South Africa: The Press and the Politics of Liberation*. London: Barbican.

Chinweizu. 1975. *The West and the Rest of Us*. New York: Random House.

———. 1987. *Decolonising the African Mind*. London: Pero.

Christian, Mark, ed. 2002. *Black Identity in the 20th Century: Expressions of the US and the UK African Diaspora*. London: Hansib.

Clarke, John Henrik., ed. 1974. *Marcus Garvey and the Vision of Africa*. New York: Random House.

Cronon, Edmund. 1968. *Black Moses*. Madison: University of Wisconsin Press.

Cross, Theodore. 2003/2004. "The Good News That the Thernstroms Neglected to Tell." *Journal of Blacks in Higher Education* 42 (Winter).

Davis, David Brion. 1966. *The Problem of Slavery in Western Culture*. Ithaca, NY: Cornell University Press.

Dawson, Michael C. 2001. *Black Visions: The Roots of Contemporary African American Political Ideologies*. Chicago: University of Chicago Press.

Dei, George Sefa. 1996. *Anti-Racism Education: Theory and Practice*. Halifax, NS: Fernwood Publishing.

Diawara, Manthia. 1998. *In Search of Africa*. New York: Oxford University Press.

Diop, Cheikh Anta. 1974. *The African Origin of Civilization*. New York: Lawrence Hill.

———. 1978. *The Cultural Unity of Black Africa*. Chicago: Third World Press.

DuBois, W. E. B. 1903. *The Souls of Black Folk*. Repr., New York: Bantam Books, 1989.

Fanon, Frantz. 1965. *The Wretched of the Earth*. New York: Grove.

Feagin, Joe. 2000. *Racist America: Roots, Current Realities, and Future Reparations*. New York: Routledge.

Fisher, Miles Mark. 1990. *Negro Slave Songs in the United States*. Secaucus, NJ: Carol Publishing Group.

Forbes, Jack. 1993. *Native Americans and Africans*. Urbana: University of Illinois Press.

Freire, Paulo. 1970. *Pedagogy of the Oppressed*. Repr., New York: Continuum Books, 1993.

Garnet, Henry Highland. 1843. "An Address to the Slaves of the United States." In *Afro-American Primary Sources*, ed. Thomas Frazier. New York: Harcourt Brace Jovanovich, 1971.

Gasset, Ortega y. 1976. *Dehumanization of Art*. New York: Norton.

———. 1994. *The Revolt of the Masses*. New York: Norton.

Gilroy, Paul. 2000. *Against Race*. Cambridge: Harvard University Press.

Glaude, Eddie. 2000. *Exodus!* Chicago: University of Chicago Press.

Gordon, Lewis R. 2000. *Existential Africana: Understanding Africana Existential Thought*. New York: Routledge.

Habermas, Jürgen. 1971. "Vorbereitende Bemerkungen zu einer Theorie der kommunikativen Kompetenz." In *Theorie der Gesellschaft oder Sozialtechnologie—Was leistet die Systemforschung?* ed. Jürgen Habermas and N. Luhmann. Frankfurt: Suhrkamp.

Hacker, Andrew. 1992. *Two Nations*. New York: Simon & Schuster.

Harding, Vincent. 1981. *There Is a River*. New York: Harcourt Brace Jovanovich.

Hudson-Weems, Clenora. 1993. *Africana Womanism: Reclaiming Ourselves.* Boston: Bedford.

James, George G. M. *Stolen Legacy.* 1956. Repr., Chicago: African American Images, 2001.

Jones, Absalom, and Richard Allen. 1794. *A Narrative of the Proceedings of the Black People during the Late Awful Calamity in Philadelphia in the Year of 1793.* Philadelphia.

Karenga, Maulana. 1990. *Introduction to Black Studies.* Los Angeles: University of Sankore Press.

———. 1993. "Towards a Sociology of Maatian Ethics: Literature and Context." *Journal of African Civilizations* 10, no. 1 (Fall): 352–95.

———. 1994. "The Moral Ideal in Ancient Egypt: A Study in Classical African Ethics." PhD diss., University of Southern California.

———. 2003. "The Pan African Initiative in the Americas: Culture, Common Struggle, and the Odu Ifa." In *Race and Democracy in the Americas,* ed. Georgia A. Persons. Vol. 9 of *National Political Science Review.* New Brunswick, NJ: Transaction.

King, Martin Luther, Jr. 1958. *Stride toward Freedom.* New York: Harper.

———. 1964. *Why We Can't Wait.* New York: Harper & Row.

Kotkin, Joel. 1994. *Tribes.* New York: Random House.

Lefkowitz, Mary. 1991. *Not Out of Africa: How Afrocentrism Became an Excuse to Teach Myth as History.* New York: Basic Books.

Levine, Lawrence. 1977. *Black Culture and Black Consciousness.* New York: Oxford University Press.

Malcolm X. 1965. *The Autobiography of Malcolm X.* Ed. Alex Haley. New York: Grove Press.

Marcuse, Herbert. 1971. *An Essay on Liberation.* Boston: Beacon.

Mazama, Ama, ed. 2003. *The Afrocentric Paradigm.* Trenton, NJ: Africa World Press.

McLuhan, Marshal. 1964. *Understanding Media: The Extensions of Man.* Repr., Cambridge: MIT Press, 1994.

Moore, Brooke Noel, and Kenneth Bruder. 1995. *Philosophy: The Power of Ideas.* Mountain View, CA: Mayfield.

Moore, Carlos, Tanya Saunders, and Shawna Moore. 1995. *African Presence in the Americas.* Lawrenceville, NJ: Africa World Press.

New York Times, June 13, 2001, p. A-14.

Obenga, Theophile. 1980. *Pour une nouvelle histoire.* Paris-Dakar: Presence Africaine.

Paz, Octavio. 1961. *The Labyrinth of Solitude: Life and Thought in Mexico.* New York: Grove Press.

Quarles, Benjamin. 1964. *The Negro in the Making of America*. New York: Collier Books.

Raboteau, Albert. 1981. *Slave Religion*. New York: Oxford University Press.

Reddings, J. Saunders. 1950. *They Came in Chains: Americans from Africa*. New York: Doubleday.

Richberg, Keith. 1997. *Out of America*. New York: Basic Books.

Robinson, Randall. 2000. *The Debt: What America Owes to Blacks*. New York: Dutton.

Rodney, Walter. 1986. *How Europe Underdeveloped Africa*. Washington, DC: Howard University Press.

Sarich, Vincent, and Frank Miele. 2004. *Race: The Reality of Human Differences*. Cambridge: Westview Press, Perseus Group.

Schuchter, Arnold. 1970. *Reparations: The Black Manifesto and Its Challenge*. Philadelphia: Lippincott.

Smith, Arthur (aka Molefi Kete Asante). 1969. *The Rhetoric of Black Revolution*. Boston: Allyn & Bacon.

———. 1973. *Transracial Communication*. Englewood Cliffs, NJ: Prentice-Hall.

Smith, Arthur, and Stephen Robb. 1971. *The Voice of Black Rhetoric*. Boston: Allyn & Bacon.

Smith, Robert C. 1995. *Racism in the Post–Civil Rights Era: Now You See It, Now You Don't*. Albany: State University of New York Press.

Stuckey, Sterling. 1987. *Slave Culture*. New York: Oxford University Press.

Stummer, Helen. 1994. *No Easy Walk, No Easy Walk*. Philadelphia: Temple University Press.

Thernstrom, Abigail, and Stephan Thernstrom. 2003. *No Excuses: Closing the Racial Gap in Learning*. New York: Simon & Schuster.

Thiong'o, Ngugi wa. 1986. *Decolonising the Mind. The Politics of Language in African Literature*. London: Currey.

Walker, David. 1829. *An Appeal to the Colored Citizens of the World*. Boston.

Walker, Tshombe. 1997. "An Afrocentric Analysis of the Hip Hop Movement." PhD diss., Temple University.

Washington, Booker T. 1901. *Up from Slavery*. New York: A. L. Burt.

Wegner, Daniel. 2002. *The Illusion of Conscious Will*. Cambridge: Bradford Books.

West, Cornel. 1992. *Race Matters*. Boston: Beacon Press.

Willhelm, Sidney. 1983. *Black in a White America*. Boston: Schenkman.

Williams, Chancellor. 1974. *The Destruction of Black Civilization*. Chicago: Third World Press.

Williams, Eric. 1961. *Capitalism and Slavery*. New York: Russell & Russell.

Wilmore, Gayraud. 1972. *Black Religion and Black Radicalism*. Garden City, NY: Doubleday.

Wilson, William Julius. 1979. *The Declining Significance of Race*. Chicago: University of Chicago Press.

———. 1999. *The Bridge Over the Racial Divide*. Berkeley: University of California Press.

Winbush, Raymond, ed. 2003. *Should America Pay?* New York: Harper-Collins.

Woods, Donald. 1978. *Biko*. London: Paddington Press.

Woodson, Carter G. 1991. *The Miseducation of the Negro*. Trenton, NJ: Africa World Press.

INDEX

Abernathy, Ralph, 52
Adorno, Theodore, 169
African Benevolent Societies, 43
African Free School, 43
Africanity, 200
African Methodist Episcopal Church,
43
Africanness, the renunciation, 46
Afro-American Poetics (Baker), 181
Afrocentric Idea, The (Asante), 177
Afrocentricity, 24, 185, 200
Afro hairstyle, 52
Afro-pessimism, 213
Alaafin of Oyo, 59
Alkebulan, Adisa, 17
Allen, James, 223
Allen, Richard, 43, 228
Allen, Troy, 17
Amanitore, 195
America, Richard, 221
American Colonization Society, 42
American Revolution, 147
Amistad (ship), 33, 230
Ani, Marimba, 173

antiracism, 32
*Appeal to the Colored Citizens of the
World, An* (Walker), 45, 228
Appiah, Kwame Anthony, 135, 213
architecton, definition, 11
assegai, 117
Attica (movie), 142

Baker, Houston, 181, 216
Baldwin, James, 142
Bankole, Katherine, 9, 17
Baraka, Amiri, 153, 217
Bearden, Romare, 180
Bell, Derrick, 33
Bernal, Martin, 149
Big Black, 142
Biko, Bantu Steve, 163
bin Laden, Osama, 136
"Black Is Beautiful," 52
Black Nationalism, 26
blackness, 27
Black Power, 37
Blackstone Rangers, 38
Black Visions: The Roots of Contempo-

rary African American Political Ideologies (Dawson), 109n2
Blake, Cecil, 17
Blues People (Baraka), 217
Boer, 163
Bonhoeffer, Dietrich, 135
Boston Gazette, 62
Botwe-Asamoah, Kwame, 17
Bridge over the Racial Divide, The (Wilson), 109
Brown, Jasbo, 46
Brown, John, 32
Bryant, Kobe, 33
Bush, George W., 53
Bush (George W.) administration, 136
Byrd, James, 164

Cabral, Amilcar, 9
Cape Town Die Burger (newspaper), 166
Carmichael, Stokeley. *See* Toure, Kwame
Carter, Jimmy, 101
Césaire, Aimé, 21
Chaka, 117, 118
Chimutengwende, Chen, 9, 57, 161–62
Chinweizu, 154
Christian, Mark, 17
Church of England, 147
cities, 114–15
civilization, 137
Clake, John Henrik, 215
collective will, 51
colonization, 42
colored people, 28
Colored People (Gates), 208
Common, 46

communication, 117–19
traditional modes, 167
Conde, Maryse, 194
Conrad, Joseph, 182
Conyers, John (congressman), 233
Creole (ship), 230
Crips, 38
Cross, Theodore, 66
Crucible, The (Miller), 194
cyberspace, 116
cybertime, 116

Dalits, 148
Damas, Léon, 21
Daniel, Jack, 9
Daniels, Ron, 229
Dawson, Michael, 26, 109
Dead Prez, 46
Debt: What America Owes to Blacks, The (Robinson), 222
Declining Significance of Race, The (Wilson), 97, 109
Decolonizing the African Mind (wa Thiong'o), 159n1
Decolonizing the Mind (Chinweizu), 159n1
Dehumanization of Art (Ortega), 95
Dei, George Sefa, 67
Delany, Martin, 26, 36
Derrida, Jacques, 14
Dewey, John, 93
Diawara, Manthia, 207–19
Do the Right Thing (movie), 184
Douglass, Frederick, 107
DuBois, W. E. B., 12, 19–24, 43, 51, 59, 64
duels, 86–87
Dunham, FeFe, 17

education, dynamic, 70
Egypt, 140, 141
Elements of Logic (Whatley), 88
empiricism, 103
exile, 207
Exodus! (Glaude), 203

Fanon, Frantz, 9, 107
Farrakhan, Louis, 55, 153
fatalism, African American, 35
Faulkner, William, 182
Ferreira, Ana Monteiro, 17
Feyerabend, Paul, 172
Fire Next Time, The (Baldwin), 54
Firestone, Cindy, 142
Forten, James, 42
Foucault, Michel, 14, 187
Fourth Lateran Council, 87
Freire, Paulo, 9, 145
Fromm, Erich, 169
Fuller, Charles, 45

Gandhi, Mahatma, 148
Garcia, Jorge, 29
Garden of Remembrance, 163
Garnet, Henry Highland, 230
Garvey, Marcus, 36, 47, 50, 51, 54, 107
Gasset, Ortega y, 120
gender, 189–93
General, 75
Gerbner, George, 9
Gilroy, Paul, 202
Glaude, Eddie, 203–206
globalization, 133
Gorbachev, Mikhail, 146
Gordon, Lewis, 25, 97
Graterford Prison, 84
Group of Eminent Persons, 234
Gyekye, Kwame, 9

Habermas, Jürgen, 14, 169–77
Hacker, Andrew, 224
Hamer, Fannie Lou, 153, 195
Hatshepsut, 195
Hawthorne, Nathaiel, 194
Hegel, Georg Wilhelm Friedrich, 174
Hegelian idea, 21
Henry, John, 153, 156
Herodotus, 149n1
historical processes, 25
Histories (Herodutus), 149n1
Holiday, Billie, 46
hooks, bell, 202
Horkheimer, Max, 169
Hudson-Weems, Clenora, 190
human equality, 226
humanness, 138

Ifa, 145
initiative against marginality, 35
In My Father's House (Appiah), 208
Innocent (pope), 87
In Search of Africa (Diawara), 207–11
instrumentalization, 109
Introduction to Black Studies (Karenga), 199
Iraq War, 136
iwa, 112

Jackson, Jesse, 52
James, George G. M., 149
Jasper, John, 153
Jefferson, Thomas, 143
Jehovah's Witnesses, 147
Jensen, Arthur, 68
Ji, Yuan, 17
Joan of Arc, 195
Johnson administration, 136
Jones, Absalom, 228

Kant, Immanuel, 143
Karenga, Maulana, 9, 37, 50, 153, 199, 219, 225
Kaunda, Kenneth, 142
Keita, Salif, 208
King, Clemon, 101
King, Martin Luther, Jr., 50, 52, 53, 63, 107, 108, 109, 148, 153, 162
Kissinger, Henry, 105
Knowledge and Human Interests (Habermas), 171
Kotkin, Joel, 208
KRS One, 46
Kurtz, Paul, 9
Kwanzaa, 37

Las Casas, Bartholomew de, 104
Laye, Sidime, 208
Leadbelly, 46
Lee, Spike, 184
Lefkowitz, Mary, 149
Lenin Peace Prize, 142
Lincoln, Abraham, 145
linearity, 134
location, 180
L'Ouverture, Toussaint, 230
Lu, Xing, 9
Lundy, Benjamin, 36

Maat, 10, 187–88, 232
Magna Carta, 88
Mandela, Nelson, 161, 166
Mangcu, Xolela, 164
Mao Tse-tung, 147
Marable, Manning, 53
Marcuse, Herbert, 9, 169, 171, 176
Marx, Karl, 145
Mayan society, 138
Mays, Benjamin, 158

Mazama, Ama, 9, 149
Mazrui, Ali, 234
Mazwai, Thami, 57
McLuhan, Marshall, 9, 28, 29–31, 85, 134
media institutions, 129–31
mediator, 75–76, 78–80
Memory of Justice, The (Ophuls), 155
menticide, 44
messianism, 47–50, 51, 52
collective messianism, 52
metaphor, architectonic symbol, 112
Miike, Yoshitaka, 17
Militant Labor Forum, 157
Miller, Arthur, 194
Million Man March, 55
monoethnicity, 69
Monroe Doctrine, 143
Monterey Institute of Technology, 29
Moon, Reverend Sun Myung, 162
Mother Teresa, 135
Mott, Lucretia, 32
MOVE organization, 147
Muhammad, Elijah, 45, 107, 153
Mulder, Connie, 162
mutuality, 226
myth, 152–53, 158

Nanny, 195
narcissism, 141
nation, a (concept), 25
National Black Independent Political Party, 62
Nationalist Party, 164
N'COBRA (National Coalition of Blacks for Reparations), 230
Negritude philosophers, 21
Negroes, becoming, 27
Newton, Huey, 50, 52

Niane, Djibril Tamsir, 217
Nixon administration, 136
Njoya (king), 59
Nkrumah, Kwame, 215
Nobel Prize, 141, 142
Nobles, Wade, 9
No Excuses: Closing the Racial Gap in Learning (Thernstrom and Thernstrom), 65
nomenclature, 28
Nzingha, 195

oaths, 87
Obasanjo, Olusegun, 234
Obenga, Theophile, 59
Oduduwa, 145
Ogun, 159
Ophuls, Marcel, 155
Opoku, Kofi Asare, 9, 212
Opubor, Alfred, 9
ordeals, 86–87
Orwell, George, 53
Ostrogoths, 86
Out of America (Richburg), 20

Parchman's Farm, 142
Paying the Social Debt: What White America Owes Black America (America), 221–22
Paz, Octavio, 133
Peters, Karl, 211
Phillips, Wendell, 36
Poe, Daryl Zizwe, 17
politics, 145
process, a dynamic analogue, 92
proofs, pagan, 86
psychology of oppression, 154
public sphere, 169–72
Pulitzer Prize, 142

Qoboza, Percy, 161
Quaid-e-Azam Human Rights International Award, 142

Rabaka, Reiland, 17
Race: The Reality of Human Difference (Sarich and Miele), 222
racism, 51, 56, 99–101
racism, process, 102, 106
Radical Democrats, 53
Ragnarok, 151
Rainey, Ma, 46
Rand Daily Mail (newspaper), 161
Randolph, A. Philip, 107
refusers, 74–75
Remond, Charles, 107
reparations, 226, 230, 231, 232–36
Revolt of the Masses, The (Gasset), 120
Richburg, Keith, 20
Robeson, Paul, 142
Robinson, Randall, 222
Rogers, Everett, 9
Roman architecture, 138
Rosenthal, Paul, 9
Rushton, J. Phillipe, 68
Russian Revolution, 146

Sassine, William, 208
Scarlet Letter, The (Hawthorne), 194
Schiller, Herbert, 85
School Daze (movie), 192
Seale, Bobby, 50, 52
Sengbe, 230
Senghor, Léopold, 21
sentinel statements, 201
separation anxiety, 210
Shange, Ntozake, 45
Shine, 153
Should America Pay? (Winbush), 222

signifiers, 75
Simpson, O. J., 33
Slater, Philip, 85
Smith, Bessie, 46
Smith, Robert C., 163
Sobeknefru, 195
Sostre, Martin, 142
souls, 21
Souls of Black Folk, The (DuBois), 12, 19–24, 27
South Africa, 13, 14
South Africa: The Press and the Politics of Liberation (Chimutengwende), 161
South African Daily Dispatch (newspaper), 163
Spielberg, Stephen, 33
spirit of nations, 21
Stagolee, 153, 156
stereotyping, 31
Structural Transformation of the Public Sphere (Habermas), 169
Stummer, Helen, 224
survival, 41

technological society, 151
television, social goals, 63, images, 121–28
Temple, Joey, 84
Thernstrom, Abigail, 65–66
Thernstrom, Stephen, 65–66
Third Reich, 91, 139
Thompson, Dudley, 234
Toure, Kwame, 37, 50
Toward A Rational Society (Habermas), 171
transactionalism, 74
Tribes (Kotkin), 208
Troy (movie), 117

Tubman, Harriet, 153, 156, 157, 195
Tupahache, Asiba, 229
Turner, Henry, 36
Turner, Nat, 48–50, 64
Two Nations (Hacker), 224

Understanding Media (McLuhan), 28
Unification Church, 162
Up from Slavery (Washington), 20

Vandals, 86
Vietnam War, 137
violence, 109
Visigoths, 86

Walker, David, 32, 45, 54, 228
Walters, Ronald, 9
Washington, Booker T., 20
Washington, Madison, 230
Washington Times (newspaper), 162
Weaver, Robert C., 156
Weber, Max, 177
Welsh, Kariamu, 155
West, Cornel, 9, 202
West and the Rest of Us, The (Chinweizu), 159
Whatley, Richard, 88
Whipple, William, 53
whiteness, 27
Williams, Chancellor, 140
Williams, Peter, 42
Wilson, August, 45
Wilson, William Julius, 97
Winbush, Raymond, 222
Without Sanctuary (Allen), 223
Woods, Donald, 163, 166
Woodson, Carter, 67
World (newspaper), 161
Wright, Richard, 82, 215–16

X, Malcolm, 20, 50, 135, 157

Yaa Asantewa, 195
Yeltsin, Boris, 145

Yenenga, Ana, 84
Yurugu, 173